Tender Grassfed Barbecue

Traditional, Primal and Paleo

Also by Stanley A. Fishman:

Tender Grassfed Meat: Traditional Ways to Cook Healthy Meat

Tender Grassfed Barbecue

Traditional, Primal and Paleo

By Stanley A. Fishman

Tender
Grassfed
Barbecue
Traditional, Primal and Paleo

Stanley A. Fishman

Published by Alanstar Games, 3000 Danville Blvd., #205, Alamo, CA 94507
grassfedmeat@sbcglobal.net
www.tendergrassfedmeat.com

Book design and illustration by Keren Fishman
Edited by Keren Fishman
Proofread by Alan Fishman

ISBN: 978-0-9823429-1-6

Library of Congress Control Number: 2011911042

PRINTED IN THE UNITED STATES OF AMERICA

Dedication and Gratitude

The creation of this cookbook owes much to the inspiration, help, and support of many people. While promoting my first book, *Tender Grassfed Meat*, I had the joy of making many new friends over the Internet, who provided invaluable help in promoting *Tender Grassfed Meat*, great advice, and terrific support for this book, *Tender Grassfed Barbecue*.

I am honored to dedicate this book to all who inspired, helped, and supported me in the making of this book. This book is dedicated to:

Roy Johnson, who gave me that chicken wing.

My father, Saul Fishman, whose stories about the wonderful grassfed meat he had eaten as a young man inspired me to believe that grassfed meat could be tender and delicious.

My mother, Ann Fishman, a magnificent cook, who taught me that every meal should taste wonderful.

My chief recipe taster, Ken Pritikin, whose heartfelt and intelligent appreciation of my cooking consistently inspired me to become a better cook.

And to the many people who gave me invaluable help, whether by generously promoting *Tender Grassfed Meat*, providing inspiration, sharing precious knowledge, giving encouragement, providing good advice, and in some cases all of the above:

Sheri Ross Fogarty, Jimmy Moore, Kimberly Hartke, Kelly the Kitchen Kop, Ann Marie Michaels, Jon Payne, Cathy Payne, Chris Kerston, Mary Graese, John Wood, Sarah Pope, Raine Saunders, Joan Grinzi, Jennifer Wood, and Sally Fallon Morell.

And to the best butcher crew I know, Brian, George, Robert, and everyone in the crew, for teaching me about the many cuts of meat and leaving the fat on!

My son, Alan Fishman, who made my writing better with his valuable suggestions and superb proofreading.

The many readers of *Tender Grassfed Meat* who praised the book in many forums, and wrote me appreciative letters.

And, most of all, my wife, Keren Fishman, my editor, book designer, artist, typesetter, technical expert, and one true love, who made this book possible.

Contents

Appendix

Introduction

Barbecue is the oldest way of cooking meat. The flavor imparted by smoldering coals unites perfectly with the natural flavor of primal meat. The enticing smell of meat cooking in front of a fire speaks to us, promising good eating.

I fell in love with barbecue when I was 5 years old.

My family had just moved into a new house in Marinwood, California, a small suburb fairly close to San Francisco. I was exploring our new backyard, when I smelled something wonderful. I followed the smell into the neighbor's yard. I saw a big balding man, wearing glasses and an apron, bending over a black box with legs. I was fascinated by the glowing coals, the sizzling chicken on the grill, the smoky smell that was making me so very hungry. The big man smiled down at me, and picked up a plate. He used the tongs in his hand to pick up a piece of chicken. He put the chicken on the plate. He handed the plate to me. There was a chicken wing on the plate. The wing was a beautiful orange color, and smelled so good. I picked up the wing and bit into it. The wing was smoky, juicy, tender, wonderful. It was the best thing I had ever eaten.

Our new home had an indoor charcoal barbecue that was somehow safe to use inside. I begged my mother to use the barbecue. One day, she finally did. She barbecued some chicken, which she basted with butter. There was a lot of flame and smoke, but the chicken was wonderful. My mother never barbecued again.

There wasn't much barbecue in Northern California at that time. There was a local barbecue restaurant, but it was not nearly as good as that chicken wing. Finally, when I was grown, I got a covered kettle grill, a barbecue cookbook, and tried my hand at barbecuing. I learned how to cook just so I could have barbecue. I got to be pretty good at barbecuing factory meat, either by grilling directly over hot factory charcoal, or by cooking over a drip pan with factory charcoal to either side. This barbecue was good, but not great. I just could not equal that chicken wing.

Years passed, I moved to places where there was no space for a barbecue, and the dream of making great barbecue slowly faded away. Then I met my one true love, and we got married. Our first apartment had a space where we could put a barbecue. We did not have much money then, and my wife wasn't sure that we could afford a covered kettle grill. I tried to convince her that it was worth it, that she just did not know how good barbecue could be. Eventually she did agree to get a covered kettle grill, because I wanted one so much. Fortunately, I found a book on Kansas City barbecue.

I learned about traditional American barbecue, the barbecue of the Deep South, Kansas City, Memphis, and Texas. I studied the art of cooking low and slow, using the magic of dry rubs, using wood chunks and wood chips for flavoring. I began to make the best barbecue I had ever cooked. My wife often referred to our covered kettle grill as the best investment we ever made. As our economic situation improved, I bought more barbecues, always trying to do better at traditional American barbecue, cooking low and slow. I still could not equal that chicken wing.

Years later, my health collapsed, and I eventually restored it by following the nutritional principles of Dr. Weston A. Price. As part of that process, I began to switch to eating grassfed and grass-finished meat.

The result was a culinary disaster. I ruined a lot of fine meat. The dry rubs lost their magic. Low and slow resulted in stringy and tough. I came across a number of studies and articles that warned against eating barbecued meat, because of toxins created by the process of barbecue. It looked like my barbecue dream would end, that I would have to give up barbecue just like I gave up ice cream, soda pop, and many other foods I used to love.

I finally learned how to cook grassfed meat, by studying and adapting traditional cooking methods. I finally realized that traditional cooking methods might work for barbecue as well. I also realized that traditional barbecue methods must have produced safe food, because all of the traditional peoples barbecued, and all of them were free of chronic illness when they ate their traditional diet.

I read everything I could find about traditional barbecue methods, going as far back as the Iliad. I learned that traditional barbecuers cooked very differently than modern ones. They used different fuels. They never let flame hit the meat. They cooked the meat in front of the heat source — not over it — or they placed the meat so far above the heat source that there was no chance of a flame ever touching the meat. They started their cooking temperature high and finished low. They did not use dry rubs, but used marinades and bastes that lubricated the meat.

I learned how to adapt these principles to my barbecuing, and I learned how to barbecue grassfed meat. This barbecue was the best of all. I finally not only equaled that chicken wing, but surpassed it.

This book contains the methods I learned and a number of my favorite barbecue recipes. Get ready to eat the best, healthiest barbecue you've ever had.

Part 1:
Benefits of Traditional Foods and Barbecue

Joy of Traditional Barbecue

The Joy of Barbecued Food

You are what you eat. Traditional peoples knew this. Traditional peoples knew how to eat and how to cook. They loved to eat, and ate without fear or guilt. They didn't count calories. They ate delicious meals full of nutrients that made their bodies strong and healthy, calmed the mind and the soul, and filled them with energy. They paid great attention to the quality of their food. They knew the farmer who raised their wheat, the rancher who raised the cows they ate, and the gardener who grew their vegetables. They paid great attention to the quality of their ingredients and they prepared their food with great care. This wonderful food gave them strong immune systems and brought pleasure and health into their lives.

Barbecue, which can be described as cooking with wood and/or charcoal, is perhaps the most traditional method of cooking. It is also the most delicious.

We can still prepare and enjoy these good traditional foods. This book will give you knowledge and methods to prepare healthy, traditional food that will taste wonderful, nourish your body, and leave you feeling better and energized after each meal.

The ingredients, recipes, and cooking methods have been carefully chosen to be healthy, nourishing, and delicious. This is the food that I and my family eat.

The barbecue techniques in this book are based on the ways people traditionally cooked with fire, using the same kind of fuel. Traditional peoples ate grassfed meat, and traditional barbecue methods were designed to cook grassfed meat. Traditional barbecue methods and grassfed meat go together perfectly, resulting in tender, absolutely delicious meat.

Too many modern people have forgotten what to eat, how to eat, and how to cook. Learning how to prepare traditional barbecue is good, but eating it is even better. With this book, you can do both.

Barbecuing Advantages of Grassfed Meat

Grassfed meat has many cooking advantages over other meat:

- Grassfed meat is tender and tastes much better than other meat.
- Grassfed meat is often easier to cook than other meat.
- Grassfed meat is easier to barbecue.

Surprised? All of these statements are absolutely true, if you know how to cook grassfed meat.

Grassfed Meat Is Different

Grassfed meat, coming from animals that have been fed the diet they were designed to eat, is quite different from other meat. It is denser, with considerably less water in it, and leaner. It has much more flavor, right in the meat. These differences mean that grassfed meat can be cooked at lower temperatures, shrinks much less in cooking, cooks much faster, needs little or no seasoning, and is much more satisfying, so you are satisfied with a smaller amount.

No More Scorching the Meat

Conventional steaks are almost always cooked over very high heat, creating much smoke and often flames in the process. The high heat is necessary to deal with the large amount of water in the meat. Various studies have found that direct grilling of meat over very high heat can create carcinogenic substances in the meat, especially when it is touched by flames. Grassfed meat browns beautifully in front of a medium hot fire, and should not be cooked directly over the heat source, as high direct heat makes it tough.

Grassfed Meat Shrinks Much Less in Cooking

Grassfed meat retains most of its volume when properly barbecued. A conventional roast or steak will shrink dramatically in size when barbecued. Grassfed meat will shrink much less, because it is denser, with much less water.

Grassfed Meat Cooks Much Faster On the Grill

Grassfed meat cooks much faster than conventional meat. You can barbecue a delicious roast in about 30 minutes. Steaks also cook much faster. This saves time and fuel costs, and is much more convenient.

Grassfed Meat Needs Less Seasoning

Grassfed meat, when properly cooked, has great natural flavor right in the meat and fat. This flavor is so good that it does not need much in the way of seasoning to be outstanding, especially when barbecued. The recipes in this book are designed to bring out the great natural flavor of the meat by using just a few traditional ingredients and flavor combinations, along with the magic of barbecue. Conventional meat has a bland, uniform taste that needs all kinds of seasonings and sauces to provide flavor.

Grassfed Meat Is Much More Satisfying

Grassfed meat and fat are full of nutrients, and have much less water in the meat. This makes grassfed meat very satisfying. When your body gets the nutrients it needs, hunger stops and you lose the desire to keep eating. Now that I eat grassfed meat, I eat half the amount of meat I used to. I did not make a decision to eat less meat, it just happened because grassfed meat is so satisfying.

Grassfed Meat Is Tender and Easy to Cook

I ruined the first grassfed meat I cooked, because I tried to cook it like conventional meat. After much research, I learned how to adapt the knowledge of our ancestors and developed several methods of making grassfed meat tender and delicious. I have found that cooking grassfed meat with these methods is easy. This is particularly true with my barbecue methods, because there is no need for direct high heat. Direct high heat on a barbecue can result in flames, smoke, and meat that is burned on the outside and raw on the inside.

Grassfed Meat Is Particularly Good for Barbecue

Grassfed meat takes on a better and more intense barbecue flavor, which is not diluted by excess water in the meat, unlike conventional beef. The combination of grassfed meat and charcoal is thousands of years old, and our taste buds know and welcome that particular taste.

Traditional Barbecue Methods Avoid Risk Factors

Is barbecue safe? There are a number of studies that conclude that barbecuing meat creates carcinogenic substances. However, traditional peoples barbecued constantly and were free of cancer.

The studies all focused on meat grilled with modern methods, using very high direct heat. The traditional methods are very different. No study bothered to contrast the difference between modern grilling methods and traditional methods. In fairness, the researchers were almost certainly unaware of the dramatic difference in cooking methods.

The researchers' solution is to stop eating barbecue. My solution is to change the cooking method to avoid the risk factors by barbecuing the way our ancestors did.

What the Researchers Found

The studies showed that grilling meat over direct high heat can cause the formation of substances that are considered carcinogenic. These substances are formed when meat is cooked with very high direct heat, especially when flames hit the meat and a hard crust is formed by the searing heat.

Some studies also found that fat dripping from the meat directly on to the heat source could result in the formation of other substances considered carcinogenic.

What is crucial to understand is that all of these substances are created by grilling the meat directly over a very hot heat source, either gas or composite charcoal briquets.

Factory meat, including a variety of processed meats full of preservatives and chemicals, was used in the studies.

As far as I could tell, the barbecued meat used in the studies was cooked with modern fuels like composite charcoal briquets and propane gas.

Some researchers found that marinating meat reduced the amount of some carcinogenic substances by as much as one hundred percent.

How Traditional Barbecue Methods Avoid the Risk Factors

Traditional peoples did not barbecue over direct high heat. In fact, they did not barbecue directly over any heat source, unless the meat was so high over a low fire that there was no chance of flames hitting the meat, and the meat only received low heat.

The prerequisites for forming the carcinogenic substances found by the studies — direct high heat, and fat dripping directly onto a very hot heat source — did not occur.

Meat was almost always cooked in front of, never over, the fire. The fire was always allowed to burn down to smoldering coals — nobody cooked directly over leaping flames. This method did not create hard charred crusts or grill marks, but a delicious, tender, browned coating.

Cooking grassfed meat over direct high heat will make it tough and inedible. Grassfed meat can be very tender when grilled by moderate to low indirect heat, which is how our ancestors grilled it.

Traditional peoples almost always marinated their meat before barbecuing it.

Traditional Peoples Used Different Fuels

Almost all barbecue cooked in the United States today is made over a very hot fire fueled by propane gas or composite charcoal briquets. Traditional peoples never used these fuels.

Composite charcoal briquets were invented by Henry Ford as a way to make money from the scrap wood left over from making automobiles. These briquets included many other ingredients besides wood scraps, such as anthracite coal, petrochemicals, and various binding materials and chemicals. They were never used by humans before the 20th century.

The use of propane gas as a barbecue fuel also began in the 20th century.

Traditional peoples used various natural substances as fuel. The most common was wood, which was always burned down to coals before the cooking began, or hardwood lump charcoal, which was made by partially burning wood in a way that caused it to form charcoal. The art of charcoal burning goes back thousands of years.

Traditional Barbecue Is Better for Grassfed Meat

Factory meat contains much more water than grassfed meat, which means that it can withstand direct high heat. The most common way to ruin grassfed meat is to cook it over direct high heat. Grassfed meat can be wonderfully tender when cooked with traditional methods.

The methods in this book avoid the risk factors.

The recipes in this book never use direct high heat, which would ruin grassfed meat. These recipes can be made with hardwood lump charcoal, 100% charcoal briquets (which contain only hardwood and a starch binder), or wood burned down to coals, which are very similar or identical to the fuels used by our ancestors.

Most of the recipes in this book call for a traditional marinade.

Benefits of Traditional Foods and Barbecue

Who Was Dr. Weston A. Price?

This book is consistent with the nutritional principles taught by Dr. Weston A. Price. While you certainly do not need to follow his principles to use and enjoy this book, this article will explain a bit about him. The copious use of animal fat in this book, which may surprise some people, is based on the research of Dr. Price. The research of Dr. Price is also the basis for the avoidance of most vegetable oils, most sweeteners, and all modern processed foods in this book. The traditional cooking methods and food combinations that form the basis of this book are also consistent with the teachings of Dr. Price.

Dr. Price was a dentist in Cleveland, Ohio. He was a very distinguished dentist who was also the research director of the American Dental Association. After many years of practice, Dr. Price realized that the teeth and health of his patients were getting worse from year to year. Even more disturbing was the fact that each generation of his patients had worse teeth and was sicker than their parents. Dr. Price decided to find out why.

The Question

After several years of research, Dr. Price decided that the problem was caused by problems with the modern diet. But he did not know what those problems were. Dr. Price did know that many so-called "primitive" peoples had excellent teeth. In fact, these "primitives" had much better teeth than the "civilized" peoples who had far superior technology. Dr. Price decided to study those "primitive" peoples who had excellent teeth.

The Search

Dr. Price decided to travel directly to where these healthy peoples lived, so he could study them first-hand and learn why they were healthy. Dr. Price traveled all over the world during the 1920s and early 1930s. He visited isolated, healthy peoples from Switzerland, the Scottish islands, Australia, Africa, Polynesia, Peru, Native Americans in Canada, and others. He also studied the close relatives of each of these peoples, who were not isolated and lived in more "civilized" circumstances, eating modern foods.

The Answer

In every case, Dr. Price learned that the traditional peoples who ate the diet of their ancestors, which consisted of unprocessed foods from hunting, gathering, herding, fishing, and natural farming, had excellent teeth, without cavities, even though they had no dentists. Not only did these people have excellent teeth, they were free of the chronic diseases that were common in civilization. They did not have cancer, heart disease, diabetes, tuberculosis, and they had none of the chronic diseases that plagued the so-called "civilized" world. They also did not have crime or mental illness. They had no need for police or psychiatrists. Their children were born healthy, without defects. Dr. Price also found that members of the same group of people, when they ate a modern diet, had terrible teeth and were plagued by every one of the chronic diseases that were common in more advanced countries. The only difference was what they ate.

The Solution

Dr. Price discovered that the key to good health is to eat a traditional diet of unprocessed food, and to eat the same kind of food that the healthy, isolated peoples ate. These foods include natural animal fat, pastured meat, wild fish and seafood, wild game, organ meats, unprocessed dairy, various vegetables, a wide variety of traditionally fermented foods, and some grains prepared by traditional methods, and other foods. Dr. Price discovered that while the diets of these widely scattered peoples were quite different, they had many elements in common. Dr. Price discovered what these elements were, especially the dietary factors that were essential for good health. He recorded his findings in a book entitled *Nutrition and Physical Degeneration*, which was published in 1939. This book described exactly what people should and should not eat in order to be well nourished.

Ignored and Rediscovered

Unfortunately, Dr. Price's work was largely ignored. However, his work was preserved by the Price-Pottenger Nutrition Foundation, which devoted itself to keeping his book in print, and keeping his knowledge alive. The Weston A. Price Foundation was founded in 1999. They have done a magnificent job of spreading Dr. Price's knowledge all over the world and the Internet. Sally Fallon Morell, the founder of the Weston A. Price Foundation, wrote *Nourishing Traditions: The Cookbook that Challenges Politically Correct Nutrition and the Diet Dictocrats*, a comprehensive cookbook which teaches the reader to cook traditional food in traditional ways. *Nourishing Traditions* also explains the teachings of Dr. Price in a way that is easy to understand. I highly recommend this book.

There is another benefit to the use of traditional foods as taught by Dr. Price. They are absolutely delicious and satisfying, when properly cooked.

Benefits of Grassfed Meat

Grassfed meat is a completely different product from conventional meat. The natural food of cattle, bison, and lamb is grass and meadow plants. When the animals are raised on grass, their meat is packed full of nutrients in the perfect proportion for good health, and in a form that can be easily assimilated by the human body.

Meat that is not 100 percent grassfed and grass-finished has been fed a mixture of grain, soy, and many other things that were never a part of the natural diet of these animals. The "other things" can include rendered restaurant waste, various animal parts, cement dust, plastic balls, and many other unsavory ingredients. Some producers only feed a 100 percent vegetarian diet to their animals. However, even these diets usually consist of a large amount of grain and soy, which are not part of the natural diet of grass-eating animals.

Omega-3 Essential Fatty Acids

The meat of grain-finished animals is very different in composition than the meat of grassfed animals. For example, the natural balance of omega-6 fatty acids to omega-3 fatty acids should be no more than four-to-one. In grassfed meat, the ratio is usually one-to-one. In meat that is not exclusively grassfed, the ratio of omega-6 to omega-3 is often twenty-to-one. The omega-6 excess in the American diet has been associated with a greatly increased risk of cancer, heart disease, obesity, rapid aging, and many other health problems. Many doctors advise their patients to take fish oil capsules to try to help with the imbalance. Grassfed meat has the same ratio of omega-6 to omega-3 as wild fish.

The Benefits of CLA

In addition to having the proper ratio of omega-6 to omega-3 fatty acids, grassfed meat contains a large amount of CLA (Conjugated Linoleic Acid). The amount of CLA goes down when the animal is fed grain. The more grain that is fed to the animal, the less CLA. Various studies have shown that CLA:

- Increases the metabolic rate

- Increases muscle mass while reducing fat

- Decreases abdominal fat

- Strengthens the immune system

- Reduces the risk of cancer

- Reduces the risk of heart disease

- Reduces the risk of diabetes

- Reduces the risk of hyperthyroidism

- Normalizes thyroid function

More Nutrients in Grassfed Meat

But that is not all. Grassfed meat contains a full complement of substances known as cofactors, which help our bodies absorb and use other nutrients.

Grassfed meat also provides a wide variety of vitamins, minerals, and amino acids. All of these nutrients are present in proper proportion to each other, along with the cofactors needed for your body to properly assimilate them.

Grassfed Meat and Fat are Ideal for Paleo Diets

The Paleo diet has been adopted by many people, and the numbers are growing. The idea that we should eat like our ancestors makes complete sense, as our bodies have evolved to eat and process the foods they used over tens of thousands of years. While there are different variations of Paleo diets, one thing is true for all of them — grassfed meat is ideal, especially when barbecued.

What is Paleo?

I did not know about the Paleo diet when I wrote my first cookbook, *Tender Grassfed Meat*. As I followed news of my book on the Internet, I came across a number of comments on Paleo websites that praised my book and talked about how it was great for people following a Paleo diet. These comments inspired me to learn about Paleo.

The Paleo concept is both simple and profound. The idea is that we should eat the same foods that our distant Paleolithic ancestors ate, before agriculture was developed. The argument is a powerful one — agriculture is only a few thousand years old, but humanity has existed for tens of thousands of years, or much longer.

The foods eaten by humanity over these tens of thousands of years included the meat and fat of ruminant animals, the meat and fat of other animals such as wild boar, the meat and fat of a huge variety of birds, wild fish, and seafood. Nuts, berries, wild roots, and plants were also eaten. Meat was eaten on the bone whenever possible, and bones were cracked open for their marrow, and formed the basis of early broths. Because humans have been eating these foods since the beginning, they are ideal for our bodies, since we have evolved to eat and digest them.

The foods of agriculture, such as grains and dairy, as well as all of the modern processed foods, are new to our bodies and can cause problems with digestion and absorption, as well as allergies and other problems.

Therefore, a true Paleo diet would avoid all modern foods, and many traditional foods, including all grains and dairy.

I personally eat lots of dairy, but only in its traditional forms. Humans have been eating traditional dairy for about ten thousand years, and my body does fine with it. I avoid most grains, and find that I can easily do without them. I avoid all modern processed foods. But the food I enjoy and crave the most is Paleo — grassfed meat and fat, cooked in front of burning coals.

But it is not enough just to eat meat and fat. Modern industrial meat has a totally different nutritional content from the meat eaten by our ancestors. Grassfed meat and fat is as close as we can get to the meat that nourished our ancestors (with the exception of wild game).

The Price–Paleo Connection — Modern Examples of a Real Paleo Diet

Three of the healthy peoples studied by Dr. Weston A. Price were eating a Paleo diet, in that they had no agriculture and no dairy. They lived completely from hunting and gathering. Their traditional diets had not changed for many thousands of years. These peoples included Alaskan Eskimos (Inuit), Australian Aborigines, and Canadian Native Americans.

When these peoples ate their traditional Paleo diet, they were healthy. When they ate modern foods, they were riddled with all kinds of chronic disease, and died in large numbers from diseases such as tuberculosis.

These peoples all ate the meat, organs, and fat of grass-eating animals, as well as other animals. Those who lived by the sea also ate huge amounts of wild seafood and fish. While all of these peoples gathered and ate a variety of nuts, berries, and plants, their diets focused heavily on meat, organs, and fat, from both land and sea animals. All of the animals they ate were eating a species-appropriate diet such as grass and meadow plants for herbivores.

Grassfed and Paleo — a Perfect Match

Most of the foods eaten by early humans are not readily available to us. But we can find and eat foods that have a similar nutritional profile. The major food of these people was the meat and fat of animals, especially ruminant animals. We can get an almost identical set of nutrients by eating plenty of grassfed meat and fat, as well as the organs of grassfed animals.

Grassfed bison meat, from bison grazing their natural habitat, is just about identical with the bison that was eaten by early humans.

Grassfed beef is very similar, even though the breed and characteristics of the animals have changed from the wild varieties available before agriculture.

Grassfed lamb and goat also have similar nutritional profiles.

Grassfed Barbecue and Paleo — an Even Better Match

While the peoples studied by Dr. Price ate some of their meat raw or fermented, much of their meat was cooked, and it was almost always cooked in front of a fire.

I do not know if any nutrients are enhanced by the barbecue process, but the taste certainly is. The mouthwatering smell and taste of charcoaled meat appeals to most people on a primal level. The smell of meat roasting in front of a fire, the flavor added by the burning coals, is one of the oldest human pleasures, one that has been enjoyed for ages.

By barbecuing grassfed meat in a traditional manner, we can enjoy this primal taste, as did our ancestors.

Using this Book While on a Paleo Diet

This book has a number of recipes that use the fat of grassfed and pastured animals. While a number of recipes call for butter, you can substitute melted animal fat such as natural lard, beef tallow, duck fat, goose fat, lamb tallow, bison suet, and chicken fat. These fats, if they are from grassfed or pastured animals, give a wonderful flavor to meat. This kind of fat was treasured by every Paleo people, whether it was the peoples studied by Dr. Price or the peoples who lived long ago.

It should be kept in mind that while grassfed meat is much leaner than factory meat, traditional peoples always ate meat with fat, and that is how our bodies are programmed to digest it.

The overwhelming majority of the meat recipes in this book are completely consistent with the Paleo diet. A few hamburger recipes include some bread crumbs, or bread, and/or cheese, as this was a tradition in Europe. But many hamburger recipes do not include these ingredients.

Why I Eat Organic or the Equivalent

I strongly recommend the use of organic ingredients or the equivalent. The reason is simple. I want to eat the most nutritious food I can, and the tastiest food I can. Dr. Weston A. Price discovered that people eating the traditional diet of their ancestors were healthy. All of the food contained in these traditional diets was organic or the equivalent. My health was restored by trying to copy the diets described by Dr. Price. After I restricted my diet to organic or the equivalent, I learned something. The food tasted better — much better.

The Human Body Is Made to Process Natural, Unaltered Food

The methods that the human body uses to sustain, nourish, and rebuild itself are many, and very complex. Nutrients are not processed in isolation, but together. For example, it is now known that an oversupply of one B vitamin can actually cause a deficiency in other B vitamins, because the body is set up to process these nutrients together, the way they are present in food. When you get your nutrients from unaltered food, everything is present that is needed to fully assimilate the nutrients. Our ancestors learned which foods were good to eat, and all of the nutrients and cofactors in those foods are necessary to properly assimilate the nutrients. Our ancestors also learned to combine foods to ensure proper nutrition. While they could not identify specific vitamins, minerals, amino acids, and fatty acids, they knew what to eat. This knowledge was passed from generation to generation, over thousands of years.

Non-Organic Foods Are Altered and Different from Traditional Foods

Modern food-raising practices have altered the very chemistry of food. For example, feeding grain and other non-grass substances to cattle changes the balance of omega-6 to omega-3 fatty acids dramatically, from one-to-one to twenty-to-one. When you eat meat from an animal made to eat grass, your body expects the food to have the proper ratio of omega-6 to omega-3. When the meat does not have the proper ratio, your body is not getting what it is ready to process. We do know that an excess of omega-6 fatty acids can cause inflammation and a host of illnesses.

Vegetables that are sprayed regularly with pesticides, which they absorb, are different from the vegetables humankind has eaten for most of history. Artificially fertilized soil lacks many of the nutrients and minerals present in naturally rich soil, and food grown with artificial fertilizers is different from food grown in naturally rich soil. This forces your body to process substances that either have never existed before (artificial chemicals and pesticides), and/or lack the substances the body expects to find in the food, which may be necessary to properly process and assimilate the nutrients.

GMOs Did Not Exist in Nature and Were Not Eaten by Our Ancestors

None of the healthy peoples studied by Dr. Price ever ate GMOs (Genetically Modified Organisms), because GMOs did not exist at the time. GMOs are plants that are changed in a laboratory, having foreign genes added to them. This presents your body with substances that it does not expect. Most GMO crops are designed with an internal pesticide, or designed to absorb and tolerate huge amounts of pesticides, amounts that might kill a normal plant. The presence of these pesticides in the crops forces your body to deal with a substance it does not expect, or know what to do with.

Modern Science Has Identified Only Some of the Nutrients and Cofactors Needed by Our Bodies

Scientists keep discovering new nutrients as time goes on, including vitamin K2 (which used to be unknown), omega-6 and omega-3 fatty acids (which were also unknown decades ago), and a number of other substances. Vitamin K2, omega-6 and omega-3 fatty acids are very important nutrients. The point is that there are dozens, maybe hundreds of nutrients and substances necessary to process nutrients that are currently unknown. Since conventional agricultural practices change the very chemistry of food, it is impossible to know what nutrients are altered or missing, since an unknown number of nutrients have not yet been discovered.

How to Get All the Nutrients and Cofactors

How can we get all of the nutrients and cofactors we need, if science has not identified all of them? The answer is very simple and I know it works because I have done it. Eating the nutrient-dense foods of our ancestors will give us all the nutrients and cofactors we need. The foods of our ancestors were organic and natural.

What Is the Equivalent of Organic?

The phrase "organic or the equivalent" is often used. "Equivalent" means food that has been raised according to organic food practices, but has not been certified organic by an authorized agency. The food is the same, it just doesn't have the stamp of approval, which can be quite expensive and time-consuming to obtain. Food meets my definition of "organic or the equivalent" if it is raised without the use of pesticides, artificial fertilizers, chemicals, or ionizing radiation. It cannot be GMO. Animals must be raised without the use of growth hormones or antibiotics. I add another requirement to the meat that I eat. The food that is fed to the animals must be species-appropriate, meaning that it is very similar to the natural diet of the animal. For ruminant animals, such as cattle, bison, and lamb, this means 100 percent grassfed.

Organic Food Tastes Much Better

There is another benefit to using ingredients that are organic or the equivalent. They will make your food taste much better. Vegetables grown in good soil, without the use of pesticides or artificial fertilizer, have much more flavor. You can really taste this when you use a recipe that has only a few ingredients. Organic spices grown in good soil that contains the full range of minerals and nutrients have a depth of flavor that is far superior to the conventional varieties. The meat of grassfed animals who have eaten lush green grass, grown in good soil, has a deep, wonderful flavor that no feedlot meat can equal.

Part 2:
How to Barbecue Grassfed Meat and Pastured Pork

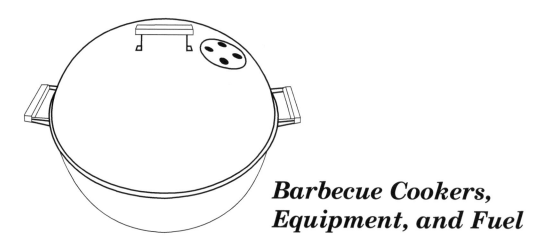

Barbecue Cookers, Equipment, and Fuel

The Right Kind of Barbecue Cooker

There are so many different kinds of barbecue cookers on the market today. They behave differently in cooking, and vary greatly in price and method. The right kind of cooker will make a huge difference in the quality of your barbecue.

Methods Traditional Peoples Used for Cooking with Fire

- They would cook in front of an open fire, fueled by charcoal or wood burned down to coals, though some used more exotic fuels.

- They would also cook their meat in various kinds of ovens fueled with charcoal or wood burned down to coals.

- They would also cook meat in a pit dug in the ground, fueled by burned-down wood or hot rocks.

However, it is just not practical for most people to burn wood down to coals. It takes a lot of skill to cook in front of an open fire, due to wind and weather. Digging a pit is not practical for most people, and is too much work for me. But it is easy to adapt a modern covered charcoal cooker to traditional methods.

My Goal Was to Find a Barbecue Cooker with the Following Qualities:

1. Compatible with the traditional barbecue methods used in this book.

2. Capable of using traditional barbecue fuels.

3. Easy to use. This means easy to control the temperature, and capable of maintaining a steady temperature. It should be easy for the average home cook to use and control.

4. Affordable.

5. Well made of quality materials, nontoxic, and should last a very long time.

6. Reasonably safe when properly used.

The Barbecue Cooker I Chose

There are very few barbecue cookers that meet all of these criteria. The type of barbecue cooker I recommend is a covered kettle grill that uses charcoal.

Why I Use a Covered Kettle Grill:

1. Ideal for the methods in this book, because it works very much like traditional charcoal ovens.

2. Capable of using traditional barbecue fuels like hardwood lump charcoal, and wood burned down to coals.

3. Very easy to use. The vents on the cover make it simple to control the temperature, which can be modified by adjusting the vents.

4. Very affordable and widely available. There are several models of the covered kettle grill, all of which will work.

5. The better models are made of enameled steel, with a stainless steel cooking grill grate. None of these materials give off toxins, and the materials are high quality and durable. With simple care, a high-quality covered kettle grill will last for decades, even longer if you replace worn-out parts.

6. When the manufacturer's safety recommendations are followed, these grills are usually reasonably safe to use.

7. An added convenience is that some of these grills come with a hinged grill grate. A hinged grill grate is important because it makes it much easier and safer to add more fuel to the fire.

There are many grills of this type. Some of them are better than others, but several high-quality models are available.

Why Not Gas?

Most of the barbecue grills in the United States use propane gas as a fuel. I have never cooked on this kind of grill, as it never seemed like barbecue to me. Our ancestors did not cook over propane gas, and it is not traditional in any way. The gas-cooked meat I have sampled lacked the taste and texture of true barbecue. If you do have a gas grill, you can still use these recipes, but it is important to be careful of the temperature. (See *What If You Only Have a Gas Grill?* on page 27.)

Why Not Open Grills?

Food cooked on these kinds of grills can be wonderful, but controlling the temperature and avoiding flare-ups takes considerable skill, which most people do not have. Timing is much harder to predict because these grills are heavily affected by wind and weather. It takes great skill to do anything but the simplest grilling on such a cooker. A covered cooker is so much easier to use and control.

Wood Pellet Grills

I have mixed feelings about this type of grill. These grills use small pellets made of wood (and sometimes other additives) as fuel. The pellets are fed into the fire by an auger, and the temperature can be controlled by adjusting the speed of the auger. I've had a wood pellet grill for many years, along with my covered kettle grill, and have achieved wonderful results with it. If you choose to use such a barbecue, the recipes in this book will work on it.

Some models of wood pellet grills are well made and reliable, and others have been troublesome and unreliable, generating many complaints on the Internet. I suggest that you carefully research the model before you buy it.

It is equally important to research the pellets you use, to make sure that they are made only from clean wood, and do not contain artificial flavors and chemicals. It used to be that the wood pellets were made only from wood that had been ground and washed to remove polluting substances. Unfortunately, technology reared its ugly head, and many wood pellets are now made with artificial chemical flavors and soybean oil, as well as wood.

Ceramic Cookers

Ceramic cookers, traditionally made of baked clay, are very old and have been used as charcoal ovens for thousands of years. They usually use lump charcoal as fuel. Modern ceramic cookers are much more durable than the fireclay that was traditionally used. I do not own a ceramic cooker, and I have no experience with them, at least not yet. However, people who have them seem to love them. I think that the recipes will work with such a cooker, though owners will have to use their own knowledge about how to control the desired temperatures.

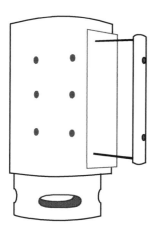

Barbecue Equipment

There are a lot of barbecue accessories sold these days. Most of them are not particularly helpful, but some of them are vital. This is what I use:

Chimney Barbecue Starter

This is a large metal cylinder with a heat shield that has been designed specifically to start barbecue fires. The cylinder is perforated with a number of holes for ventilation. It is one of the best ways I know to light any kind of charcoal. (See *Lighting the Fire* on pages 20 - 22.) There are several versions available. The best ones are made to last. Whatever model you choose should have a good heat shield to protect your hand.

Hinged Grill Grate

A hinged grill grate allows you to raise the part of the grill that is over the fire easily, without having to lift the entire grill grate. This is very useful, because it makes it easy for you to add charcoal, smoking herbs, or wood chunks to the fire.

Two Pairs of Long Tongs

I use one pair to handle the food, and another pair to pick up and move pieces of charcoal or wood.

The tongs should have wooden grips to protect your hands, be sturdily made, and easy to manipulate. They should be made of wood and stainless steel. They should be spring loaded. Since you will be squeezing the tongs to close them around an object, I suggest testing them in the store to make sure you are comfortable with them before buying. It is worthwhile getting a quality product, both for safety and longevity.

Long Handled Barbecue Fork

This should have a long handle, sturdy construction, and a wooden grip. It should be made of stainless steel and wood. It is often easier to turn food by piercing it with the fork and flipping it over. I know that many cookbooks and culinary authorities state that you should never pierce cooking meat with a fork, but this is not a problem when you are cooking grassfed meat.

Drip Pan

A good drip pan is one of the best investments you can make, since all the food in this book is cooked in front of, but not over, the heat source, All the drippings from the cooking meat will fall into the pan, which keeps your barbecue clean and functional. It is important to measure your barbecue before you buy the pan to make sure that the pan will fit. I use a high-sided stainless steel roasting pan, which is cleaned after each use. There are many different kinds of pans available, but the key is to find one that fits in your barbecue and will cover all of the area under which you place the meat.

Basting Brush

A quality basting brush with a long wooden handle makes basting much easier. Many of the recipes call for regular basting of the meat, and this is a very useful tool for this purpose.

Instant-Read Meat Thermometer

This is one of the most useful tools you can have when you are learning how to barbecue. Barbecue is more of an art than a science, and the time that it takes to cook meat (especially longer-cooking recipes) can vary greatly due to such factors as the outside temperature, wind, moisture in the fuel, and other factors. When you are an experienced barbecuer, you will know when the meat is done just by the way it looks and smells. It takes years to develop this kind of intuition, and a good instant-read meat thermometer will be invaluable while you are learning the art.

An instant-read meat thermometer allows you to read the internal temperature of the meat by sticking the pointed end of the thermometer into the meat and reading the temperature on the dial. There are many brands available. Some are very inaccurate. It is worth spending the money to get a quality instant-read meat thermometer that will give you an accurate temperature reading and last.

Heat-Resistant Gloves

It is very important to have a pair of well insulated heat-resistant gloves. You need to protect your hands from the heat of the fire and the coals when you are starting the fire and moving coals around. Again, it is worth it to buy a high-quality pair, as the cheapest ones may not work well.

Fire Extinguisher

A small fire extinguisher is a wise investment. While you can almost always keep a fire under control with normal safety precautions, things can go wrong, and it is best to be prepared.

Choosing the Right Fuel

Choosing the right fuel is crucial for great barbecue. The goal is to use a traditional fuel that will work well in cooking, and is widely available. This would have been a real challenge even 10 years ago. Fortunately, 100 percent hardwood lump charcoal has become widely available. Briquets made from 100 percent hardwood charcoal and a binder such as natural starch have become widely available in the last couple of years, and are also excellent and easier to use.

Wood can be burned down to coals, but this adds a lot of time and effort, so I usually use lump charcoal or briquets made from 100 percent hardwood charcoal and a starch binder. I never use conventional composite charcoal briquets, which is still the most common kind of charcoal.

Traditional Fuels

Traditional peoples used a number of fuels for cooking. This included lump charcoal, wood burned down to coals, small branches, and more unusual types of fuel, such as peat. They most certainly did not use conventional composite charcoal briquets.

The Different Types of Coals

100 Percent Hardwood Lump Charcoal

To me, this is the fuel of choice. It is produced by burning wood in a limited-oxygen environment. The toxins and impurities burn off during production, leaving a clean fuel. Humans have used this fuel for thousands of years. It is easy to use, easy to light, and it can be added to a fire that has already been started. It provides wonderful flavor.

The problem with lump charcoal is that the pieces are different sizes. The size can range from tiny pieces that will fall through the bars of your fire grate to huge pieces that are hard to light and use. This depends mainly on the manufacturer. There is a huge difference between brands in quality. I try to use charcoal that was made from actual wood and branches, rather than industrial waste such as scraps from flooring mills. I prefer brands where most of the pieces range in size from one-half to two times the size of ordinary charcoal briquets. Since these pieces burn well together when in a pile, they work very well for the recipes in this book.

Lump charcoal, especially mesquite charcoal, can give off a lot of sparks when burning, often with a loud crackling noise.

100 Percent Hardwood Charcoal Briquets

This fuel has almost all the benefits of lump charcoal, with the added benefit that all the pieces are the same size, unless broken. They are easier to use in cooking. The other thing that is different is that they contain one binding material, usually some kind of starch.

It is wise to be careful when buying this fuel, because of deceptive labeling. The words "hardwood charcoal" are often used on the labels of conventional composite charcoal briquets. This only means that the wood used in the briquet is hardwood, the briquet can still contain many other ingredients. I make sure the briquets I buy have nothing but hardwood and one binder in the list of ingredients.

Charcoal briquets work in traditional barbecue because they are almost entirely made from lump charcoal, crushed and formed into briquet shapes. I have used this fuel many times, and it works great. It is easier to use than lump charcoal.

Conventional Composite Charcoal Briquets

This is what most people think of and use when they barbecue with charcoal. They were invented by Henry Ford, as a way to make money from the scrap wood from his automobile factories. They contain not only wood, but a number of other substances, including various chemicals, often borates and anthracite coal. Traditional people did not use them, and neither do I.

Wood Coals

Hardwood was often used for cooking by traditional peoples. Logs and branches were burned down until they became glowing coals, and the coals were used for cooking. This can be a very long process, and I rarely bother with it. The wood coals can give great flavor, but I am happy with the flavor I get from 100 percent hardwood charcoal.

There are some issues in using wood coals. First, it takes a lot of wood, which can be expensive. It is crucial not to use wood that contains artificial chemicals, and this can be hard to find from a trusted source. Finally, you need more wood coals, as they do not last as long as charcoal.

The recipes in this book have been tested with 100 percent hardwood lump charcoal and 100 percent hardwood charcoal briquets (with a starch binder).

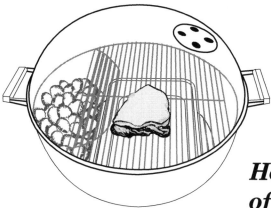

How to Cook in Front of the Fire

Indirect Cooking — the Traditional Way

All of the recipes in this book are designed for the indirect barbecue method, which means that the food is never cooked directly over the fire. Most American grilling is done with the direct method, where the food is cooked directly over the heat source, either gas or charcoal.

Most traditional peoples did all their barbecuing by the indirect method. This has a number of advantages:

1. The food is very unlikely to be scorched or burned;

2. Blinding, choking smoke is not created by fat dripping directly on the fire;

3. Carcinogenic substances are not created by direct high heat or by fat dripping on the fire;

4. It is much easier to control the fire, because you do not have to deal with flames caused by drippings or flare-ups;

5. It is much easier to cook at medium high to low heat with this method;

6. The drippings go right into the drip pan, rather than the coals and the barbecue. This avoids a grease buildup in the barbecue, and the combination of charcoal dust and grease that can bake on to a barbecue. In other words, you have much less chance of a grease fire and the barbecue is much easier to clean.

Lighting the Fire

You cannot have a barbecue without fire, and you cannot have a fire unless you light it.

When I was a child, every barbecuer used some kind of lighter fluid to start the fire, except for those who used gasoline. Neither method was used by traditional peoples.

Traditional peoples usually kept a fire burning somewhere at all times, usually because they did not want to go to the trouble of starting a new one, which was quite difficult, involving rubbing sticks together, or striking flints, or other work-intensive methods. The invention of matches made lighting a fire much easier.

I do not use lighter fluid, and have never used gasoline, which is very dangerous. In fact, there is danger whenever you light a fire, though the danger can be easily controlled by the use of common sense and basic safety precautions.

I also do not want petrochemicals in my food, and certainly do not like the flavor of those substances.

Three Methods to Light a Barbecue Fire

1. **First Method.** This is the method I almost always use.

Fill a chimney barbecue starter that is designed for lighting charcoal about one-half to two-thirds full of lump charcoal, or hardwood charcoal briquets (about 40 charcoal briquets).

Place two large sheets of crumpled newspaper (full sheets, not half sheets) in the bottom of the chimney, then light the newspaper with a match.

This will eventually ignite the coals in the chimney, starting slowly at first, and speeding up as the lit coals light their neighbors, until most of the coals are lit. After about 10 minutes, when there are some flames near the top of the chimney, carefully pour the coals in a pile on one side of the cooker, making sure that all pieces of the coals are out of the chimney. Also, make sure that the bottom vents are completely open. Then place the hot, empty chimney in an out-of-the-way fireproof location.

Some of the coals will inevitably tumble away from the pile and be scattered on the bottom grate of the cooker. Use the tongs to pick up these pieces and add them to the pile, and to adjust the pile of burning coals so there is room for the drip pan (wearing gloves to protect your hands).

At this point, let the pile burn down for 10 minutes or so, until the fire is ready.

The fire is ready when most of the coals are white or red hot in color, and there is little or no flame.

When the fire is ready, place the drip pan next to, but not touching, the coals.

Place the food over the drip pan, never over the fire. Place the cover on the cooker, with the fully open vents directly opposite the fire. This type of indirect cooking is used for all the recipes in this book. *(See illustrations below.)*

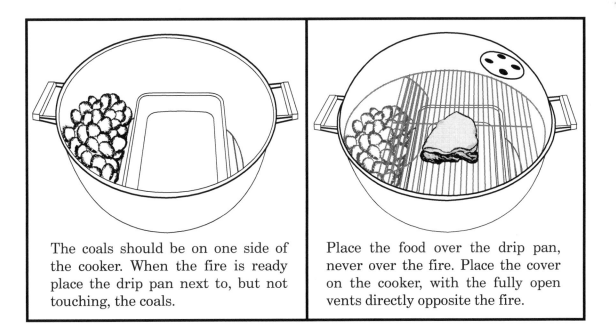

| The coals should be on one side of the cooker. When the fire is ready place the drip pan next to, but not touching, the coals. | Place the food over the drip pan, never over the fire. Place the cover on the cooker, with the fully open vents directly opposite the fire. |

2. **Second Method.** The advantage of the second method is that you do not have to pour burning coals out of a chimney. This method can take a lot longer than using a chimney. This method does not work well with lump charcoal, but works fine with hardwood charcoal briquets.

    Make sure that the bottom vents of the cooker are completely open. Build a pile of unlit charcoal on one side of the cooker, using about 40 hardwood charcoal briquets. Then place several fire starter cubes evenly in and around the pile, then light them with a long match. This will result in the coals lighting, after a while. The lit coals will ignite the unlit coals.

    At this point, let the pile burn down for 10 minutes or so, until the fire is ready.

    The fire is ready when most of the coals are white or red hot in color, and there is little or no flame.

    When the fire is ready, place the drip pan next to, but not touching, the coals.

    Place the food over the drip pan, never over the fire. Place the cover on the cooker, with the fully open vents directly opposite the fire. This type of indirect cooking is used for all the recipes in this book. *(See illustrations on previous page.)*

    Cubes for starting charcoal fires are sold in a number of stores. Some cubes are made of paraffin, and some are made of wood soaked with vegetable oil. Both kinds work.

3. **Third Method.** Make sure that the bottom vents of the cooker are completely open. Build a pile of unlit charcoal on one side of the cooker. Take an electric rod which has been designed for starting fires, and use it according to the manufacturer's instructions. This method is too "modern" for me, but it does work if you have the tool.

    At this point, let the pile burn down for 10 minutes or so, until the fire is ready.

    The fire is ready when most of the coals are white or red hot in color, and there is little or no flame.

    When the fire is ready, place the drip pan next to, but not touching, the coals.

    Place the food over the drip pan, never over the fire. Place the cover on the cooker, with the fully open vents directly opposite the fire. This type of indirect cooking is used for all the recipes in this book. *(See illustrations on previous page.)*

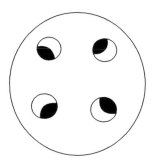

Playing with Fire — How to Control the Temperature

Controlling the temperature of your fire is one of the keys to great traditional barbecue.

Controlling the temperature is quite difficult with an open grill, which is why all the cooking in this book is done with a covered cooker, with the cover on.

In a covered cooker it is much easier to control the temperature, but it requires some skill. This is because the wind and the outside temperature have an effect, even when cooking with a covered cooker. We cannot control the weather, but we can adjust to it.

The recipes in this book often tell you to use "medium high heat," "medium low heat," "low heat," or "reduce the heat as low as possible." How do you do this?

You control the temperature in a covered cooker by adjusting the vents on the top of the cover. The vents on the bottom of the cooker are usually kept fully open, except when you want a really low temperature.

You can also control the temperature by the size of the fire, but the recipes in this book are all designed to work with a medium amount of charcoal, the amount necessary to fill up one-half to two-thirds of a chimney barbecue starter, or about 40 hardwood charcoal briquets. I have found it is easier to adjust the temperature this way, as a big fire requires more oxygen, burns hotter, and is harder to adjust.

Medium High Heat

When all the top and bottom vents are fully open, the fire is getting as much oxygen as possible, which causes the fire to burn hotter. This is the normal setting for "medium high heat."

The heat is medium high because the food is cooked in front of, not over, the fire, and because only a moderate amount of charcoal is used.

On a day that is very windy, or hot, or both, keeping the vents fully open can result in a fire that is too hot. Closing the top vents slightly, to where they are three-quarters to seven-eighths open, is the way to solve this.

Medium Low Heat

Adjusting the top vents until they are half-closed is the way to achieve medium low heat. On a windy or hot day, closing the top vents somewhat more may be needed. On a cold day, opening the vents a little more may be advisable.

Low Heat

Closing all the top and bottom vents until they are only one-quarter inch open is the way to achieve low heat.

Reducing the Heat as Low as Possible

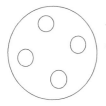

Reducing the heat as low as possible means closing all the top and bottom vents until they are completely closed. This may cause the fire to really die down, but that is exactly what is intended.

If Your Cooker Has a Built-In Thermometer

There are some cookers that come with thermometers and even have a temperature gauge like an oven that you can set to a particular temperature. If your cooker has a built-in thermometer:

Medium High Heat	350 to 400 degrees
Medium Low Heat	250 to 300 degrees
Low Heat	200 to 250 degrees

"Reduce the Heat as Low as Possible" means setting the temperature control to the lowest setting.

Ways to Test the Temperature

A classic way to test the temperature of your fire is to hold your hand a couple of inches above the top vents. If you can hold your hand there for only 2 seconds before it gets too hot, the temperature is medium high. If you can hold your hand there for 4 seconds before it gets too hot, the temperature is medium low. If you can hold your hand there for 6 seconds before it gets too hot, the temperature is low. If you can hold your hand there indefinitely, the fire is out. If it is windy, this method does not work, as the wind will blow the heat away.

Remember when I said that barbecue is an art, not a science? This is one of the areas where the art comes in. The exact adjustment of the vents to control the temperature on your cooker, in your backyard, with the weather of the day, is something you will have to learn with experience. Eventually, you will get the knack of knowing your cooker, and how hot it cooks when the vents are in a particular position, and what adjustments you need to make for weather. The above suggestions for closing the vents are suggestions rather than definite instructions.

This is actually much easier than it sounds. All you have to do is pay attention to what happens. You will quickly learn how your cooker responds to adjustments just by cooking with it.

Don't worry about ruining the meat, because a meat thermometer will be used to test doneness, and this works well. Remember, we are looking for a general temperature range, rather than an exact temperature, and the recipes will work within that range.

If you are cooking a roast that requires a long time, it is wise to add some coals to the fire. This is really easy with a hinged grill grate, which is why I recommend one. After an hour or so, add two handfuls of lump charcoal or hardwood briquets to the fire. You can add more than this if you think it is necessary. Check every hour to see if you need to add more.

One of the many nice things about this natural fuel is that you can add it unlit to a burning fire, as there are no chemical additives that have to be burned off first.

Start with the guidelines above, learn your cooker, and you will soon control the temperature of your barbecue like the artist you will become.

When Is It Done?
Developing Your Barbecue Instinct

Barbecue is more of an art than a science. Every fire you light will be different in its composition, heat, duration, smokiness, and other factors. The cooking process is also affected by the outside temperature, the wind, the humidity, the elevation, and many other factors.

You usually have no control over these variables, and they all have an effect on how long it takes to cook your meat. All of the recipes in this book include suggested cooking times, but you may find that the actual cooking time is longer or shorter than the recommended time, because of these variables.

As you gain experience, you will develop a sense of how fast the meat is cooking, when to adjust the temperature, when it is time to turn the meat, when it needs basting, and when it is done.

You can develop this sense faster by paying careful attention to your cooker and the meat cooking on it. Notice the color of the meat, how it smells, and the heat of the cooker. Pay attention to how the meat looks when it is done, and to everything else that happens during the cooking process. Your mind will analyze this information, store it, add to it, and you will reach a state where you just know exactly what to do when you barbecue.

It takes some time to reach this state of knowing, however, and there are some immediate steps you can take to know when the meat is done.

Tips for Knowing When It's Done

One of the most effective things you can do is to buy a high-quality instant-read meat thermometer. This thermometer can be inserted inside the meat at any time during the cooking process and will give you the internal cooking temperature of the meat.

I cannot emphasize enough how important it is to get a high-quality thermometer. The lower quality versions will not give you an accurate reading and can easily cause you to ruin the meat.

The following charts will give you a guide for the doneness of meat by temperature: I should mention that the government recommends different temperatures, and it is your choice as to which recommnedations to follow. These charts were developed for grassfed and pastured meats, and I make no recommendations as to safety.

Doneness for Grassfed Beef	
Rare	115 – 120 degrees
Medium Rare	121 – 130 degrees
Medium	131 – 140 degrees
Well Done	141 degrees and up

Doneness for Grassfed Bison

Rare	110 – 120 degrees
Medium Rare	121 – 125 degrees
Medium	126 – 130 degrees

Bison is at its best when rare, or medium rare.

Doneness for Grassfed Lamb

Rare	125 – 130 degrees
Medium Rare	131 – 140 degrees
Medium	141 – 150 degrees
Well Done	151 degrees and up

Doneness for Pastured Pork

The temperature to which pastured pork should be cooked varies greatly, depending on the cut.

Pork must be cooked to at least 140 degrees, to avoid the danger of trichinosis.

- More expensive cuts such as loin, rib, sirloin, and tenderloin, are best at a temperature of about 150 to 160 degrees.

- Classic barbecue cuts, such as spareribs and pork shoulder, can be absolutely wonderful at higher temperatures, even up to 180 degrees, if cooked slowly on a barbecue for a long time.

However, the meat thermometer will not work for steaks, chops, or other thin cuts of meat. Another way of judging temperature is to stick a metal skewer or roasting fork into the meat, withdraw it, and test the temperature of the metal with your finger. If it is cool, the meat is not ready. If it is somewhat warm, it is rare. If it is slightly hot, it is medium rare. If it is hot, it is medium. Once you have enough experience at comparing the temperature of the metal with the doneness of the meat, you will know how done the meat is, according to your standards.

The ease with which the skewer or fork goes into the meat will give you a good idea of its tenderness. Steaks can toughen if they are cooked too long.

Many cooking authorities will tell you to never pierce the meat while cooking, or you will "lose valuable juices." I have never found this to be true for grassfed meat. Yes, sometimes some juice comes out, but it does not hurt the taste or juiciness of the meat.

If the meat looks done to you, or seems to be cooking faster than you expect, do not hesitate to check the temperature.

What If You Only Have a Gas Grill?

I learned from a reader of my Facebook page for *Tender Grassfed Meat*, that some towns only allow the use of gas grills (not charcoal grills) in apartment complexes. While I am a huge advocate of wood and charcoal fires, and the book was designed for such fires, a gas grill can be used for most recipes. This is done by using the gas grill to simulate the use of a traditional fire.

The recipes in this book were not tested with a gas grill, for two simple reasons. Gas grills are not traditional; and I do not have a gas grill.

However, most of the recipes in this book can be made on a gas grill, though they will lack the flavor given by charcoal and wood. Some people use a small box with wood chips when using a gas grill.

The main principles to keep in mind are:

- The cooking must be done with indirect heat.

- The cooking temperature must range from moderate to low, depending on the recipe.

- Indirect cooking on a gas grill is done by putting the meat on a rack set into a drip pan, and placing the rack and drip pan over a burner that is turned off. One of the other burners is used to provide the heat source.

- The burner that is on should be adjusted to medium, which is the equivalent of "medium high" as referred to in the recipes. If the recipe calls for "medium low," the burner should be set to low.

- There are many kinds of gas grills, with differing numbers of burners, and you will have to experiment with your grill to reach a setting that creates the specified temperatures. Some of the larger grills may require the use of more than one burner. Keep in mind that medium high is roughly 350 degrees, and medium low is roughly 250 degrees.

- Cooking should be done with the cover on, just like it is with a charcoal grill, as the recipes were all designed for this.

Traditional Barbecue Flavors

The Ancient Art of Basting

There is an old barbecue method that has been used for thousands of years, but is largely abandoned today. The method is very easy to use, and it improves the flavor and tenderness of barbecued meats immensely.

The method is basting. This involves nothing more complicated than making a baste from a few simple ingredients, and brushing the meat with it. The meat is brushed with the baste before cooking and brushed a few times during cooking. So simple, and yet, the improvement in taste and flavor is immense. It is important to choose the right ingredients, especially the secret ingredient.

Why did people stop basting? My own experience provides an answer. When I first started barbecuing, I remembered that my favorite barbecue restaurant used to boast about its secret baste. I tried a recipe for a baste I found in a modern cookbook, used it once, and never basted again, until I learned how to cook grassfed meat, decades later.

Why did I stop basting? I used a modern recipe that was mostly wine, fruit juice, a long list of spices, and some modern vegetable oil, probably corn oil. The baste did almost nothing to improve the meat. That is why I gave up on it. I did not know that the baste was missing the secret ingredient.

The secret ingredient makes all the difference, making the meat tender, enhancing its flavor, giving the meat an almost glossy coating which keeps it from drying out, and making it smell even better as it cooks.

What Is the Secret Ingredient?

The secret ingredient is melted animal fat. That's right, melted animal fat. Butter, unhydrogenated natural pork lard, grassfed beef tallow, duck fat, ham fat, chicken fat, even grassfed bison fat. Animal fat. The most feared and demonized of foods is what traditional peoples from the Native Americans to the Europeans used as the main ingredient of their bastes. Because of the pathological fear of animal fat in the modern world, people stopped using it.

The healthy peoples studied by Dr. Weston A. Price all ate plenty of natural animal fat, and they were all free from chronic disease. Modern research has shown that the fat from grassfed and pastured animals is a vital nutrient that improves the natural functioning of the body. It is one of the oldest foods, and our bodies know how to digest and use it.

Most of the bastes in this book are based on some kind of animal fat as the main ingredient. While you may never have seen a modern recipe for a baste like this, you will not believe how good it will make the meat taste. These bastes are easy to make and easy to use. Best of all is the fact that they keep the meat moist and make it tender, while adding incredible flavor.

The sparerib recipes in this book depend on these bastes for success, and these ribs are so good that you will be astonished when you bite into them.

The basted, barbecued roasts are in a class by themselves when it comes to depth of flavor and primal goodness.

There is a reason why old-time bastes were used for thousands of years, all over the world. They make the food so tender and delicious.

Herbal Smoke

The Ancient Greeks would roast lamb and goats as a sacrifice to their gods, to placate the wrath of the gods and avoid disaster. The Greek gods were believed to be cruel, and enjoyed tormenting humankind. But even these cruel immortals were vulnerable to the joy of barbecued meats. These meats were always roasted in front of fires made aromatic with sweet smelling herbs, such as thyme, rosemary, bay, and myrtle. The tempting smell of aromatic smoke and roasting meat would make the gods hungry, and please them.

These ancient people knew something about barbecue, because the smoke from aromatic herbs can give incredible flavor to meat. Many other traditional peoples would throw some herbs or aromatic wood on the fire when roasting meat. I decided to try this. Putting some herbs on the fire was one of the tastiest decisions I ever made.

Three Methods to Add Herbs to the Fire

1. **First Method.** The herbs can be soaked in water for an hour or so, drained, and a handful or two can be added to the fire once the fire is ready. While soaked herbs take longer to burn, and produce smoke for a longer period of time, the water will reduce the temperature of the fire.

2. **Second Method.** The herbs can be added to the fire dry. They will burst into flames almost immediately, and will quickly burn into the coals. Covering the cooker will stop the flames, even with the vents open, and there will be some aromatic smoke. The herbs will burn into the coals and provide a subtle but delicious flavor as the meat cooks.

3. **Third Method.** This is my favorite method, which gives the best flavor of all, in my opinion. I choose a recipe that includes plenty of aromatic herbs in the marinade. After I brush the herbs and vegetables off the meat, I reserve them. When the fire is ready, just after I put the meat on the grill, I add the herbs and vegetables to the fire and quickly close the lid. The herbs and vegetables have been coated by olive oil and meat juices, and they give absolutely incredible flavor to the meat. Since the meat has been marinated in the same ingredients, the smoke complements the flavor of the marinated meat perfectly, providing an incredible depth of flavor.

Whichever method you choose, it is important not to smother the fire. A handful is the right amount, though you can use less. After the herbs have completely burned down, and there is no more herbal smoke, you can add another handful for a truly intense smoky herbal flavor.

Best Herbs for Smoke Flavor

The best herbs for smoke flavor are rosemary, thyme, sage, bay leaf, and Mediterranean myrtle, which is my favorite. Try to get these herbs with the stems, as the woody stems give great flavor. You can use these herbs fresh or dried. The dried herbs burn faster and give a more intense flavor, but the fresh herbs are wonderful as well.

It is important to only use organic (or the equivalent) herbs for this purpose. The reason is that herbs that have been sprayed with pesticides will have the flavor of the pesticide to a certain degree, especially when burning, and I prefer the pure flavors of the natural herb. I also do not want to breathe the smoke of burning pesticides, or have pesticides in my food.

Using herbal smoke to flavor barbecued meats is one of the oldest flavoring techniques, and is utterly delicious.

Wood Smoke

Traditional peoples generally tried to avoid smoke and flames when they were barbecuing. They would let the wood or charcoal burn until the flames were gone, and little or no smoke was produced. Meat that tasted too much of smoke was described as having a "noisome stink," and was the mark of a poor cook. While wood smoking was common, it was done at very low temperatures to preserve meat or fish, not to cook them. I have followed this tradition in developing the main cooking method used in this book.

However, the United States of America has a tradition of enjoying barbecued meats with a heavier smoky flavor. I must confess that I often love this kind of smoky taste. When I want a smokier taste in my meat, I add some wood chunks to the fire as it starts. Here is how I do it.

Selecting the Wood Chunks

The type of wood used is very important. The wood should be natural, unprocessed hardwood. The wood should not have been sprayed with pesticides.

The wood should be cut into chunks, with a two inch square being the ideal size, though the chunks will never be exact. Chunks with a lot of bark should be avoided, as the bark can give a very bitter taste to the meat. Wood chunks made specifically for barbecue are widely sold in the U.S., though you could cut your own, especially if you are handy with an ax. The size of the chunks will vary, even in the same bag.

Many kinds of wood are sold for this purpose. Some my favorites are:

*   Mesquite
*   Hickory
*   Oak
*   Pecan
*   Apple
*   Cherry

I have used and enjoyed all of these, and they all give a different taste to the meat.

Using Wood Chunks in a Charcoal Fire

Most bags of barbecue wood chunks will instruct you to soak the chunks in water before using them, so their smoke will last longer. I never soak the wood chunks. It seems wrong, somehow, to put wet wood on a fire. I doubt very much that any of our ancestors did this.

I use anywhere from one to four wood chunks for a charcoal fire. The bigger the chunk, the longer it will take to burn down, and the hotter it will be. Using a larger amount of chunks will result in a hotter and smokier fire.

I place a few hardwood coals on the bottom of a chimney barbecue starter, then add the chunks. I cover the chunks with the rest of the hardwood charcoal I would normally use, and light the fire. When it is time to empty the can, I use tongs to surround the chunks with coals. The chunks may still be flaming, and it may take a few minutes for the flames to burn out. When all the wood is black or grey, covering the barbecue with the vents open should end the flames.

Wood chunks make for a hotter fire, so your food may be readier sooner, or you may want to cool the fire by adjusting the vents. You should be able to see some smoke coming from the vents as the meat cooks, which will give a deep smoky flavor to your barbecue.

Wood chips for smoking are also sold. These do not work in a chimney barbecue starter, because of their small size, and have to be added to the coals after the coals are poured out of the chimney, and piled into a firebed. Then the wood chips have to burn out. I find chunks easier to use.

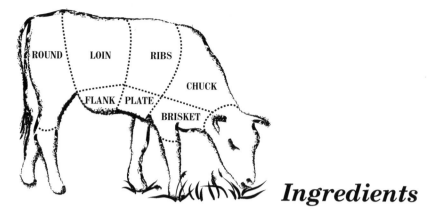

Ingredients

Quality Matters

The quality of the ingredients you use in barbecue is one of the most important factors in the quality of the finished meal. There is an old saying "You cannot make a silk purse out of a sow's ear."

The same is true in cooking. You cannot make nourishing, delicious food out of poor ingredients.

I have read literally hundreds of old cookbooks in learning how to recreate traditional cooking methods. All of the authors stressed the importance of getting the best ingredients.

Our ancestors understood this. They would go to great efforts to buy the best quality food they could afford. It was much easier for them, because they lived in a time where it was easy to tell the quality of food just by examining it. This is no longer true, because technology has enabled manufacturers to disguise the poor quality of many ingredients. The use of packaging, marketing, chemicals, nanites, irradiation, and many other techniques have made it very difficult to judge the quality of food.

The only solution I have come up with is to only buy products that are organic or the equivalent, from a seller I trust. You can still tell the quality of unmodified, unprocessed ingredients just by examining them.

Just because something is certified "organic" does not mean it is good. Some organic products are great, but others are terrible. You have to examine the product and its ingredients to be sure.

Much of what I buy is not certified organic, but is the equivalent of organic, in that it is produced without chemicals, without drugs, and without modified ingredients.

I encourage you to use the best ingredients you can afford. This will make a huge difference in the taste and nutritional value of your food.

Why Organic and Natural?

I call for organic vegetables, fruits, and spices in all of my recipes. You can also use the equivalent of organic, which is food that has been grown by organic methods, but has not received organic certification. Foods that are the equivalent of organic are just as good, sometimes better. Foods that are the equivalent of organic are usually less expensive than foods that have received organic certification.

Organic foods are usually considerably more expensive, spoil much faster, and are often harder to find. So why use them? The simple answer is because they taste better and are healthier.

Organic foods behave differently in cooking than the so-called conventional foods. You will not get the same results if you try to substitute conventional ingredients for the organic ones. Conventional vegetables often contain pesticides and chemicals intended to prolong their shelf life, are almost always grown through the use of artificial fertilizers, and have been designed for their appearance and shelf life. These characteristics have an impact on taste and nutrition. U.S. government agencies have stated that conventional fruits and vegetables are safe for human consumption.

I consider the best source of nutritional information to be the Weston A. Price Foundation, which maintains an excellent website full of vital information about nutrition and health. I highly recommend that you visit their website at www.westonaprice.org.

Selecting Grassfed Meat

First, make sure the meat is grassfed and grass-finished.

Just about every cow, bison, and lamb is fed grass at some point in its life. The meat we call grassfed is also grass-finished, which means that it is not finished on grains and other feed, and does not go to a feedlot.

The meat does not need to be certified organic to be grassfed. The animals should be fed living grass and meadow plants right in the pasture when the weather allows, and dried grass and forage in the winter. If they are fed anything else, they are not grassfed. (It's fine if calves and lambs get milk from their mothers.) The animals should not be given growth hormones, antibiotics, or any kind of growth promotant. The point is that the animals should be eating what they have been designed to eat: grass, meadow plants, and dried grass, and that's about it.

It should be understood that meat can be certified organic without being grassfed, and that most of the "organic" beef, bison, and lamb sold in the U.S. is fed soybeans, grains, and other substances that are not grass.

About Grassfed Fat

Grassfed beef is much leaner than factory beef. The best grassfed beef has some marbling. Marbling is the tiny flecks of white fat that you should be able to see in the meat. The more marbling, the more tender and tasty the beef. It should be noted that fat from grassfed beef is extremely healthy, as well as flavorful. A nice fat cap on a roast or steak adds great flavor, and really helps in cooking.

Grassfed bison does not have marbling. Neither does grassfed lamb. A fat cap for lamb and bison really helps, both for flavor and cooking.

Pastured Pork

This refers to pork that is raised by traditional methods, from heritage breeds that have plenty of fat. The pigs are often allowed to roam woodlands (which is their natural habitat), root through harvested orchards, and are often fed the skim milk left over from making cream and butter. Pigs are omnivores, and it is completely natural for them to eat meat, insects, grains, and fruits along with plants. Pastured pigs are not fed GMO feeds full of soy.

Cooking Oil

Most of the cooking oils used today are a product of modern food technology. They were not eaten for most of history. Modern cooking oils do not tenderize meat, or add good flavor to food. They are not used in this book.

It is crucial to use only unfiltered olive oil for marinating, because it contains the enzymes that help tenderize the meat.

I only use four traditional vegetable oils for marinating and cooking:

1. **Extra Virgin Olive Oil, Unfiltered and Organic.** This is the oil of choice for marinating meat. It lubricates and tenderizes meat without making it mushy. It carries other marinade flavors deep into the meat. The oil must be unfiltered, as filtering removes the very part of the oil (lipids and enzymes) that tenderizes the meat. My favorite brand is sold by Chaffin Family Orchards, made from trees grown on land that has never been sprayed with chemicals.

2. **Extra Virgin Olive Oil, Organic.** This oil is great for all cooking purposes, such as sautéing, browning, or frying. It will not tenderize meat, as the lipids and enzymes have been removed by filtering.

3. **Extra Virgin Coconut Oil, Organic.** This oil is very good for cooking purposes. It does have a distinctive flavor, which can really change the taste of meat. Since I prefer marinades that bring out the natural taste of the meat, I rarely use it in marinades.

4. **Unrefined Toasted Sesame Oil, Organic.** This oil has a strong, nutty, aromatic flavor. It is often used to flavor Asian dishes. This flavor goes particularly well with beef. I use it in barbecue marinades for Asian-style dishes.

A number of traditionally made European olive oils are the equivalent of organic.

Oils to Avoid

The wrong oil can ruin any dish. All modern vegetable oils should be avoided. The following non-traditional oils ruin the taste of meat, in my opinion, and I never use them:

Canola Oil

Corn Oil

Cottonseed Oil

Soybean Oil

It does not matter if some of these modern vegetable oils are organic, or cold pressed, or expeller pressed, I still avoid them.

Animal Fat

The very words "animal fat" invokes fear in most people. This fear has been created by a huge and pervasive marketing campaign. The truth of the matter is that we need to eat fat to be healthy, and the very best fat you can eat is the right kind of animal fat and fish fat. Traditional peoples knew this and ate huge quantities of good animal fat. This is explained in detail at the website of the Weston A. Price Foundation.

Traditional peoples almost always used animal fat to flavor and baste their grassfed or wild meat. These fats keep the meat moist and tender, and give it incredible flavor. Butter is a traditional animal fat that has been used for basting and flavoring in hundreds of cuisines.

Natural animal fats include: the fat of grassfed animals, including milk fats like butter and ghee; the fat from pastured pork, including natural, unhydrogenated lard and bacon; and the fat of naturally raised poultry such as chickens and ducks.

Pastured Butter

It is important to use only the right kind of butter. Most of the butters available have been made from factory milk. They are full of water, which causes them to spatter when cooking. Many of these butters are mixed with vegetable oils such as canola oil, and have various chemicals added to them.

The right kind of butter comes from organic milk. It should be pure butter, with no added oils, chemicals, or water. However, just being organic is not enough. The cows should be raised on pasture. Pastured butter tastes much better, and melts and cooks without spattering. It is ideal for basting any meat.

Pastured butter was what our ancestors used.

Beef Fat

Beef fat is one of the tastiest and most nutritious fats you can use, as long as it comes from grassfed cattle.

The best place for beef fat to be is right on the meat as you cook it. A one-quarter inch fat cap will do wonders for flavor and tenderness. (Thicker is better.) Unfortunately, many producers super-trim their meat, slicing off the very fat that provides flavor and tenderness. Replacing this fat is often desirable for barbecuing. The best replacement for beef fat is — beef fat. Fortunately, many producers sell beef fat in the form of suet and tallow.

Beef Suet is composed of little pieces of fat. This is usually sold in large containers, but you can freeze what you do not use, and thaw as necessary.

Beef Tallow is beef fat and/or beef suet which has been melted and strained. In its solid form, it is hard and brittle. My refrigerator always has a jar of beef tallow.

Whether suet or tallow, beef fat has many uses, which include replacing a trimmed-off fat cap, basting, roasting, frying, and sautéing.

Finally, you can substitute beef tallow for butter in any recipe that calls for butter.

Lamb Fat

Grassfed lamb fat is sold in the form of suet or lamb tallow. It is less versatile than beef fat or pork lard, but can provide wonderful flavor when properly used. Lamb fat is excellent for replacing a trimmed-off fat cap, and for basting.

Lamb fat can have an unpleasant, greasy texture when it congeals, so food cooked with lamb fat should be served hot. Lamb fat has a low smoking point, and can smell bad when it gets too hot. Lamb fat should be used for frying only at low to medium temperatures.

Lard

Lard was once the most common cooking fat in America. (It is still the most popular cooking fat in much of the world, including China.) The reputation of lard was destroyed by a clever marketing campaign. Most people switched to hydrogenated oils and vegetable oils. It is now almost impossible to find natural, unhydrogenated lard in any grocery store.

Hydrogenated lard (which is usually all that is available) should never be used in cooking because it has had its very structure chemically altered — which ruins its taste.

Lard should come from naturally raised pigs, and must be unhydrogenated. Lard is excellent for basting, frying, sautéing, stir-frying, providing fat to meats, adding flavor, and baking. It has a soft, spreadable consistency that makes it easy to work with. It behaves well in the pan, and can withstand high temperatures without breaking down.

Bacon

Bacon is used in several recipes in this book for its fat and flavor. I use only uncured bacon, because I am wary of chemical preservatives, such as nitrates.

Lean bacon is an absurdity. The main purpose of using bacon is for its fat, which aids in cooking and provides great flavor. Be sure to inspect each package carefully to make sure that the bacon strips are mostly fat. Lean bacon just won't work in these recipes.

If you do not want to use bacon, you can substitute butter or beef tallow.

Salt

The kind of salt you use will have a dramatic effect on your cooking, not to mention your health.

There are those who say all salt is sea salt, and that there is no difference. While it is true that all salt originated at some time from the sea, there is a tremendous difference in how it is processed, and what else is included in the salt. This makes a huge difference in taste, and how the salt affects the food.

Refined salt is bleached with chemicals, and has had just about all of the minerals that are in natural salt removed. This results in a product so bitter that sugar or some other sweetener is added to make it palatable. Manufacturers of refined salt often add other ingredients, such as aluminum products and artificial iodine. The effect of these refined salts on the cooking process, not to mention taste, is terrible.

Unrefined salt that has been harvested by traditional methods retains the natural minerals, lacks artificial additives, has a better effect on food, and just tastes better. There are many varieties.

Since these varieties are gathered in different parts of the world, and naturally include various minerals and other substances, there can be a dramatic variation in taste. There can also be quite a difference in color. Some salts are grey, some are different shades of white, one is even red. My favorite salt is unrefined sea salt.

This salt is moist, grey in color, contains trace minerals, and has a wonderful flavor. It has large crystals, which I usually crush with a rolling pin when seasoning meat, so that the salt is more evenly distributed and absorbed. These salts are considerably more expensive than factory salt, but the differences in taste, health, and cooking qualities are worth it. If you substitute an inferior salt, you will have inferior results.

Spices and Condiments

This book uses traditional flavorings in the recipes. Since these traditional flavors were created with organic ingredients, I consider it important to use herbs, spices, and condiments that are organic, or the equivalent. Organic herbs and spices have much more flavor.

Fresh Herbs

These should, without exception, be organic, or the equivalent. It is best to have these locally grown, as they do not travel well. Sage, rosemary, thyme, and Italian parsley are the ones I use most often, though I also use oregano, marjoram, cilantro, and basil.

Dried Herbs

Good quality dried herbs can add wonderful flavor. I use only organic, or the equivalent.

Spices

I only buy organic spices because the flavor is so much better. I also use some spices from different areas of Europe, such as Spain and Portugal, which while not labeled organic, have been produced by traditional methods, and grown in good soil.

Vegetables, Herbs, and Fruits

Fresh vegetables and fresh herbs can really improve the flavor and even the tenderness of grassfed meat. They are a crucial ingredient in many of my marinades.

Unfortunately, most of the vegetables available in the U.S. lack flavor. This is because most of them have been modified for purposes that have nothing to do with nutrition or taste. My solution is to buy only those vegetables, fruits, and herbs that are organic or the equivalent.

Buy Local

It is best if you can buy from a local farmer who raises organic produce, or from a grocer who sells produce from local farmers. I ask you to join me, and many others, in supporting small farmers and small producers. We'll all eat better, tastier, and healthier if we do.

About Grassfed Meat, Pastured Pork, and Good Fats

Grassfed Beef Tastes Better

Grassfed beef tastes much better, is more tender, and works much better for barbecue than conventional beef. Many people would disagree with this, claiming that grassfed beef is "tough" and does not taste good. This can be true, but only if the grassfed beef is cooked improperly. Our ancestors, for most of history, ate only grassfed beef, and developed many delicious ways to barbecue it. This book teaches traditional methods modified for modern times.

There is a great difference between grassfed beef and conventional beef.

Conventional Beef

While the cattle used for conventional beef usually start out on grass, everything changes when they are moved to a feedlot to fatten up. Conventional cattle are fed a diet that is not natural for cattle. This diet consists of processed feed made out of soy, corn, and other ingredients. This unnatural diet causes the very composition of the meat to change. For example, cattle raised exclusively on grass have a ratio of omega-3 fatty acids to omega-6 fatty acids that ranges from one-to-one to one-to-four. After a typical time in a feedlot, the ratio changes to one-to-twenty, which is completely unbalanced.

The meat of such cattle has very little flavor, with almost all the flavor being in the fat. Conventional beef has the same bland, boring taste, no matter where it is raised. This means it requires a lot of seasoning to be tasty.

Conventional beef is quite watery, and shrinks greatly in cooking as the water is cooked off. Because of the water, conventional beef is often cooked over direct high heat to deal with the water. Many studies have linked the barbecuing of meat over direct high heat to the formation of carcinogens.

Conventional cattle are almost always given artificial growth hormones, to make them grow much faster than normal. Conventional cattle are also given antibiotics regularly, even when they are not sick, because antibiotics make them grow faster. While the unnaturally fast growth created by these chemicals increases profits, it does nothing for the taste or nutritional value of the meat. Health concerns have been raised about the use of these substances.

Grassfed Beef

Grassfed and grass-finished beef are fed nothing but the living grass and meadow plants that are the natural food of cattle, sometimes with mineral supplements. Hay, which is dried grass, is fed to these cattle in the winter, when they do not have access to pasture.

Grassfed and grass-finished beef has a deep beefy flavor. This flavor comes in many variations, depending on the breed of cattle, the forage they eat, the contentment of the individual cow, the age of the animal, and many other factors. The variation in flavors can easily be tasted, and provides the consumer with a wonderful variety of delicious tastes.

The natural flavor of good grassfed beef is so outstanding that it needs very little in the way of seasoning or marinades.

Grassfed beef is not watery, and will shrink much less in cooking, giving you more meat to eat, instead of water that cooks off. Grassfed barbecue will be ruined by cooking over direct high heat, and grassfed meat cooks beautifully at medium and low temperatures, in front of, but not over, the heat source. Indirect cooking at medium high heat or less avoids the barbecuing over direct high heat that has been linked to the formation of carcinogens in meat by many studies. It is actually much easier to grill meat this way, as you do not have to worry about leaping flames and scorched meat.

Grassfed and grass-finished beef comes from cattle that are not given artificial growth hormones or antibiotics. While the government allows these substances to be used in cattle raised for grassfed beef, I have never found a grassfed rancher who uses growth hormones or daily antibiotics. Some grassfed producers will use antibiotics on a sick animal.

Grassfed beef is the same beef humanity has been eating for thousands of years, containing all the nutrients and cofactors our bodies expect to find when they digest the meat. The composition of the meat is the same as it has been for many thousands of years.

Grassfed Bison Is the Best

Bison are huge, magnificent creatures designed to roam the vast plains of North America and to graze on the native grasses. The meat of these noble animals has a wonderful flavor of its own, with a sweet, clean taste found in no other meat. I have found that bison meat is one of the most energizing and rejuvenating foods I have ever eaten.

Bison Thrive on Pasture

Once, more than 60 million bison roamed the Great Plains of the United States and Canada. These herds were so vast that it would take them days to pass a single spot. The bison ate the native plants and grasses, growing strong, healthy, and numerous. A number of Native American nations lived off the bison, getting almost all of their food from these healthy animals.

The Native Americans who lived off the bison were noted for their strength, endurance, physical beauty, intelligence, and robust good health. The bison thrived on the native grasses, and the people thrived off the bison. But this happy balance was doomed.

Industry Almost Exterminated the Bison

In the nineteenth century, the clothing industry discovered that bison hides were perfect for making warm clothing, coats, hats, and other apparel. They paid buffalo hunters to use specially designed buffalo rifles to slaughter the bison for their hides. This was made economically viable by the railroads, which could cheaply transport huge numbers of bison hides to the factories. The bison were slaughtered by the millions. The professional buffalo hunters would take only the hides and leave the rest of the bison to rot. This mass slaughter of the bison was encouraged by American industry and government, as a way to remove the main food source of the Native Americans living on the Great Plains, and as a way to clear the land of bison so it could be used for farming. By the end of the nineteenth century, there were less than 600 bison left alive in the United States. Over 60 million had been slaughtered for their hides.

The Bison Return

Fortunately, efforts were made to finally protect the bison. Their numbers increased, and bison were once again used for food. Some creative ranchers learned how to raise bison and increase their numbers — and soon there was a substantial increase in the number of bison. These early ranchers raised and finished the bison on grass. They found that bison eating their native grasses were sturdy, healthy, hardy animals, who provided wonderful meat. However, raising bison naturally required a great deal of knowledge and effort on the part of the ranchers, and it took a while to raise bison for meat. Some bison ranchers began to feed grains to their bison. These grain-fed bison grew and matured faster. However, bison were never intended to eat grain, and the very composition of their meat and fat changed.

How to Make Bison Taste Like Beef

A bison industry was formed. The industry decided that they would sell more bison if they could make bison taste like beef. The industry then developed ways of feeding unnatural diets to bison that were designed to make them grow faster, and have their meat taste like beef. The industry succeeded completely. Grain-finished bison tastes just like grain-finished beef. The sweet, clean taste of grassfed bison was lost.

Bison were meant to roam the prairie, eating the native grasses, not to be confined in a feedlot, eating food that is unnatural to them.

The Grassfed Solution

Fortunately, there are some bison ranchers who keep their animals on the pasture, and do not feed them grains, or send them to feedlots. These animals are healthy, and are free to roam the prairies as they were designed to do. Their meat is sweet, and nourishing, with the wonderful clean taste that is equaled by no other meat. This is the only kind of bison meat that I will eat. It is absolutely delicious, especially when barbecued.

Grassfed Lamb Is Delicious

Lamb is very unpopular in the United States. When I mention lamb to my friends, most of them say "I don't like lamb." This dislike is so intense that most of them will not even taste it.

Yet lamb is extremely popular and valued in all of Europe, the former Soviet Union, the Middle East, India, Australia, South America, New Zealand, and in most of the world. In fact, lamb may be the world's favorite meat.

Why do Americans dislike lamb? Why does the rest of the world love it?

The answer is very simple. The lamb eaten in the rest of the world is very different than most American lamb. There are two major differences.

First, American lamb often comes from animals that are also used for wool. Lanolin, a substance present in sheep bred for wool, gives an unpleasant taste and smell to the meat. Most of the lamb eaten in the rest of the world comes from breeds raised for meat, not wool.

Second, American lamb is usually grain-finished, while lamb in the rest of the world is almost always raised exclusively on grass.

Lamb Bred for Meat Tastes Better

Humankind has developed many breeds of sheep over thousands of years. Some breeds were developed for their wool, which was used to make clothing. The wool and meat of these breeds contain a great deal of lanolin, a substance that smells bad and gives an unpleasant flavor to meat.

Breeds that have been developed for meat do not have lanolin, and their meat smells good and lacks the unpleasant flavor given by lanolin. Many of these meat breeds have a wonderful flavor and texture of their own.

Unfortunately, much of the lamb sold in the United States comes from breeds that are used both for wool and meat. This is the cause of the unpleasant smell and taste so many Americans associate with lamb.

Meat breeds smell good and taste better.

Grassfed Lamb Tastes Better

Most American lamb is "finished" on grain, in a feedlot. "Grain" usually means a mixture of GMO corn and GMO soy. This kind of grain is not the natural food of lambs, who are ruminants designed to graze on living plants in the pasture, not processed grains.

Most of the lamb eaten in the rest of the world is fed grass only, and is never put in a feedlot.

This is a crucial difference, as the taste of lamb is heavily influenced by what the lamb is fed. For example, lambs raised in central Spain eat a number of herbs in the pasture, which gives a wonderful, herbaceous taste to their meat. Lamb raised in the salt marshes of Brittany has a slightly salty taste, from marsh plants growing in salty soil.

Grassfed lamb has a sweet, clean taste, redolent with the flavor of the living herbs and grasses eaten on the pasture. It is never greasy, and the texture is firm and tender.

The Pleasure of Pastured Pork

I used to avoid pork, even organic pork. Most pork is just too lean and lacks flavor. Nearly all the traditional ways of cooking pork were designed for fattier pork, with every roast having the skin and a thick layer of fat attached. Traditional ways of cooking pork just did not work with the modern pig.

Pastured Pork

My local farmers' market now carries real pastured pork. This pork is so much better than anything I was able to get before. The meat has incredible flavor, perfect fat content, and makes me feel good after eating it, something that never happened with any other kind of pork.

These pigs are not penned and stuffed with soy and garbage, but roam the woods, eating their natural diet of mast, which is composed of seeds and fruits fallen from trees, various plants, bugs, and the occasional small animal. They are also allowed to root in harvested organic vegetable fields and orchards, and are given the skim milk left over from making cream and butter. These pigs are from the famous Berkshire heritage breed, a breed developed for fine eating in England, long ago.

I was delighted to discover that these pigs came with a nice coating of their own life-giving fat. Now I would have a chance to taste why pork was so loved in traditional European cooking.

Roasting Pastured Pork

I made the first pork roast. I roasted it carefully in a traditional way. I was surprised to see that there was very little fat in the pan. The meat was very good, with a nice flavor, fairly tender, and tasted nothing like the soy-fed pork that I disliked.

But something was missing. It was very good, but not great. Great is my standard for grassfed meat. Good is just not good enough. It is not that I am a great cook, it is that traditional meat does taste great, when properly cooked, and anyone can learn to properly cook grassfed meat. The greatness is in the natural meat humankind has been eating for thousands of years. In other words, the greatness comes from the meat, not the cook. There is a very old saying, "God gives us good meat, the devil sends us cooks."

If I cook grassfed meat and it tastes only good, then I know I have done something wrong.

Rediscovering the Lost Art of Scoring

I did a bit of research, and learned about the lost art of scoring. Several old books stated clearly that scoring was the most important part of cooking a pork roast. Most Americans have never even heard of it. The old books assumed everybody would do it as a matter of course.

Scoring means making long parallel cuts through the skin and fat of the pork roast, stopping short of cutting into the meat. I started to score my next roast, and learned that it was not easy to cut through the tough, slippery skin. I sharpened a sturdy knife, got a glove that would give me a good grip, and set to work, being careful to angle the edge of the knife away from the hand holding the pork. This went much easier. I found that making cuts every half-inch worked well.

I roasted the pork the same way I had the previous roast, with the only difference being the scoring. The smell coming from the oven made me so hungry it was hard to wait for the meat to finish cooking. The taste was fantastic, like no pork I had ever tasted before. Very tender, juicy without being wet, rich without being greasy, with a wonderful deep flavor that makes me hungry just to think of it. I finally understood why pork roasts were so loved in the past. I felt good and renewed after eating the roast — again a new experience.

And this was a shoulder roast, one of the cheapest parts of the pig!

Finding Grassfed Fat

All too often, when shopping for grassfed meat, I find myself asking, "Where's the fat?"

The ugly truth is that far too much grassfed meat has all the visible fat trimmed off, and has very little fat in the meat.

The most nutrient-dense component of grassfed meat is the fat. The fat of grassfed animals is rich in omega-3 fatty acids, conjugated linoleic acid (CLA), and many other nutrients.

The fat also gives great flavor and enhances tenderness. The Weston A. Price Foundation advises always eating meat with fat. Traditional peoples, from the peoples of old Europe, to the Native Americans, to the ancient Chinese, always ate meat with plenty of fat.

Yet many producers and sellers of grassfed meat trim off all the visible fat from their meat, and some deliberately raise their beef to be lean. For me, the most frustrating part of buying grassfed meat is getting meat with enough fat.

The key is to buy meat that comes with enough fat, both visible and internal. This involves careful shopping and lobbying producers.

Tips for Buying Fattier Grassfed Meat

There are several indicators you can look at to find fattier grassfed meat. Here are some of them:

The Breed of Cattle

Genetics have a lot to do with the fat content in beef. Breeds that have been raised for meat, such as shorthorns and Angus, are much more likely to have more fat. Breeds that are noted for leanness, such as Galloway or Charolais, are much more likely to be very lean.

The Time of Year the Beef Is Processed

Traditionally, cattle were processed for meat in the late spring or early summer, after they had been eating the rich green grass of spring for as long as possible. This was the best natural way to put fat in the cattle, and meat processed at this time has more fat, more flavor, and more tenderness.

There are a number of ranchers and producers who only process their beef at that time of the year, and freeze it. If you have enough freezer space, that is a particularly good time to buy a large quantity of meat.

The Philosophy of the Producer

The attitude and belief of the rancher actually raising the meat animal has a huge impact, as there is much they can do to make the meat fattier or leaner. If the producer brags about how lean and fat-free their meat is, the meat is going to be very lean.

If the producer talks about the benefits of grassfed fat and why it is good to leave some fat on the meat, then your chances of getting fattier grassfed meat are a lot better.

Ask!

Many producers and butchers carry both lean and fattier grassfed meat. I have found that just asking for the fattiest grassfed cuts makes a huge difference. Asking for fattier meat also tells a wise producer that the demand is out there, and may well increase the supply of fattier grassfed meat.

How to Add Good Fat to Lean Grassfed Meat

Often, no matter what I do, the grassfed meat available is just too lean. Fortunately, our ancestors often faced the same problem, and developed some solutions. Here are some of the solutions I use:

Pastured Butter

Pastured butter is the best friend of lean meat. You can coat the meat with softened butter before cooking. You can baste the meat with butter. You can put butter directly on the hot meat when it is served at the table. All of these methods will improve the meat.

Grassfed Tallow and Suet

Tallow can be placed directly on roasting meat, so it can baste the meat as it cooks. You can melt some tallow and use it to baste the meat as it cooks. You can use suet, whether beef, bison, or lamb, in the same way.

Bacon

You can place fat slices of bacon directly on a roast, or render the fat from bacon and use it for basting.

Natural, Unhydrogenated Lard

You can rub softened lard all over the meat prior to cooking. You can place lard directly on top of a roast. You can use melted lard as a baste.

Part 3:
Recipes

Bone Broth

Beef
Bone Broth

About Bone Broth for Barbecue

What is a section about broth doing in a book about barbecue? Traditionally made broth is a vital ingredient in most of the bastes in this book. You cannot get a broth like this from a can or a cube. True homemade broth adds wonderful taste to the bastes, giving a depth of flavor that just cannot be equaled by a commercial broth. The substances in traditional broth keep the meat moist, improve the texture, and help give a beautiful, glossy finish to the meat once it is done.

Homemade broth is by far the best. This is because properly made broth will have many substances from the bones and cartilage that were used to prepare it, as well as many minerals and nutrients. All of these factors are completely missing from an improperly made broth.

No commercial broth is simmered long enough to get the proper nutrients, gelatin, and other necessary substances out of the bones and cartilage. It takes at least 12 hours of simmering for these substances to leave the bones and become part of the broth.

I include recipes for **Beef Bone Broth, Bison Bone Broth,** and **Barbecue Bone Broth.** Any of these broths can be used in any of the bastes. I am very grateful to Sally Fallon Morell of the Weston A. Price Foundation for the wonderful knowledge of broth that she has provided. All of these recipes are based, at least in part, on the knowledge and techniques she provided in her cookbook, *Nourishing Traditions.*

My first cookbook, *Tender Grassfed Meat,* has a number of other recipes for broth. One difference is that the recipes in that book call for a small amount of vinegar. The recipes in this book do not include vinegar. While a true homemade broth can be excellent with or without vinegar, leaving the vinegar out works better for a broth that is also used for basting.

In addition to being a superb cooking ingredient, these broths are loaded with minerals, natural gelatin, and other nutrients that make them extremely healthy and nourishing. Traditional peoples all ate plenty of bone broth when they could get it. I and my family have some broth twice a day.

Simple Steps to Broth

Making your own broth may seem intimidating, especially if you have not done it before, but it is really simple.

1. Put a bunch of ingredients (meat, bones, meat trimmings, assorted vegetables, and some salt) in a large stainless steel stockpot. Cover the ingredients with filtered water.

2. Heat the contents to boiling, skim off the scum, add the salt, cover the pot, and let simmer for at least 12 hours.

3. Strain the broth into glass jars, let cool, and refrigerate so the fat rises to the top.

Broth Cooking Tips

1. Use the proper equipment. You'll need a large stainless steel stockpot, a large stainless steel skimmer, lots of quart-sized Mason jars, and a fine mesh stainless steel strainer that covers the opening of a Mason jar.

2. Use only filtered water. Unfiltered water is full of chemicals (such as chlorine and fluoride) that will ruin the taste of your broth.

3. Use only bones, meat, and trimmings from grassfed animals. They will give a much better flavor to your broth.

4. Use only organic (or the equivalent) vegetables. Non-organic vegetables are often full of pesticides, which will go right into your broth, ruining the taste. Organic (or the equivalent) vegetables will give a much better flavor to your broth.

5. Use only good, natural, unrefined sea salt. Factory salts have been stripped of their minerals, and often have other ingredients added to them, such as sugar and aluminum, which have no place in your broth. Natural, unrefined sea salt will add natural minerals to your broth, and tastes so much better.

6. Be sure to remove the scum from the broth as it rises to the top with a skimming spoon designed for that purpose. Scum has no place in your broth.

7. When the broth is ready and has cooled somewhat, strain it through a fine mesh stainless steel strainer into quart-sized Mason jars, then refrigerate overnight. The fat will rise to the top, solidify, and act as a seal that will help preserve the broth. Remove the fat before heating the broth.

8. Fresh broth should be kept in the refrigerator and used within a week of the time it is made. It is safest to bring the broth to a full boil when reheating it.

Beef Bone Broth

Traditional barbecuers have used beef bone broth as a baste for a very long time. This broth, which has an intense beefy flavor, also contains many substances from the bones and cartilage that help make the meat tender, while enhancing its taste. You cannot get flavor like this from a can or a cube. In addition to being a wonderful baste ingredient, this broth makes one of the most nutritious drinks you can possibly have, being full of life-giving nutrients.

The long simmering time is based on the wisdom of traditional peoples, who knew that it took a very long time to get the precious nutrients from the bones.

You will need a large stockpot for this one. Make sure that it is stainless steel, not aluminum.

Makes 6 to 8 quarts

4 to 6 pounds assorted grassfed beef bones, scraps and trimmings, cartilage and sinew, including some marrow bones. Beef oxtails are ideal. Leftover bones from roasts are fine.

Enough filtered water to cover the bones by 2 to 3 inches

Assorted Root Vegetables

1 large organic onion, peeled and coarsely chopped

4 stalks of organic celery, coarsely chopped

4 large organic carrots, peeled and coarsely chopped

4 cloves organic garlic, peeled and coarsely chopped

For Simmering

2 tablespoons coarse unrefined sea salt

1. Put the beef into a large stainless steel stockpot. Add the water. Add all the vegetables. Heat the pot until the water begins a strong simmer. This will take a while due to the large volume of ingredients and water.

2. When the water is close to boiling, remove all the scum that rises to the top with a skimming spoon. This can also take a while, but is necessary.

3. Once the scum is gone, add the salt.

4. Cover and simmer gently for 12 hours.

5. Using a ladle, strain into jars, cover, and refrigerate once the bottles have cooled down. The fat will rise to the top, and will solidify in the refrigerator. This fat will help preserve the broth. The fat should be removed before the broth is reheated. It can be used as cooking fat in all kinds of dishes.

Bison Bone Broth

The Native Americans used to take the bones of bison, crush them with heavy rocks, and simmer the crushed bones for many hours to make a broth that was incredibly rich in minerals and nutrients. I have not been able to find crushed bison bones anywhere, but this recipe also makes great broth, and is so much easier than crushing massive bones with heavy rocks.

This broth works beautifully as part of a baste, adding many substances that really help make the meat taste wonderful, while making the meat more tender. This broth not only works wonderfully for bastes, but is delicious and refreshing.

You will need a large stockpot for this one. Make sure that it is stainless steel, not aluminum. The long cooking time is necessary to combine the flavors, and get the nutrients out of the bones.

Makes 6 to 8 quarts

4 to 6 pounds assorted grassfed bison bones with cartilage and meat. Bison oxtails are excellent.

Enough filtered water to cover the bones by 2 to 3 inches

Assorted Root Vegetables

6 organic green onions, coarsely chopped

4 stalks of organic celery, coarsely chopped

4 large organic carrots, peeled and coarsely chopped

2 cloves organic garlic, peeled and coarsely chopped

For Simmering

2 tablespoons coarse unrefined sea salt

1. Put the bison into a large stainless steel stockpot. Add all the vegetables. Heat the pot until the water begins a strong simmer. This will take a while due to the large volume of ingredients and water.

2. When the water is close to boiling, remove all the scum that rises to the top with a skimming spoon. This can also take a while, but is necessary. For some reason, bison seems to have even more scum to be removed than other meats. It's worth the extra work.

3. Once the scum is gone, add the salt.

4. Cover and simmer gently for 12 hours.

5. Using a ladle, strain into jars, cover, and refrigerate once the bottles have cooled down. The fat will rise to the top, and will solidify in the refrigerator. This fat will help preserve the broth. The fat should be removed before the broth is reheated. It can be used as cooking fat in all kinds of dishes.

Barbecue Bone Broth

This recipe is unusual, and gives a lot of barbecue flavor to your broth. When you use this broth for basting, the flavor goes right into the meat, which is also being flavored by the coals. This results in a deep barbecue flavor that enhances any meat.

The secret? Using bones and scraps from meat that has already been barbecued. I save up bones and leftovers from barbecued meat, and freeze them until I have enough to make broth. This is also a great way to use up leftovers, but there is nothing leftover about the taste!

Makes 6 to 8 quarts

4 to 6 pounds assorted bones, scraps and trimmings, including leftover barbecued bones and meat. Any kind or combination of grassfed meat will do, and it is fine to mix the bones and meat from different animals.

Enough filtered water to cover the bones by 2 to 3 inches

Assorted Root Vegetables

6 organic green onions, coarsely chopped

4 stalks of organic celery, coarsely chopped

4 large organic carrots, peeled and coarsely chopped

4 cloves organic garlic, peeled and coarsely chopped

For Simmering

2 tablespoons coarse unrefined sea salt

1. Put the meat and bones into a large stainless steel stockpot. Add the water. Add all the vegetables. Heat the pot until the water begins a strong simmer. This will take a while due to the large volume of ingredients and water.

2. When the water is close to boiling, remove all the scum that rises to the top with a skimming spoon. This can also take a while, but is necessary.

3. Once the scum is gone, add the salt.

4. Cover and simmer gently for 12 hours.

5. Using a ladle, strain into jars, cover, and refrigerate once the bottles have cooled down. The fat will rise to the top, and will solidify in the refrigerator. This fat will help preserve the broth. The fat should be removed before the broth is reheated. It can be used as cooking fat in all kinds of dishes.

Grassfed Beef

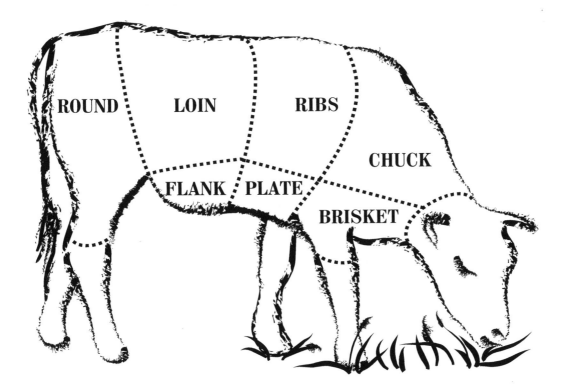

ROUND   LOIN   RIBS

CHUCK

FLANK   PLATE

BRISKET

Judging Doneness in Grassfed Beef

Not all grassfed beef is the same. Different producers raise different breeds and crossbreeds. The plants which the cattle graze upon differ greatly from region to region, as does the quality of the soil. Some producers try to raise cattle with good fat content, while others try to raise very lean cows. Some producers dry age their meat, some wet age it, and others do not age it at all.

All of these variables affect the taste, tenderness, and cooking time of the meat. The cooking times given in this book are an estimate, based on experience. This is why variable times are given for so many recipes. These times should give excellent results for most grassfed beef. Do not be afraid to change the cooking times, based on your experience. In time, you will get a feel for your barbecue cooker, and the particular kind of beef you are cooking. Remember, barbecue is more art than science.

Judging Doneness

If you are cooking a roast, or a thick steak, a good quality instant-read meat thermometer can really help you judge the doneness of the meat, and how fast it is cooking. The ease with which the thermometer goes into the meat can also give you a good idea of how tender the meat is.

Doneness for Grassfed Beef	
Rare	115 – 120 degrees
Medium Rare	121 – 130 degrees
Medium	131 – 140 degrees
Well Done	141 degrees and up

A meat thermometer does not work for thin steaks, because the meat is not thick enough.

Another way of judging temperature is to stick a metal skewer or roasting fork into the meat, withdraw it, and test the temperature of the metal with your finger. If it is cool, the meat is not ready. If it is somewhat warm, it is rare. If it is slightly hot, it is medium rare. If it is hot, it is medium. Once you have enough experience at comparing the temperature of the metal with the doneness of the meat, you will know how done the meat is, according to your standards.

The ease with which the skewer or fork goes into the meat will give you a good idea of its tenderness. Steaks can toughen if they are cooked too long.

Many cooking authorities will tell you to never pierce the meat while cooking, or you will "lose valuable juices." I have never found this to be true for grassfed meat. Yes, sometimes some juice comes out, but it does not hurt the meat.

Lean Steak with Tenderizing Asian Marinade

Not all grassfed beef is the same. All grassfed beef has much less fat than conventional beef. I have found that the more fat and marbling in grassfed beef, the more tender and flavorful the meat. So I always try to buy grassfed beef that has at least some fat, and some marbling, the more, the better. Sometimes, however, I wind up with a piece of extremely lean grassfed beef that has little or no fat and marbling. That is when I use this marinade, which I developed to deal with very lean grassfed beef. This marinade is based upon the traditional Asian seasoning combination of ginger, garlic, and green onions. I have added two kinds of tenderizing oils. This marinade will make even very lean grassfed beef tender and delicious.

Serves 2 to 4

1 lean bone in grassfed rib steak, about 1½ inches thick, (or any steak that does not have too much connective tissue, such as ribeye, T-bone, New York tip, strip, top sirloin, sirloin tip, center cut shoulder, or flat iron)

For the Marinade

2 (1 inch) pieces organic ginger, chopped, and crushed

2 large cloves organic garlic, chopped, and crushed

2 organic green onions, chopped, and crushed

2 tablespoons unrefined organic toasted sesame oil

2 tablespoons unfiltered organic extra virgin olive oil

1. The day before you plan to cook the steak, combine all ingredients to make the marinade. Mix well. Place the steak in a glass bowl, and coat all surfaces with the marinade. Cover, and let rest at room temperature for at least 1 hour. Refrigerate overnight.

2. Take the meat out of the refrigerator at least 1 hour before you plan to cook it, so it can reach room temperature.

3. Build a charcoal fire on one side of the cooker only. Bring your cooker to medium high heat, with all vents fully open.

4. Brush the marinade off the meat. It's okay if a few bits remain. Place the meat on the grill in front of, but not over, the heat source. Cover, and cook for 7 minutes.

5. Turn the meat over. Cover, and cook for another 7 minutes.

6. Reduce the heat to medium low by adjusting the top vents to half-closed, and cook for another 5 minutes, or until done to your taste.

Serve and enjoy this tender meat.

The Mighty Porterhouse Steak

A thick barbecued steak has been the ideal of great eating for a good part of America's history. The noted 19th century writer Mark Twain ordered a steak in a Parisian restaurant. Mr. Twain was so disappointed with the small, unappealing steak he was served, which he described as being the size, shape, and thickness of a man's hand, that he wrote an ode "To the Mighty Porterhouse Steak."

The Porterhouse is a bone in cut that contains both tenderloin and strip loin, providing a wonderful contrast of flavors and textures. The flavor of the meat is very much enhanced by the bone. Unfortunately, most Porterhouses cut today are anything but mighty, being cut so thin that the unique advantages of this cut are lost.

The Porterhouse in this recipe is truly mighty, being three inches thick. Thick grassfed steaks are particularly wonderful with the unique cooking qualities of grassfed meat, which allow you to get a nicely browned exterior, along with a perfectly rare interior. The contrast between the brown outside and the deep interior of the meat is dramatic, yet complementary, providing a wonderful range of tastes and textures.

This is a cut for a truly special occasion, being large not only in size but in price. However, I doubt that you could have a steak experience at any steakhouse that could even come close to this one.

The Mighty Porterhouse was made for the barbecue. There are very few ingredients in this recipe and I defy you to come up with anything that tastes better than this.

Serves 2 to 4

1 bone in grassfed Porterhouse steak, cut 3 inches thick
3 tablespoons unfiltered organic extra virgin olive oil

Mighty Porterhouse Rub
1 teaspoon coarse unrefined sea salt, crushed
1 teaspoon organic granulated garlic powder
½ teaspoon freshly ground organic black pepper

1. At least 1 hour before you plan to cook the meat, cover all surfaces of the steak with the olive oil. Let marinate at room temperature for at least 1 hour.

2. Build a charcoal fire on one side of the cooker only. Bring your cooker to medium high heat, with all vents fully open.

3. When the cooker is ready, sprinkle the seasoning lightly over each side of the Porterhouse. Place the Porterhouse in front of, but not over, the heat source. Cover, and cook for 8 minutes.

4. Turn the Porterhouse over. Cover, and cook for another 8 minutes.

5. Carefully move the Porterhouse to the center of the cooker, and place the Porterhouse on the large flat bone at the top of the steak. The steak will look like a one-sided pyramid at this point. Cover, and reduce the heat to medium low by adjusting the top vents to half-closed. Cook for 25 minutes.

6. Reduce the heat as low as possible by closing all the top and bottom vents completely, and leave the steak in the cooker for another 5 minutes.

Charcoaled Porterhouse Steak

The combination of good charcoal and good meat can produce wonderful flavor and tenderness. Very little else is needed. In fact, in some countries, steaks are seasoned very simply so as not to dilute the incredible flavor marriage of charcoal and beef. One such country is Brazil, where beef is actually referred to as a "noble meat," one that needs very little seasoning on the grill. The Porterhouse steak was born in the United States of America and has often been considered the most desirable of all steaks. This steak contains two wonderful cuts of meat, the tenderloin and the strip loin, joined by a flavor-giving bone that makes both of them more tender and delicious.

This recipe is for a more conventionally cut Porterhouse steak. It is different in taste and texture from the **Mighty Porterhouse Steak** (see page 56), because it is a thinner cut. But it is just as good in its own right, because cutting it thinner gives it more flavor from the charcoal. This is yet another example of how a few carefully chosen quality ingredients are all that is needed for an incredibly tender and delicious steak.

Serves 4

2 grassfed Porterhouse steaks, approximately 1 inch thick

3 tablespoons unfiltered organic extra virgin olive oil

1 teaspoon coarse unrefined sea salt, crushed

1. At least 1 hour before you plan to cook the steaks, coat all meat surfaces with the olive oil and place in a glass bowl.

2. Build a charcoal fire on one side of the cooker only. Bring your cooker to medium high heat, with all vents fully open.

3. Sprinkle all sides of the meat with the salt. Place the steaks in front of, but not over, the heat source. Cover, and cook for 5 minutes on each side. This should give you a medium rare steak. (You can cook 4 minutes on each side for a rare steak, or 6 minutes on each side for a medium steak.)

Serve and enjoy the tender, flavorful meat.

Romantic Porterhouse for Two

Sharing a big steak as part of a special meal can be very romantic. Thick Porterhouse steak is perfect for such a meal, as it contains two wonderful cuts of meat, strip loin and tenderloin, which are held together by a central bone. The bone also provides great flavor to the meat. I made this steak as part of a special romantic dinner, which also included sautéed potato hearts. The combination was both delicious and romantic. My wife and I enjoyed it very much.

Serves 2

1 grassfed Porterhouse steak, 1½ to 2 inches thick

3 tablespoons unfiltered organic extra virgin olive oil

1 teaspoon freshly ground organic black pepper

4 cloves organic garlic, crushed

2 tablespoons fresh organic Italian parsley leaves, finely chopped

1 teaspoon coarse unrefined sea salt, crushed

1. At least 1 hour before you plan to cook the meat, place the Porterhouse in a glass bowl. Coat all sides of the meat with the olive oil. Sprinkle the pepper on all sides of the meat. Combine the garlic and parsley, and press the mixture into all sides of the meat. Cover, and let rest at room temperature for at least 1 hour.

2. Build a charcoal fire on one side of the cooker only. Bring your cooker to medium high heat, with all vents fully open. After the meat has rested for 1 hour and when your cooker is ready, scrape the garlic and parsley off the meat. Sprinkle all sides of the meat with the salt. Place the steak in front of, but not over, the heat source, with the fat side of the meat facing the heat source. Cover, and cook for 7 minutes.

3. Turn the steak over, keeping the fat side of the meat facing the heat source. Cover, and cook for another 7 minutes.

4. Check for doneness. If the meat is not done to your taste, turn the steak over. Cover, and reduce the heat to medium low by adjusting the top vents to half-closed. Cook for a few more minutes (turning the steak over after 2 minutes), until done to your taste.

Serve and enjoy this romantic dinner.

Transylvanian Garlic Bandit's Steak

It has been known in Transylvania for a long time that the combination of garlic, beef, and charcoal is delicious. Transylvania, like so much of the Balkans, had a large number of bandits, who were often also known as freedom fighters. Any dish that cooked very quickly is likely to be called a robber's or a bandit's dish, since the bandits depended on their speed to avoid capture. The bandits often marinated their meat, which does not sound quick. They must have marinated the meat the night before and carried it in their saddlebags, while on the run, so it would be ready to cook immediately.

There are many variations on this dish throughout the Balkans. The reason for the garlic is the taste, though I hear it's supposed to repel vampires. I have also added some unfiltered extra virgin olive oil, which is not Transylvanian. The olive oil does make the meat more tender and carries the flavor of the garlic deep into the meat.

Serves 2 to 4

2 grassfed T-bone steaks, approximately 1 inch thick

4 cloves organic garlic, finely chopped

2 tablespoons unfiltered organic extra virgin olive oil

1 teaspoon coarse unrefined sea salt, crushed

1. At least 2 hours before you plan to cook the steaks, combine the garlic with the olive oil. Rub this mixture into all sides of the steaks. Cover the steaks. Let them rest at room temperature for 2 hours. (Or let rest at room temperature for 1 hour, then refrigerate overnight.)

2. If you have refrigerated the meat, remove the steaks from the refrigerator at least 1 hour before you plan to cook them, so they can come to room temperature.

3. Build a charcoal fire on one side of the cooker only. Bring your cooker to medium high heat, with all vents fully open. When the cooker and the steaks are ready, scrape the garlic off the meat. Sprinkle all sides of the meat with the salt.

4. Place the steaks in front of, but not over, the heat source. Cover, and cook for 3 to 5 minutes on each side, depending on how you like your meat.

Serve and enjoy these quick, delicious steaks.

Grilled Ribeye Steak with Simple Steak Rub

Ribeye, which usually refers to a boneless steak cut from the prime rib, is one of the most common cuts of grassfed meat. It has great flavor, and a unique texture. It is ideal for barbecuing, and is at its best with simple seasoning and smoldering charcoal.

For the Steak

2 grassfed boneless ribeye steaks, cut 1½ inches thick

¼ cup unfiltered organic extra virgin olive oil

For the Rub

1 teaspoon coarse unrefined sea salt, crushed

1 teaspoon freshly ground organic black pepper

1 teaspoon organic granulated garlic powder

1. The day before you plan to cook the meat, combine the steaks with the olive oil in a glass bowl. Coat all surfaces of the steaks with the oil. Cover, and let rest for 1 hour at room temperature, then refrigerate overnight.

2. Remove the steaks from the refrigerator at least 1 hour before you plan to cook them, so they can come to room temperature.

3. Prepare the rub by crushing the salt together with the other ingredients. Mix well.

4. Build a charcoal fire on one side of the cooker only. Bring your cooker to medium high heat, with all vents fully open. Rub the steaks generously on both sides with the rub just before you put them on the grill.

5. Place the steaks on the grill, in front of, but not over, the heat source. Cover, and cook for 3 minutes on each side.

6. Move the steaks to the center of the grill, and turn them over. Cover, and reduce the heat to medium low by adjusting the top vents to half-closed. Cook for 5 minutes on each side, or until done to your taste.

7. Reduce the heat as low as possible by closing all the top and bottom vents completely, and let rest in the cooker for another 5 minutes.

Serve the steaks and enjoy some of the best beef you will ever taste.

Oregano Steak

Traditional food combinations often rely upon just a few carefully chosen ingredients. Over time, a people would learn that certain ingredients worked very well together and complemented particular foods, such as beef. This is how a food combination becomes a tradition.

In Old California, beef was king. Oregano was the favorite herb used to flavor beef, and was often combined with garlic. Steaks were always cooked with charcoal or wood coals. I decided to combine these elements and add some unfiltered olive oil. The result is this recipe, redolent with the flavor of Old California.

Serves 4

2 to 4 grassfed ribeye steaks, about 1 inch thick, totaling about 2 pounds

For the Marinade
3 tablespoons unfiltered organic extra virgin olive oil
2 organic garlic cloves, finely chopped
Leaves from 8 stems organic oregano, finely chopped

For Cooking
1 teaspoon coarse unrefined sea salt, crushed

1. At least 1 hour before you plan to cook the steaks, make the marinade. Combine all ingredients, and mix well. Place the steaks in a glass bowl, and coat all surfaces of the meat with the marinade. Cover, and let rest at room temperature for 1 hour.

2. Build a charcoal fire on one side of the cooker only. Bring your cooker to medium high heat, with all vents fully open. Sprinkle both sides of the meat with the salt, just before you put the steaks on the grill.

3. Place the steaks on the grill, in front of, but not over, the heat source. Cover, and cook for 3 to 6 minutes on each side, depending on how you like your beef.

Serve and enjoy the flavor of Old California.

Thick Strip Steak

Thick steaks used to be the ultimate luxury food. The very phrase "a meat eater" meant a person of substance and importance. The ultimate meat to eat was a thick steak. Thick steaks have fallen out of favor in the last few decades. I think one of the major reasons for the decline is that thick factory steaks are very difficult to cook. The high heat necessary to deal with the water in the steak would usually cause a really thick steak to be ruined, often being burned on the outside and raw on the inside.

Thick grassfed steaks do not have this problem. In fact, the wonderful cooking qualities of grassfed meat make it easy to cook a wonderful thick steak. The meat has a nice flavorful exterior and an interior that is so tender, flavorful, and delicious that I begin to wonder why anyone makes anything other than a thick steak. One thick steak can be cut up to serve several people.

This recipe brings back the thick barbecued steak in a very simple, yet utterly delicious way. I must warn you, once you eat a great thick steak, there is no going back.

Serves 4

1 (2 pound) grassfed strip steak, with fat cap, approximately 2 inches thick
2 tablespoons unfiltered organic extra virgin olive oil

For the Rub
¼ teaspoon coarse unrefined sea salt, crushed
¼ teaspoon organic granulated garlic powder
¼ teaspoon freshly ground organic black pepper
¼ teaspoon organic dried oregano, crushed between your fingers

1. At least 1 hour before you plan to cook the steak, coat all surfaces of the meat with the olive oil. Place in a glass bowl, cover, and let rest for 1 hour at room temperature.

2. Mix all ingredients for the seasoning.

3. Build a charcoal fire on one side of the cooker only. Bring your cooker to medium high heat, with all vents fully open. When the cooker is ready, sprinkle the seasoning lightly over all sides of the steak. Place the steak in the cooker, in front of, but not over, the heat source. Cover, and cook for 6 minutes.

4. Turn the steak over. Cover, and cook for another 6 minutes.

5. Move the steak to the center of the cooker, and turn it fat side up. Cover, and reduce the heat to medium low by adjusting the top vents to half-closed. Cook for 25 to 30 minutes, depending on how you like it.

6. Reduce the heat as low as possible by closing all the top and bottom vents completely, and let it rest in the cooker for another 5 minutes.

Serve and enjoy the luxury of a great thick steak.

Thick Strip Steak with Classic European Flavors

I have always been fascinated by how fundamentally simple a very complex cuisine can be. The flavoring combination of onions, carrots, and celery is the base for a number of the most classic and complex sauces in French and Italian cuisine. These three vegetables are also used as the flavor base for a huge number of stews, soups, and other classic dishes in many European countries. I decided to use this flavor combination as the basis of a simple marinade for charcoal steak. The enzymes and juices of the vegetables really made the meat tender, while carrying their flavors deep into the meat. The results were absolutely delicious, as well as easy.

Serves 4

1 (2 pound) grassfed strip steak, about 2 to 3 inches thick, with fat cap

For the Marinade

1 medium organic onion, cut into coarse chunks

1 medium organic carrot, cut into coarse chunks

1 stalk of organic celery, cut into coarse chunks

¼ cup filtered water

1. At least 2 hours before you plan to cook the steak, prepare the marinade. Combine all ingredients in a blender and blend until the vegetables are completely crushed, and are partially liquefied. Pour the mixture into a glass bowl large enough to hold the steak. Place the steak in the bowl and coat all sides of the steak with the mixture. Cover, and let rest at room temperature for at least 2 hours, or refrigerate overnight.

2. If you have refrigerated the meat overnight, remove from the refrigerator at least 1 hour before cooking so the meat can come to room temperature.

3. Build a charcoal fire on one side of the cooker only. Bring your cooker to medium high heat, with all vents fully open. Scrape all the marinade off the meat. Place the meat in the cooker, in front of, but not over, the heat source. Cover, and cook for 8 minutes.

4. Turn the steak over. Cover, and cook for another 8 minutes.

5. Move the steak to the middle of the grill, and turn it fat side up. Cover, and reduce the heat to medium low by adjusting the top vents to half-closed. Cook for 10 minutes. This should give you a medium rare steak. If the steak is not done to your taste, cover, and cook for a few more minutes.

Serve and enjoy the classic beefy flavor.

Steak in the Style of Ancient China

Chinese cuisine has spread far beyond China and is one of the oldest and greatest cuisines our planet has ever known. While current Chinese cuisine is famous for its emphasis on rice, vegetables, and extensive spicing and seasoning, this was not always true. The food of choice in ancient China (at least for the nobles) was meat. Meat was often cooked with the fat of another animal, which created interesting flavor variations. While some of this meat was fried with the fat of a different animal, some was certainly grilled, and most likely basted with such fat.

This recipe honors this ancient Chinese cooking technique by using bison fat as a baste for beef steak. The recipe is very simple, but the taste is absolutely wonderful. The bison fat makes the beef taste a little bit like bison, but it still retains its beefy flavor. This steak is so good that I suspect only a meat shortage could have caused the Chinese to abandon this type of cookery.

Serves 4

2 grassfed strip steaks, totaling approximately 2 pounds
2 tablespoons unfiltered organic extra virgin olive oil
3 tablespoons melted grassfed bison fat, (or melted grassfed bison suet)
1 teaspoon coarse unrefined sea salt, crushed

1. At least 1 hour before you plan to cook the meat, place the meat in a glass bowl large enough to hold it. Rub all surfaces of the steaks with the olive oil. Cover, and let rest at room temperature for at least 1 hour, or refrigerate overnight.

2. If you have refrigerated the meat overnight, remove it from the refrigerator at least 1 hour before cooking so it can come to room temperature.

3. Build a charcoal fire on one side of the cooker only. Bring your cooker to medium high heat, with all vents fully open. When the meat has been marinated and is at room temperature, and the cooker is ready, brush both sides of the steaks with the melted bison fat (or suet). Sprinkle the salt over both sides of the steaks. Place the steaks in the cooker, in front of, but not over, the heat source. Cover, and cook for 5 to 8 minutes on each side, depending on how you like your meat.

Serve and enjoy the wonderful flavors of this ancient way of cooking.

Portuguese Butter Steak

Butter and steak go together in Portuguese cooking. The Portuguese, like most of the people in Southern Europe, really appreciate butter, rather than only using olive oil. Often they use both in the same recipe. Steaks are often sautéed in butter, and sometimes they are grilled with butter. There are many different versions of these steaks. This is mine, with my own unique basting method. This steak is so delicious that just thinking of it makes me hungry. I will try to hold my hunger at bay long enough to write this recipe.

Serves 2 to 4

2 grassfed strip steaks, about 1¼ inches thick, totaling about 2 pounds

2 tablespoons unfiltered organic extra virgin olive oil

For the Garlic Butter Baste

4 cloves organic garlic, very finely chopped and crushed

2 imported bay leaves, preferably Turkish, crushed and crumbled

1 teaspoon coarse unrefined sea salt, crushed

1 teaspoon freshly ground organic black pepper

4 tablespoons softened pastured butter

1. At least 1 hour before you plan to cook the steaks, coat all surfaces with the olive oil, and let rest in a covered glass bowl at room temperature.

2. Prepare the garlic butter baste by thoroughly mixing all ingredients together until they are very well combined. A sturdy fork is a good tool for this job.

3. Build a charcoal fire on one side of the cooker only. Bring your cooker to medium high heat, with all vents fully open.

4. When the cooker is ready, place one-quarter of the garlic butter baste on the top of each steak, spreading the butter so it completely covers the top side of each steak. (This will use up half of the baste.)

5. Place the steaks on the grill, butter side up, in front of, but not over, the heat source. Cover, and cook for 4 to 5 minutes, depending on how you like your steak.

6. Turn the steaks over, and spread half the remaining garlic butter baste on the top side of each steak (which will use up the remaining baste). Cover, and cook for 4 to 5 minutes.

7. Reduce the heat as low as possible by closing all the top and bottom vents completely, and let rest for another 4 to 5 minutes.

Serve and enjoy the rich buttery flavor.

Strip Steak with Pear Marinade

Marinating a steak with pears may sound strange, but different fruits have been used to marinate meat for a very long time. It is actually traditional in Korea to use the Asian pear as part of a marinade for beef. Lemons and lemon juice are very commonly used in marinades in Europe, Asia, and the Middle East. Fruits have enzymes that can make meat tender.

I decided to try using a sweet pear as the basis of a marinade. I decided to add raw unheated honey and ginger to provide even more tenderizing enzymes. The result is one of the most tender steaks I have ever tasted, and one of the most delicious.

Serves 2 to 4

2 grassfed strip steaks, 1¼ to 1½ inch thick, totaling approximately 2 pounds

For the Marinade

1 very ripe organic pear, peeled, seeded, and crushed, with juice

1 teaspoon organic fresh ginger, finely chopped

1 tablespoon raw organic unheated honey

2 tablespoons unrefined organic toasted sesame oil

1 tablespoon Thai fish sauce

2 cloves organic garlic, finely chopped

1 teaspoon freshly ground organic black pepper

1. At least 1 hour before you plan to cook the steaks, prepare the marinade. Combine all the marinade ingredients, and stir constantly until the honey has dissolved into the rest of the marinade. Place the steaks in a glass bowl, pour the marinade over the steaks, and stir to make sure that all sides of the meat are coated with the marinade. Cover, and let rest at room temperature for 1 hour.

2. Build a charcoal fire on one side of the cooker only. Bring your cooker to medium high heat, with all vents fully open. When the meat has marinated for 1 hour and the cooker is ready, place the steaks in front of, but not over, the heat source. Cover, and cook for 5 to 7 minutes, depending on how you like your meat.

3. Turn the steaks over. Cover, and cook for another 5 to 7 minutes.

Serve and enjoy the exotic flavor of this tender meat.

Romanian Garlic Strip Steak

Romania has one of the tastiest cuisines on the planet. Most Americans have never even heard of Romania, but many are familiar with Transylvania. Transylvania is famous as the home of the infamous vampire, Count Dracula. Transylvania is actually part of Romania, and has a wonderful cuisine of its own. I don't know if Romanians still use garlic to ward off vampires, but they do use plenty of it in their flavorful cooking. This steak is absolutely wonderful, being flavored with a garlic-studded, Romanian-style baste which goes perfectly with the wood flavors of barbecue. The olive oil keeps the baste from solidifying, and really unites the flavors. This is the perfect steak for anyone who loves garlic.

Serves 4

1 grassfed strip steak with fat cap, approximately 2 to 2½ inches thick

1 tablespoon unfiltered organic extra virgin olive oil

For the Baste

2 tablespoons pastured butter

¼ cup homemade bone broth, preferably *Beef Bone Broth* (page 50)

4 cloves organic garlic, very finely chopped

1 tablespoon unfiltered organic extra virgin olive oil

½ teaspoon freshly ground organic black pepper

1. At least 1 hour before you plan to cook the meat, rub 1 tablespoon of olive oil all over the steak. Place in a glass bowl, and let rest at room temperature while you prepare the baste.

2. Combine the butter, broth, and garlic in a small saucepan. Heat over low heat just until the butter melts completely. Remove from the heat, and pour the mixture into a bowl. Add the olive oil and black pepper. Stir well. Brush a coating of this baste all over the meat, and let rest at room temperature for at least 30 minutes, or until the meat has been out of the refrigerator for at least 1 hour.

3. Build a charcoal fire on one side of the cooker only. Bring your cooker to medium high heat, with all vents fully open. Place the meat in the cooker, in front of, but not over, the heat source. Cover, and cook for 8 minutes.

4. Turn the steak over, brushing all sides with the baste, cover, and cook for another 8 minutes.

5. Move the steak to the middle of the grill, fat side up, and baste. Cover, and reduce the heat to medium low by adjusting the top vents to half-closed. Cook for 10 minutes. This should give you a medium rare steak. If the steak is not done to your taste, cover, and cook until done.

Serve and enjoy the Romanian flavors.

Barbecued Tenderloin Steak

Tenderloin is one of the most prized cuts on any meat animal. The meat is very tender, and has a wonderful, buttery texture, if cooked properly. Smoldering charcoal really enhances the flavor of this tender meat, and provides the main flavor in this simple recipe, which includes the traditional American flavors of salt and pepper.

Serves 4

4 grassfed tenderloin steaks, 6 to 8 ounces each
3 tablespoons unfiltered organic extra virgin olive oil
1½ teaspoons coarse unrefined sea salt, crushed
1 teaspoon freshly ground organic black pepper

1. At least 1 hour before you plan to cook the steaks, place them in a glass bowl, and coat all surfaces with the olive oil. Cover, and let rest at room temperature for 1 hour.

2. Build a charcoal fire on one side of the cooker only. Bring your cooker to medium high heat, with all vents fully open. Sprinkle the salt and pepper on all sides of the steaks.

3. Place the meat on the grill, in front of, but not over, the heat source. Cover, and cook for 3 to 5 minutes on each side, or until done to your taste.

Serve and enjoy the classic grilled flavor.

Barbecued Tenderloin with Porcini Mushroom Butter

This tenderloin combines traditional European flavors for tenderloin with the magic of the barbecue, resulting in a deep, complex flavor that is both exotic and satisfying. Porcini mushrooms, known by many names in Europe, provide a deep, woodsy flavor to meat. The powdered form is perfect for combining with butter. The use of onions to marinate the meat is an old Polish tradition, and the onion flavor combines beautifully with the porcini butter.

Serves 4

4 grassfed tenderloin steaks, 5 to 8 ounces each

1 large organic onion, sliced, and crushed

4 tablespoons pastured butter, melted

1 teaspoon porcini mushroom powder

1 teaspoon coarse unrefined sea salt, crushed

1. At least an hour before you plan to cook the steaks, place the meat in a glass bowl and cover all surfaces with the onions. Cover the bowl, and let rest for 1 hour.

2. Build a charcoal fire on one side of the cooker only. Bring your cooker to medium high heat, with all vents fully open. Combine the melted butter with the porcini mushroom powder. Scrape the onions off the steaks, then brush one side of the steaks with the butter. Sprinkle half the salt over the buttered side of the steaks.

3. Place the steaks on the grill, in front of, but not over, the heat source, buttered side up. Cover, and cook for 3 to 5 minutes, depending on how you like your steaks.

4. Turn the steaks over, brush with the remaining porcini mushroom butter, and sprinkle the rest of the salt on the steaks. Cover, and cook for another 3 to 5 minutes, depending on how you like your steaks.

Serve and enjoy the rich traditional flavors.

Hawaiian Steak

People rarely think of Hawaii when they think of beef, but Hawaii has a long tradition of raising grassfed cattle, longer than Texas!

Cattle were introduced to Hawaii in 1795 by Captain George Vancouver, who left five of them as a gift. Within a few decades, there were over 15,000 cattle in Hawaii, and they were a problem. They reverted to being wild, and would actually eat the thatched roofs of people's houses. They also intimidated and attacked the people. The King of Hawaii decided to turn this problem into a resource, and sent one of his wisest advisors to California in 1832. California was part of Mexico at the time, and its economy was based completely on raising huge herds of cattle. The cattlemen of California were experts in managing cattle. The Hawaiians hired three California cowboys, who went to Hawaii, trained horses and people, and got the cattle under control within a few years. The Hawaiian cowboys were called Paniolos, and they raised excellent grassfed cattle. Mesquite was brought to Hawaii, and planted so cattle could graze on it. Mesquite adapted to the new soil and climate, and evolved into a plant known as kiawe, which makes an excellent natural charcoal. Beef became part of the Hawaiian diet, and the descendants of those original five cattle still graze on the big island of Hawaii.

This recipe is based on traditional Hawaiian methods of flavoring steak. The crushed garlic helps tenderize the meat, while providing wonderful flavor. The unfiltered olive oil is my addition. This steak is simple and delicious. It really does taste best cooked in front of a kiawe fire.

Serves 2 to 4

1 (1¾ to 2½ pound) grassfed top sirloin steak, approximately 2 inches thick, (or ribeye steak of similar size)

3 tablespoons unfiltered organic extra virgin olive oil

4 to 6 cloves organic garlic, crushed

1½ teaspoons coarse unrefined sea salt, crushed

1. The day before you plan to cook the steak, place the meat in a glass bowl. Cover all surfaces of the meat with the olive oil. Press the crushed garlic into all sides of the meat. Cover, and let sit at room temperature for 1 hour, then refrigerate overnight.

2. Remove the meat from the refrigerator at least 1 hour before you plan to cook it, so it can come to room temperature.

3. Build a charcoal fire (preferably with kiawe charcoal) on one side of the cooker only. Bring your cooker to medium high heat, with all vents fully open. Sprinkle the salt all over the meat. Place the meat on the grill, in front of, but not over, the heat source. Cover, and cook for 5 minutes.

4. Turn the meat over. Cover, and cook for another 5 minutes.

5. Turn the meat over. Cover, and reduce the heat to medium low by adjusting the top vents to half-closed. Cook for another 5 minutes at medium low heat.

6. Turn the steak over once more, cover, and cook for another 5 minutes. This should give you a rare steak. If you prefer a less rare steak, continue cooking at medium low heat, turning every 2 minutes, until done to your taste.

Steak Vidalia

One of the best qualities of grassfed meat is that it has a wonderful taste of its own and needs very little in the way of seasoning. Sometimes, however, just one seasoning can deeply enhance the taste and tenderness of the meat, making a great thing even better. This recipe is based almost entirely on the seasoning qualities of the Vidalia onion.

Vidalia onions are grown near the town of Vidalia, Georgia. There is something special in the soil there that makes these onions unbelievably sweet and flavorful. They also have a surprising ability to make meat more tender. The combination of grassfed steak, crushed Vidalia onions, and smoldering charcoal resulted in a steak so flavorful and tender that I had to try the recipe several times just to confirm how good it was.

Serves 4

1 (2 pound) grassfed top sirloin steak, about 1½ inches thick

3 tablespoons unfiltered organic extra virgin olive oil

1 large organic Vidalia onion, finely chopped

2 cloves organic garlic, finely chopped

1. At least 1 hour before you plan to cook the steak, coat the meat with the olive oil and place it in a glass bowl. Press half the onions, garlic, and any juices into one side of the meat. Turn the meat over and press the remaining onions and garlic into the other side of the meat. Cover the bowl, and let rest at room temperature for at least 1 hour.

2. Build a charcoal fire on one side of the cooker only. Bring your cooker to medium high heat, with all vents fully open. When the cooker is ready, brush the onions and garlic off the steak. You may reserve the onions and sauté them in butter as a side dish.

3. Place the steak in front of, but not over, the heat source. Cover the grill, and cook for 5 minutes on each side. This will give you a rare steak. If you prefer a less rare steak, cook for 7 minutes on each side, or to taste.

Serve and enjoy some of the most flavorful and tender meat you will ever taste.

Baltic Steak

The nations surrounding the Baltic Sea are more famous for their freezing winters than their barbecue, but they do cook outdoors during the short, cool summers. Baltic barbecue sometimes involves the use of softwoods (such as pine) for fuel, in contrast to the rest of the world, which prefers hardwood. I still prefer hardwood charcoal, which I think goes wonderfully with the traditional Baltic flavors. This steak has a very tasty, somewhat different flavor.

Serves 4

1 (2 pound) grassfed top sirloin steak, approximately 1½ inches thick

For the Marinade

¼ cup unfiltered organic extra virgin olive oil

1 medium organic onion, coarsely chopped

1 medium organic carrot, coarsely chopped

1 teaspoon organic dried mustard powder

1 teaspoon freshly ground organic black pepper

For Cooking

1 teaspoon coarse unrefined sea salt, crushed

1. The day before you plan to cook the meat, make the marinade. Combine all marinade ingredients in a bowl, and mix well. Place the steak in a glass bowl, and add the marinade. Coat all sides of the meat with the marinade, pressing the vegetables into the meat. Cover, and let rest at room temperature for 1 hour, then refrigerate overnight.

2. Remove the meat from the refrigerator at least 1 hour before you plan to cook it, so it can come to room temperature.

3. Build a charcoal fire on one side of the cooker only. Bring your cooker to medium high heat, with all vents fully open.

4. Scrape the vegetables off the steak with a spoon, and sprinkle all sides of the meat with the salt just before you put the meat on the grill.

5. Place the meat on the grill, in front of, but not over, the heat source. Cover, and cook for 7 to 9 minutes on each side, depending on how you like your steak.

Serve and enjoy the flavor of the Baltic.

Shashlik Steak

Shashlik is one of the most popular foods in Russia. This is very interesting, because shashlik is not a Russian dish. It comes from the Caucasus, a mountain area that was conquered by the Russians in the 19th century. Now, most of the area is independent, but the Russian love for shashlik remains.

Traditionally, shashlik is made from beef or lamb, cut into cubes of various sizes, and cooked on skewers, being very similar to the more widely known shish kabob. The meat is always marinated, and there are many different marinades. I was curious how a steak would taste when marinated like shashlik, and the result of my curiosity was fantastic.

Serves 4

1 grassfed top sirloin steak, about 2 pounds, about 1¼ to 1½ inches thick

For the Marinade

1 medium organic onion, puréed in a blender

¼ cup unfiltered organic extra virgin olive oil

4 organic garlic cloves, very finely chopped

2 tablespoons organic fresh basil leaves, finely chopped

2 tablespoons organic fresh cilantro leaves, finely chopped

1 teaspoon freshly ground organic black pepper

For Cooking

1 teaspoon coarse unrefined sea salt, crushed

1. The day before you plan to cook the steak, prepare the marinade. Combine all of the marinade ingredients, and mix well. Place the meat in a glass bowl, and pour the marinade over the meat, making sure that all surfaces of the meat are coated by the marinade. Cover, and let rest at room temperature for 1 hour, then refrigerate overnight.

2. Remove the meat from the refrigerator at least 1 hour before you plan to cook it, so the meat can come to room temperature.

3. Build a charcoal fire on one side of the cooker only. Bring your cooker to medium high heat, with all vents fully open. When the cooker is ready, scrape the marinade off the meat with a spoon, and sprinkle all sides of the meat with the salt. Place the meat in front of, but not over, the heat source. Cover, and cook for 5 to 8 minutes on each side, depending on how you like your meat.

Serve and enjoy this flavorful steak.

Top Sirloin Steak with Korean Flavors

The Korean genius for seasoning barbecued beef is usually applied to small, quickly cooked slices of meat. I have found that these seasonings work very well with a nice, thick steak, especially on the barbecue. I have substituted naturally fermented fish sauce for soy sauce and organic Grade B maple syrup for other sweeteners.

The wood flavors from the barbecue and this marinade work beautifully together, giving nice, slightly exotic flavor to the tender meat.

Serves 4

1 grassfed top sirloin steak, approximately 2 pounds

For the Marinade
1 (1 inch) piece organic ginger, crushed and finely chopped

2 large cloves organic garlic, finely chopped

2 organic green onions, finely chopped

1 tablespoon Thai fish sauce

1 tablespoon organic Grade B maple syrup

2 tablespoons unrefined organic toasted sesame oil

1 teaspoon freshly ground organic black pepper

1. At least 1 hour before you plan to cook the steak, make the marinade by combining all ingredients and stirring well.

2. Place the steak in a glass bowl, and coat all surfaces of the meat with the marinade, pressing the chopped vegetables into the meat with the back of a spoon. Let rest at room temperature for 1 hour. At this point, you can cook the meat or refrigerate it overnight.

3. If you refrigerated the meat, take it out of the refrigerator at least an hour before cooking, so it can come to room temperature.

4. Build a charcoal fire on one side of the cooker only. Bring your cooker to medium high heat, with all vents fully open. When the cooker is ready, scrape the marinade off the meat with a spoon, and place the steak in front of, but not over, the heat source. Cover, and cook for 5 to 8 minutes on each side, depending on how you like your steak.

Serve and enjoy the exotic Korean flavors.

"R&R" Steak with Thai flavors

During the Vietnam War, American soldiers often went to Thailand when they were granted some "R&R" (Rest and Recreation) time off from the deadly business of soldiering. Enterprising Thai businesspeople quickly learned that what the soldiers wanted to eat was barbecued steak, so they came up with a form of barbecued steak. The meat was usually water buffalo, and it was well marinated so it would be tender. I have been told that some of these steaks were absolutely delicious. I thought maybe these steaks tasted better than they actually were, because the guys who ate them had been eating World War II Era C Rations. Nevertheless, the idea intrigued me, so I gave it a try. I am really glad I did.

This recipe is my version, based on a description of such a steak from a friend who was there. It is very tender and has a wonderful Asian flavor.

Serves 4

1 (1½ to 2 pound) grassfed top sirloin steak, about 1¼ inches thick

For the Marinade
1 (2 inch) piece organic fresh ginger, chopped, and crushed
2 large organic garlic cloves, chopped, and crushed
2 organic green onions, chopped, and crushed
2 dried organic hot peppers, chopped, and crushed
1 teaspoon freshly ground organic black pepper
3 tablespoons Thai fish sauce
2 tablespoons unfiltered organic extra virgin olive oil
2 tablespoons unrefined organic toasted sesame oil
1 tablespoon organic peanut butter

1. The day before you plan to cook the steak, combine all the ingredients for the marinade, and mix well. Use a spoon to crush and stir the peanut butter until it blends with the other ingredients. Place the steak in a glass bowl just large enough to hold it, and coat all surfaces with the marinade. Let rest at room temperature for 1 hour, then refrigerate overnight.

2. Take the steak out of the refrigerator at least 1 hour before you plan to cook it, so it can come to room temperature.

3. Build a charcoal fire on one side of the cooker only. Bring your cooker to medium high heat, with all vents fully open. Scrape the marinade off the steak with a spoon. It's okay if a few bits cling to the steak. Place the steak in front of, but not over, the heat source. Cover, and cook for 5 to 8 minutes on each side, depending on how you like your steak.

Serve and enjoy the unusual and delicious flavors of this tender steak.

Butter Steak

People rarely think of center cut shoulder as being perfect for a thick steak. In fact, center cut shoulder is usually condemned to the slow cooker, or used to make stews or pot roasts. But a properly prepared thick center cut shoulder steak is wonderfully tender, and has a rich beefy flavor. This steak is particularly delicious, as it is cooked with butter. The combination of butter and barbecue is heavenly.

Serves 4

1 (2 pound) thick grassfed center cut shoulder steak, 2 to 2½ inches thick

3 tablespoons unfiltered organic extra virgin olive oil

1 small organic onion, sliced, and crushed

½ teaspoon coarse unrefined sea salt, crushed

½ teaspoon freshly ground organic black pepper

4 tablespoons softened pastured butter

1. The day before you plan to cook the meat, place the steak in a glass bowl, and coat all surfaces with the olive oil. When the steak is coated with the olive oil, cover all surfaces of the meat with the crushed onion. Cover the bowl, and let rest at room temperature for 1 hour, then refrigerate overnight.

2. Take the meat out of the refrigerator at least 1 hour before you plan to cook it, so it can come to room temperature.

3. Combine the salt and pepper with the softened butter, mixing well.

4. Build a charcoal fire on one side of the cooker only. Bring your cooker to medium high heat, with all vents fully open. When the cooker is ready, scrape the onions off the meat with a spoon. Cover the top side of the meat with half the softened butter mixture. Place the meat on the grill, buttered side up, in front of, but not over, the heat source. Cover, and cook for 6 minutes.

5. Turn the steak over, and cover the other side of the meat with the remaining butter mixture. Cover, and cook for another 6 minutes.

6. Turn the steak over. Cover, and reduce the heat to medium low by adjusting the top vents to half-closed. Cook for 10 minutes at medium low heat.

7. Turn the steak over again. Cover, and cook for another 10 minutes, or until done to taste.

8. When the steak is done, reduce the heat as low as possible by closing all the top and bottom vents completely, and let it rest in the cooker for another 5 minutes.

Serve and enjoy this thick, tender steak.

Tender Shoulder Steak in the Style of Ancient China

This recipe uses the traditional Chinese seasoning combination of green onions, garlic, and ginger, along with the ancient Chinese technique of using the fat of a different animal to flavor the grilled meat. This steak is very tender and flavorful.

Serves 4

1 (2 pound) thick grassfed center cut shoulder steak, 1½ to 2 inches thick

For the Marinade

3 tablespoons unfiltered organic extra virgin olive oil

2 organic green onions, crushed, and finely chopped

1 (2 inch) piece organic ginger, crushed, and finely chopped

4 organic garlic cloves, crushed, and finely chopped

For Cooking

1 teaspoon coarse unrefined sea salt, crushed

2 tablespoons rendered duck fat

1. The day before you plan to cook the steak, place the steak in a glass bowl. Coat all surfaces of the meat with the olive oil. Then press the crushed green onion, ginger, and garlic into all sides of the meat. Cover, and let rest at room temperature for 1 hour, then refrigerate overnight.

2. At least 1 hour before you plan to cook the steak, remove it from the refrigerator so it can come to room temperature.

3. Build a charcoal fire on one side of the cooker only. Bring your cooker to medium high heat, with all vents fully open. With a spoon, knock the vegetables off both sides of the steak. Spread 1 tablespoon of duck fat on each side of the steak. Sprinkle the salt on both sides of the steak. Place the meat in front of, but not over, the heat source. Cover, and cook for 7 to 8 minutes.

4. Turn the steak over. Cover, and cook for another 7 to 8 minutes.

5. Reduce the heat as low as possible by closing all the top and bottom vents completely, then let the steak rest in the cooker for another 7 minutes.

Serve and enjoy this exotic, tender steak.

Thick Korean Steak

Most Korean beef marinades call for either malt syrup or corn syrup as an ingredient. I have serious reservations about using either of these substances, so I was delighted to learn that some traditional marinades use honey instead. I decided to use the most traditional honey I can get, an organic raw honey that has never been heated and contains all the original enzymes and nutrients. It is the kind of honey that humankind has eaten for millennia, before the industrial processing of honey was introduced in the 20th century. I decided to try this marinade on a very un-Korean cut of beef — a thick steak cut from the shoulder. My thought was that the unprocessed honey, which still had its natural enzymes, would be perfect for tenderizing a steak. I was right. This recipe turns an economical cut of meat into an unbelievably tender and flavorful feast.

Serves 4

1 (2 pound) thick grassfed center cut shoulder steak, 2 to 2½ inches thick

For the Marinade
2 tablespoons Thai fish sauce

2 tablespoons unrefined organic toasted sesame oil

1 heaping teaspoon raw organic unheated honey

1 (1 inch) piece organic ginger, chopped, and crushed

2 organic green onions, chopped, and crushed

2 cloves organic garlic, finely chopped, and crushed

1 teaspoon freshly ground organic black pepper

1. The day before you plan to cook the meat, prepare the marinade. Combine the marinade ingredients, and mix well. Keep stirring until the honey has completely dissolved into the rest of the marinade. The honey will thicken the marinade. Place the steak in a glass bowl large enough to hold it. Coat all the surfaces of the meat with the marinade. Cover, and let rest at room temperature for 1 hour, then refrigerate overnight.

2. Remove the meat from the refrigerator 1 hour before you plan to cook it, so it can come to room temperature.

3. Build a charcoal fire on one side of the cooker only. Bring your cooker to medium high heat, with all vents fully open. Place the steak in front of, but not over, the heat source. Cover, and cook for 8 minutes.

4. Turn the meat over. Cover, and cook for another 8 minutes.

5. Reduce the heat to medium low by adjusting the top vents to half-closed, and cook for 10 to 15 minutes, depending on how you like your meat.

6. Turn the meat over again, cover, and cook for another 10 to 15 minutes at medium low heat.

7. Reduce the heat as low as possible by closing all the top and bottom vents completely, cover, and let it rest in the cooker for another 5 minutes.

Serve and enjoy this tender steak with Korean flavors.

Steak with Thai Flavors

The traditional flavors of Thailand are unique and delicious. Traditionally, there was very little beef eaten in Thailand, and most of it was usually cooked in small pieces. Most of the "beef" was actually the meat of water buffalo. However, I like Thai flavors so much that I went ahead and created a Thai-style marinade for steak. This marinade gives a wonderful flavor to charcoal-cooked steak, really enhancing the fine flavor of the meat. This recipe is different, and delicious.

Serves 4

2 grassfed center cut shoulder steaks, approximately 1¼ inches thick

For the Marinade

1 tablespoon organic cilantro stems, chopped, and crushed

1 tablespoon natural oyster sauce

1 tablespoon Thai fish sauce

1 tablespoon raw organic unheated honey

1 tablespoon unrefined organic toasted sesame oil

1 teaspoon freshly ground organic black pepper

2 cloves organic garlic, chopped, and crushed

1 organic green onion, chopped, and crushed

1. At least 1 hour before you plan to cook the steaks, prepare the marinade. Combine all the ingredients and mix well, stirring until the honey has dissolved into the other ingredients. The honey will thicken the marinade. Place the steaks in a glass bowl, and coat all surfaces of the meat with the marinade. Cover, and let sit at room temperature for 1 hour. At this point, you can cook the meat or refrigerate overnight.

2. If the meat was refrigerated, take it out of the refrigerator at least 1 hour before you cook it, so it can come to room temperature.

3. Build a charcoal fire on one side of the cooker only. Bring your cooker to medium high heat, with all vents fully open. Place the steaks in front of, but not over, the heat source. Cover, and cook for 4 to 7 minutes on each side, depending on how you like your steaks.

Serve and enjoy these exotic, tender steaks.

Steak with the Flavors of Ancient Rome

The ancient Romans loved good food. They were very creative, and would spend huge amounts of money just to get the right ingredients. The meats favored by the Romans were pork, lamb, goat, and just about every other kind of animal they could get their hands on. Some old Roman cookbooks have survived to this day. Unfortunately, they provide very little information on cooking techniques. They often consist of nothing but a list of ingredients, with no measurements given. Nevertheless, I found the flavor combinations to be so interesting that I decided to experiment.

I found no Roman recipes for cooking beefsteak. However, I did find a number of recipes for pork, lamb, and wild game. This gave me some idea of the flavors they used with meat. I combined some of these flavors, and the result is this wonderfully tender, absolutely delicious steak.

It is important to use an unprocessed, unheated, organic honey. This is because only an unprocessed, unheated honey will have the active enzymes that will help make the meat tender. In fact, truly raw, unheated honey is a wonderful tenderizer for meat, and was used for this purpose by the ancient Romans.

Serves 4

4 grassfed flat iron steaks, approximately 1¼ inches thick

For the Marinade

1 tablespoon raw organic unheated honey

1 tablespoon white wine, Spanish sherry works well

2 tablespoons unfiltered organic extra virgin olive oil

1 teaspoon Thai fish sauce

1 teaspoon organic dried thyme

½ teaspoon dry organic coriander seeds, in powder form

½ teaspoon freshly ground organic black pepper

1. The day before you plan to cook the meat, prepare the marinade by mixing all ingredients together. Keep stirring until the honey has completely dissolved into the other ingredients. The honey will thicken the marinade. Place the meat in a glass bowl, and coat all surfaces of the meat with the marinade. Cover, and let rest at room temperature for 1 hour, then refrigerate overnight.

2. Remove the meat from the refrigerator at least 1 hour before you plan to cook it, so it can come to room temperature.

3. Build a charcoal fire on one side of the cooker only. Bring your cooker to medium high heat, with all vents fully open. When your cooker is ready, place the steaks in front of, but not over, the heat source. Cover, and cook the steaks for 4 to 5 minutes on each side, depending on how you like them.

Serve and enjoy the wonderful flavors of ancient Rome.

Petite Tenders with Traditional Rub

If you don't know what a petite tender is, you're not alone, hardly anybody does. The petite tender is an extremely tender part of the shoulder, and makes a wonderful steak. The flavor and tenderness are so good, that I decided to try a very simple and traditional marinade. The taste was outstanding and the steaks lived up to their name. They were very tender.

This recipe also works well with flat iron steak, another very tender cut.

Serves 4

2 grassfed petite tender (teres major) steaks, (or flat iron steaks), totaling 1½ to 2 pounds

2 tablespoons unfiltered organic extra virgin olive oil

1 teaspoon organic granulated garlic powder

1 teaspoon freshly ground organic black pepper

½ teaspoon coarse unrefined sea salt, crushed

1. At least 1 hour before you plan to cook the steaks, combine the olive oil, garlic powder, and black pepper. Mix well. Rub this mixture all over the steaks. Place the steaks in a glass bowl. Cover, and let rest at room temperature for at least 1 hour.

2. Build a charcoal fire on one side of the cooker only. Bring your cooker to medium high heat, with all vents fully open. Just before placing the meat on the grill, sprinkle all sides of the meat with the salt. Place the steaks in front of, but not over, the heat source. Cover, and cook for 4 minutes on each side, or a little longer, depending on how you like your steaks.

Serve and enjoy this tender meat.

Traditional English Prime Rib

The English used to be famous for their roast meat. Perhaps their favorite way of cooking meat was to put a whole prime rib on a spit and roast it in front of a wood fire, basting it with its own fat. This roast was so beloved that they even wrote poems about it. While roasting a whole prime rib on a spit is not practical for most of us, we can cook something utterly delicious that is based on this glorious old tradition. A covered barbecue can give a similar effect to a rotisserie because of the convection effect which swirls hot air over, under, and around the meat.

Serves 4 to 8

1 (4 pound) grassfed bone in prime rib roast, with fat cap
3 tablespoons unfiltered organic extra virgin olive oil
¼ cup grassfed beef suet, (or beef lard)
½ teaspoon dried thyme, either wild or organic, crushed between your fingers
½ teaspoon freshly ground organic black pepper
1 teaspoon coarse unrefined sea salt, crushed

1. The day before you plan to cook the roast, place the meat in a glass bowl. Coat all surfaces of the meat with the olive oil, cover, and let rest for 1 hour, then refrigerate overnight.

2. Take the roast out of the refrigerator at least 1 hour before you begin cooking, so it can come to room temperature.

3. Build a charcoal fire on one side of the cooker only. Bring your cooker to medium high heat, with all vents fully open.

4. Melt the beef suet over low heat in a small saucepan. Sprinkle the meat with thyme, pepper, and salt. Carefully pour half of the melted beef fat over the sides and top of the roast.

5. Place the roast on the grill, in front of, but not over, the heat source, so that one of the long meaty sides faces the heat source, fat side up. Cover, and cook for 15 minutes.

6. Pour half of the remaining fat over the roast. Rotate the roast so the other long meaty side of the roast faces the heat source. Cover, and cook for another 15 minutes.

7. Pour the rest of the fat over the top and sides of the roast. Cover, and reduce the heat to medium low by adjusting the top vents to half-closed. Cook for 30 minutes.

8. Test for doneness. If the roast is not done to your taste, add two handfuls of charcoal to the fire. Cover, and continue to cook at medium low heat, checking for doneness every 10 minutes.

Serve and enjoy this magnificent roast.

Charcoal-Roasted Prime Rib

Hardwood charcoal is one of the oldest fuels known to humankind. It has been used for thousands of years, all over the globe. It has not been improved upon yet.

Many people think that you need flames and/or smoke to get a great barbecue flavor. But our ancestors often tried to cook without flames or smoke, relying on glowing coals to flavor the meat and provide the necessary heat.

A prime rib roast is an elite cut of meat, and it really shines in this recipe. Three simple ingredients and hardwood charcoal combine to provide outstanding flavor and tenderness. This recipe is intended for a roast with a fat cap, which every prime rib should have.

Serves 4 to 8

1 (3½ to 5 pound) 2-rib grassfed prime rib roast

4 tablespoons unfiltered organic extra virgin olive oil

1 teaspoon organic granulated garlic powder

1 teaspoon freshly ground organic black pepper

1. The day before you plan to cook the roast, place it in a glass bowl large enough to hold it, and coat all surfaces of the meat with the olive oil. Sprinkle the garlic powder and black pepper over all sides of the meat. Cover, and let rest at room temperature for 1 hour, then refrigerate overnight.

2. Remove the meat from the refrigerator 1 hour before you plan to cook it, so it can come to room temperature.

3. Build a charcoal fire on one side of the cooker only. Bring your cooker to medium high heat, with all vents fully open. Place the roast fat side up, in front of, but not over, the heat source, so that one of the long meaty sides faces the heat source. Cover, and cook for 15 minutes.

4. Turn the meat so the other long meaty side of the roast is facing the heat source. The roast will remain fat side up. Cover, and cook for another 15 minutes.

5. Cover, and reduce the heat to medium low by adjusting the top vents to half-closed. Cook for 30 minutes at medium low heat.

6. Test for doneness. If the meat is not done to your taste, add two handfuls of charcoal to the fire. Cover, and continue to cook at medium low heat, checking for doneness at 5 minute intervals.

7. When the roast is done to your taste, reduce the heat as low as possible by closing all the top and bottom vents completely, and let the roast rest in the cooker for 10 minutes.

Serve and enjoy the tender meat, rich with the primal taste of hardwood charcoal.

Barbecued Prime Rib with a Garlic Marinade

The standing rib roast, often known as the prime rib, is the king of traditional English roasts.

Prime rib is almost always prepared in an oven these days, and rarely barbecued. However, it was traditionally cooked in front of a fire. Cooking it with wood or charcoal gives it great flavor. Here, we use olive oil and garlic to flavor and tenderize the roast, which they do admirably. This is one of the best roasts you will ever taste.

Serves 4 to 6

1 (3-rib) grassfed standing rib roast, with fat cap (see note below)
4 tablespoons unfiltered organic extra virgin olive oil
6 large cloves organic garlic, crushed

1. The day before you plan to cook the roast, rub the olive oil all over the meat. Press the crushed garlic into the meat. Place in a glass container, and refrigerate overnight.

2. Remove the roast from the refrigerator 1 hour before you plan to cook it, so it can come to room temperature.

3. Build a charcoal fire on one side of the cooker only. Bring your cooker to medium high heat, with all vents fully open.

4. Remove the garlic from the meaty parts of the roast and place it on top of the fat cap.

5. Place the roast in front of, but not over, the heat source, so that one of the long meaty sides faces the heat source, fat side up. Cover, and cook for 10 minutes.

6. Rotate the roast so the other long meaty side of the roast faces the heat source. Cover, and cook for 10 more minutes.

7. Reduce the heat to medium low by adjusting the top vents to half-closed. Cook for 1 hour at medium low heat. Test for doneness. If it is not done to your taste, add two handfuls of charcoal to the coals. Continue cooking, checking for doneness at 10 minute intervals.

Serve and enjoy the delicious, tender meat.

NOTE: If the roast does not have a fat cap, cover with beef tallow, or thinly sliced pastured butter, or strips of good natural bacon.

Charcoal-Roasted Prime Rib with a Basil Butter Baste

Sometimes, despite all my efforts, I end up with a roast that has no fat cap. One of the best solutions I have devised is to use a good baste, loaded with life-giving animal fat. This baste gives a wonderful flavor to charcoal-roasted meat and helps keep it moist and tender during roasting. The meat in this recipe is cooked at a relatively low temperature, which also enhances tenderness. The butter baste, enhanced by garlic and fresh basil, unites with the smoldering charcoal to create a very special taste indeed.

Serves 4

1 (2-rib) grassfed prime rib roast, (a fat cap is not necessary)

2 tablespoons unfiltered organic extra virgin olive oil

For the Baste

½ cup homemade bone broth, preferably *Beef Bone Broth* (page 50)

4 tablespoons pastured butter

2 tablespoons fresh organic basil leaves, finely chopped

4 cloves organic garlic, finely chopped

½ teaspoon coarse unrefined sea salt, crushed

½ teaspoon freshly ground organic black pepper

1. The day before you plan to cook the roast, rub the olive oil all over the meat. Place the meat in a glass bowl. Cover, and let sit at room temperature for 1 hour, then refrigerate overnight.

2. Take the meat out of the refrigerator at least 1 hour before you plan to cook the meat, so it can come to room temperature.

3. Add all ingredients for the baste to a small saucepan. Heat over low heat until the butter melts completely. Remove from the heat once the butter is melted, and mix well.

4. Let the baste cool until it is warm, not hot. Use a basting brush to paint the baste all over the meat, covering all surfaces of the roast. Let the basted meat rest for at least 30 minutes. Keep the baste warm, as you will be using it again.

5. Build a charcoal fire on one side of the cooker only. Bring your cooker to medium high heat, with all vents fully open.

6. When the cooker is ready, place the roast in front of, but not over, the heat source. Cover, and reduce the heat to medium low by adjusting the top vents to half-closed. Cook for 30 minutes at medium low heat.

7. Baste the meat. Cover, and cook for another 30 minutes.

8. Add two handfuls of charcoal to the fire, and baste the meat again. Cover, and cook for another 30 minutes, or until done to your taste.

Serve and enjoy the rich flavors.

Hawaiian Prime Rib

Prime rib is a favorite cut of meat in Hawaii. The Hawaiian tradition of roasting prime rib goes back to the 1830s, when beef was added to the traditional Hawaiian diet. Kiawe is the Hawaiian name for a plant that was brought from the American Southwest to feed cattle. Texans know this plant as mesquite. Kiawe charcoal is available on the mainland and gives a wonderful, unique flavor to meat. While the flavor of kiawe charcoal is similar to mesquite, it is different, and gives a smoky, exotic flavor to barbecued meat.

The garlic, sea salt, and kiawe combine to make a memorable and delicious prime rib roast. If you do not have kiawe, you can use any good hardwood lump charcoal.

Serves 4

1 (2-rib) grassfed prime rib roast, with fat cap

3 tablespoons unfiltered organic extra virgin olive oil

6 cloves organic garlic, crushed

1½ teaspoons coarse unrefined sea salt, crushed

2 teaspoons coarsely ground organic black pepper

1. The day before you plan to cook the roast, place the meat in a glass bowl, and coat all surfaces with the olive oil. Press the crushed garlic firmly into the meaty parts of the roast. Cover, and let rest at room temperature for 1 hour, then refrigerate overnight.

2. Remove the roast from the refrigerator at least 1 hour before you plan to cook it, so it can come to room temperature.

3. Build a charcoal fire (preferably with kiawe charcoal) on one side of the cooker only. Bring your cooker to medium high heat, with all vents fully open. Just before you place the meat on the grill, remove the garlic from the meaty parts of the roast, and place it on top of the fat cap. Sprinkle some of the salt over the meat. Take the remaining salt and all of the pepper and press it into the fat cap.

4. Place the roast in front of, but not over, the heat source, so one of the long, meaty sides faces the heat source (fat side up). Cover, and cook at medium high heat for 15 minutes.

5. Rotate the roast so the other long, meaty side faces the heat source (fat side up). Cover, and cook for another 15 minutes.

6. Reduce the heat to medium low by adjusting the top vents to half-closed, and continue cooking for another 30 minutes. Check for doneness, if the meat is not done to your taste, add two handfuls of charcoal to the coals. Cover, and continue cooking at medium low heat until the meat is done to your taste, checking for doneness at 10 minute intervals.

Serve and enjoy the wonderful flavor of this Hawaiian roast.

Smoked Ribeye Roast

The name of this recipe refers to the classic technique of cooking a roast for a long time over a low fire. You should not expect to see clouds of smoke pouring out of your cooker. What you should expect is tender meat with a reddish smoke ring around the outside, and a definite smoky flavor in the meat. A flavor that complements, but does not overwhelm the glorious natural taste.

Cooking low and slow is the basis of old-style American barbecue. The tougher and cheaper cuts of meat were often cooked by this method. Meat prepared by this method was cooked until it was very well done. It could take many hours to cook a roast. This roast is unusual in that it is cooked to a delicious medium rare, and is cut from the ribeye, a very tender piece of meat. Very little seasoning is used, as the smoldering charcoal provides the flavor.

Serves 4 to 6

1 (2 to 3 pound) grassfed ribeye roast, with fat cap if possible
¼ cup unfiltered organic extra virgin olive oil
1 teaspoon coarse unrefined sea salt, crushed

1. The day before you plan to cook the roast, place it in a glass bowl. Add the olive oil, and make sure all surfaces of the meat are coated with the oil. Cover, and let rest for 1 hour, then refrigerate overnight.

2. Take the roast out of the refrigerator at least 1 hour before you plan to cook it, so it can come to room temperature.

3. Build a charcoal fire on one side of the cooker only. Bring your cooker to medium high heat, with all vents fully open.

4. Just before you put the meat on the grill, rub the salt all over the roast.

5. Place the roast on the middle of the grill, fat side down. Cover, and reduce the heat to medium low by adjusting the top vents to half-closed. Cook for 50 minutes at medium low heat.

6. Add two handfuls of charcoal to the fire, and turn the roast over, fat side up. Cover, and cook for another 25 minutes, or until done to your taste.

Serve and enjoy the smoky, tender meat.

Smoke-Roasted Ribeye with Mediterranean Herb Crust

The Mediterranean is famous for the flavor of its herbs, which grow profusely in the area. Animals often graze on wild herbs, which give a delicious and distinctive flavor to the meat. One of the favorite ways to cook meat is to roast it in front of a fire, often made of aromatic wood. The terrific flavor comes from a combination of the aromatic woods used for the fire and the herb diet of the animal. Here in the United States, we do not have fields of herbs that animals graze on, but we can still recreate the flavor with a marinade. The use of fresh and dried herbs in the same marinade provides a deep and rounded herbal flavor.

Serves 4 to 6

1 (2½ pound) grassfed ribeye roast

Mediterranean Herb Crust

1 tablespoon organic fresh thyme leaves, finely chopped

½ teaspoon organic dried thyme

1 tablespoon organic fresh rosemary leaves, finely chopped

½ teaspoon organic dried rosemary

2 cloves organic garlic, finely chopped

½ teaspoon freshly ground organic black pepper

3 tablespoons unfiltered organic extra virgin olive oil

For Cooking

1 teaspoon coarse unrefined sea salt, crushed

1. The day before you plan to cook the roast, combine the fresh and dried thyme, the fresh and dried rosemary, and the garlic. Crush together to form a paste. Add pepper and olive oil. Mix well. Place the roast in a glass bowl. Rub this herb crust all over the prime rib so it is evenly distributed on all sides. Cover, and let rest at room temperature for 1 hour, then refrigerate overnight.

2. Take the roast out of the refrigerator at least 1 hour before you plan to cook it, so it can come to room temperature.

3. Build a charcoal fire on one side of the cooker only. Bring your cooker to medium high heat, with all vents fully open.

4. Sprinkle the salt all over the roast. Place the roast in front of, but not over, the heat source, fat side up. Cover, and cook for 15 minutes.

5. Rotate the roast so the other side is facing the fire. Cover, and cook for another 15 minutes.

6. Move the roast to the center of the grill. Cover, and reduce the heat to medium low by adjusting the top vents to half-closed. Cook for another 15 to 30 minutes, or until done to your taste.

Strip Loin Roast with
Native American Flavors

The original Native Americans do not get enough credit for their wonderful cooking and knowledge of how to combine flavors. Some of their knowledge has been passed down to their descendents, and much has been lost.

This recipe is based on a Native American seasoning combination used for bison. I decided to try it on some beef, and it gave a savory, primal flavor to the meat.

Serves 2 to 4

1 (2 pound) grassfed strip loin roast with fat cap

2 tablespoons unfiltered organic extra virgin olive oil

Leaves from 4 stalks organic fresh sage

3 organic green onions, including the tops, coarsely chopped

2 large cloves organic garlic, coarsely chopped

1. At least 2 hours before you plan to cook the roast, coat with the olive oil. Combine the sage, green onion, and garlic, and chop together until finely chopped. Place the roast in a glass bowl, and press the mixture into all sides of the meat. Marinate at room temperature for 2 hours. (Alternatively, you can let rest for 1 hour, then refrigerate overnight.)

2. If you refrigerate overnight, take the meat out of the refrigerator at least 1 hour before you plan to cook it, so it can come to room temperature.

3. Build a charcoal fire on one side of the cooker only. Bring your cooker to medium high heat, with all vents fully open. Place the roast in the cooker, fat side up, in front of, but not over, the heat source. Cover, and cook for 18 minutes.

4. Rotate the roast so the other side faces the heat source, cover, and cook for another 18 minutes.

5. Reduce the heat as low as possible by closing all the top and bottom vents completely, and let rest for 5 minutes.

Serve and enjoy this wonderful beef.

Roast Beef with the Flavor of Old California

California was once the home of huge ranchos that raised large herds of cattle. In fact, the town in which I live, which is the home of over 40,000 people, was part of such a rancho. Cattle used to graze on the very spot where I'm sitting now, as I type these words. They grazed on green, sweet grass, and they thrived. The cattle were raised mainly for their hides, which were the basis of the entire California economy in those pre-gold rush days. However, the Californios loved beef, and developed many delicious ways of cooking it. The rub for this roast is based on traditional California flavorings. This roast has wonderful flavor, showing again how tradition creates and preserves wonderful taste.

Serves 4

1 (2 pound) grassfed strip loin roast, with fat cap

For the Rub

3 tablespoons unfiltered organic extra virgin olive oil

1 teaspoon organic dried oregano, crushed between your fingers

1 teaspoon organic granulated garlic powder

½ teaspoon smoked paprika, preferably Spanish or organic

½ teaspoon freshly ground organic black pepper

For Cooking

1 teaspoon coarse unrefined sea salt, crushed

1. At least 1 hour before you plan to cook the meat, prepare the rub. Place all the rub ingredients in a bowl, and stir until they are very well combined. Place the meat in a glass bowl, and coat all surfaces of the meat and fat with the rub, pressing it into the meat. Cover, and let rest at room temperature for at least 1 hour.

2. Build a charcoal fire on one side of the cooker only. Bring your cooker to medium high heat, with all vents fully open. Place the meat in front of, but not over, the heat source, fat side up. Cover, and cook for 10 minutes.

3. Rotate the meat so the other side of the meat faces the heat source, still fat side up. Cover, and cook for another 10 minutes.

4. Reduce the heat to medium low by adjusting the top vents to half-closed, and continue to cook for another 10 to 20 minutes, or until done to your taste.

Serve and enjoy the wonderful flavors of Old California.

Beef Roast in the Style of Ancient China

This is yet another way to cook meat in the style of ancient China, by using the fat of a different animal to flavor the meat. This recipe also includes the traditional Chinese seasoning combination of ginger, green onions, and garlic. I have added unfiltered organic extra virgin olive oil, which was never used in ancient China, but really unites the flavors in a delicious way, and helps make the meat tender.

Serves 4

1 (2 pound) grassfed strip loin roast, (or tenderloin roast)

3 tablespoons unfiltered organic extra virgin olive oil

1 (2 inch) piece ginger, crushed and finely chopped

2 organic green onions, crushed and finely chopped

4 organic garlic cloves, crushed and finely chopped

3 tablespoons melted grassfed bison fat, (or melted grassfed bison suet)

1 teaspoon coarse unrefined sea salt, crushed

1. At least 1 hour before you plan to cook the meat, place the meat in a glass bowl large enough to hold it. Rub all surfaces of the meat with the olive oil. Mix the ginger, green onions, and garlic together, then press them into all sides of the meat. Cover, and let rest at room temperature for 1 hour.

2. Use a spoon to remove the vegetable pieces from the meat. Place the meat on a plate, and brush all sides of the meat with the melted bison fat (or suet).

3. Build a charcoal fire on one side of the cooker only. Bring your cooker to medium high heat, with all vents fully open. Sprinkle the salt over all sides of the meat. Place the meat on the grill, in front of, but not over, the heat source, fat side up. Cover, and cook for 25 minutes.

4. Reduce the heat to medium low by adjusting the top vents to half-closed, and cook for another 10 minutes, or until done to your taste. Check for doneness at 5 minute intervals.

Serve and enjoy this wonderful roast.

Charcoal Roasted Tenderloin

Tenderloin is one of the most expensive and tender cuts of meat. It is actually quite lean. Tenderloin has a less intense flavor than other cuts of beef, but a few carefully chosen ingredients can enhance its flavor.

Tenderloin is usually cut into small steaks. Roasting a big piece of tenderloin gives you a depth of flavor and texture that you just cannot get with a small steak. The porcini mushroom powder really enhances the flavor, (as does the onion powder if you prefer to use that). The flavor of smoldering charcoal combines perfectly with the marinade ingredients to create an unforgettable taste and texture.

Serves 4 to 6

1 grassfed tenderloin roast, approximately 2 pounds, trimmed of all silverskin

For the Marinade

3 tablespoons unfiltered organic extra virgin olive oil

2 teaspoons porcini mushroom powder, (or organic onion powder)

1 teaspoon organic granulated garlic powder

1 teaspoon freshly ground organic black pepper

For Cooking

1 teaspoon coarse unrefined sea salt, crushed

1. At least 1 hour before you plan to cook the roast, prepare the marinade. Combine the marinade ingredients, and stir well. Place the meat in a glass bowl and pour the marinade over the meat, making sure that all surfaces of the meat are coated with the marinade. Cover, and let rest at room temperature for at least 1 hour.

2. Build a charcoal fire on one side of the cooker only. Bring your cooker to medium high heat, with all vents fully open. Sprinkle the salt all over the meat. Place the meat on the grill, in front of, but not over, the heat source. Cover, and cook for 25 to 30 minutes, depending on how you like the meat.

3. Reduce the heat as low as possible by closing all the top and bottom vents completely, and let the roast rest for 5 minutes.

Serve and enjoy the luxurious texture and wonderful taste of this magnificent roast.

Roast Tenderloin with the Flavors of Korea

Beef is revered and honored in traditional Korean cuisine. The Korean people have been cooking beef for a very long time, and they have come up with some wonderful flavor combinations. Traditionally, beef for the barbecue is cut into small, thin pieces which are cooked very quickly over wood charcoal. I wondered if the traditional flavors of Korea would work with a whole roast tenderloin. They do. The traditional Korean seasonings give a deep and wonderful flavor to the whole tenderloin which is only enhanced by the barbecue process.

Serves 4

1 (1½ to 2 pound) grassfed tenderloin roast, trimmed of all silverskin

For the Marinade

2 tablespoons naturally fermented organic soy sauce

2 tablespoons unrefined organic toasted sesame oil

1 tablespoon organic Grade B maple syrup

1 teaspoon freshly ground organic black pepper

1 tablespoon sherry

2 organic green onions, finely chopped

2 large cloves organic garlic, finely chopped

A few drops thick red organic hot sauce

1. At least 1 hour before you plan to cook the roast, combine all ingredients to form a marinade. Place the roast in a glass bowl, and coat all surfaces of the meat with the marinade. Cover, and let rest at room temperature for at least 1 hour.

2. Build a charcoal fire on one side of the cooker only. Bring your cooker to medium high heat, with all vents fully open.

3. Place the roast in front of, but not over, the heat source. Cover, and cook for 20 to 30 minutes, depending on the size of the roast and how you like it cooked.

Serve and enjoy the wonderful Korean flavors.

Roast Picanha

The very best recipes are often a surprise. I read a lot about the various ways of making a particular cut, put a few ingredients together, try a technique that seems to fit, and test it. And sometimes, just sometimes, the meat turns out to be extraordinary, something that is much better than good, something that is as close to perfection as we humans ever seem to get. This is one of those recipes.

Picanha is a traditional cut in South America, particularly in the great cattle-raising countries of Argentina, Brazil, and Uruguay. Picanha is the most popular cut of meat in Brazil. Picanha is cut from the top of the sirloin. It has a beautiful fat cap, which is the key to its extraordinary flavor. I ordered some picanha, a very good decision.

This recipe is very simple, and very easy. I do not know if anything could be better. The meat had a deep beefy flavor, unusual and yet familiar, that was like magic in my mouth. The texture was firm yet very tender. It sliced easily and evenly, beautiful medium rare slices that were a joy to eat. This is an eating experience that must be tasted to be understood. I felt well-nourished and full of energy after eating this. I treat myself and my family to picanha, every now and then. Believe me, it is something to look forward to.

Serves 4 to 8

1 (3 pound) grassfed picanha (also called New York tip, or rump cover), with fat cap

3 tablespoons unfiltered organic extra virgin olive oil

1 tablespoon coarse unrefined sea salt, dissolved in 1 cup of boiling filtered water

1. At least 2 hours before you plan to cook the meat, coat all surfaces with the olive oil. Place the roast in a glass bowl, cover, and let rest at room temperature for 2 hours.

2. Build a charcoal fire on one side of the cooker only. Bring your cooker to medium high heat, with all vents fully open.

3. Sprinkle some of the saltwater mixture on both sides of the roast. Place the roast in the cooker, fat side down, in front of, but not over, the heat source. Cover, and reduce the heat to medium low by adjusting the top vents to half-closed. Cook for 30 minutes at medium low heat.

4. Sprinkle some more of the saltwater mixture over the roast. Turn the roast over so the fat side is up. Sprinkle some of the saltwater mixture over the fat. Cover, and cook for 30 more minutes.

5. Turn the heat down as low as possible by closing all the top and bottom vents completely. Let rest for 5 minutes. This should give you a medium rare roast. Picanha should not be cooked too long.

Serve and enjoy the wonderful meat.

Picanha with Californio Rub

Picanha is perhaps the favorite cut of meat in South America, especially in the great beef-eating countries of Argentina, Uruguay, and Brazil. This cut, which comes with a covering of the most delicious fat imaginable, has a unique texture and flavor that is just wonderful. Picanha is pretty much unknown in the United States, though there is often some picanha included in what is sold as top sirloin steak. Picanha in the United States used to be called New York tip, and was popular among those who knew meat. Now it is called rump cover, a totally unappealing name that obscures the wonderful qualities of this magnificent cut of beef.

Picanha has such a wonderful flavor of its own that South Americans usually cook it with nothing but salt, or a saltwater baste. I decided to try a rub based on the seasonings of Old California. I am sure the expert cattlemen there must have appreciated this fine cut, though this is just a guess.

The combination of picanha, smoldering charcoal, and the flavors of Old California, is exquisite.

Serves 4 to 8

1 (3 pound) grassfed picanha (also called New York tip, or rump cover), with fat cap

For the Wet Rub

3 tablespoons unfiltered organic extra virgin olive oil

1½ teaspoons organic dried oregano, crushed between your fingers

1 teaspoon organic granulated garlic powder

1 teaspoon freshly ground organic black pepper

For Cooking

1 teaspoon coarse unrefined sea salt, crushed

1. The day before you plan to cook the roast, make the wet rub by combining all ingredients and stirring until well mixed. Place the meat in a glass bowl, and rub the mixture all over the meaty side, pressing it in with your fingers (or a spoon). Cover, and let rest at room temperature for 1 hour, then refrigerate overnight.

2. Remove the roast from the refrigerator at least 1 hour before you plan to cook it, so it can come to room temperature.

3. Build a charcoal fire on one side of the cooker only. Bring your cooker to medium high heat, with all vents fully open.

4. Sprinkle the salt all over the meat side of the picanha. Place the meat on the grill, fat side down, in front of, but not over, the heat source. Cover, and reduce the heat to medium low by adjusting the top vents to half-closed. Cook for 20 minutes at medium low heat.

5. Turn the meat over, so it is fat side up. Cover, and cook for another 20 to 40 minutes, or until done to your taste.

High-Low Barbecued Roast Beef

This recipe came about as a result of my reading many descriptions of roasting meat in various histories, old cookbooks, and even some historical novels. It seemed that everybody would build a good hot fire of burning coals and roast the meat in front of the fire. They would let the fire burn down during the cooking process, which meant that it would first cook at a high heat, which would get cooler as the fire burned down until the meat was finished over a very low fire. I decided to see if I could recreate this effect in a covered barbecue using natural charcoal. The result was so outstanding that it needs to be tasted to be believed. The only ingredient besides the beef in this recipe is some olive oil. Nothing else is needed.

Serves 4 to 6

1 (2 pound) grassfed sirloin tip roast, (or center cut shoulder roast), with fat cap (see note below)

3 tablespoons unfiltered organic extra virgin olive oil

1. At least 2 hours before you plan to cook the meat, place it in a glass bowl and coat all surfaces of the meat with the olive oil. Cover, and let rest at room temperature.

2. Build a charcoal fire on one side of the cooker only. Bring your cooker to medium high heat, with all vents fully open. Place the roast in front of, but not over, the heat source, fat side up. Cover, and cook for 12 minutes.

3. Rotate the roast so the other side is facing the heat source. Cover, and cook for another 12 minutes.

4. Move the roast to the center of the grill. Cover, and reduce the heat to medium low by adjusting the top vents to half-closed. Let the roast cook for another 30 minutes, then check for doneness. If the roast is not done to your liking, continue cooking, checking for doneness at 10 minute intervals.

5. When the roast is done to your taste, reduce the heat as low as possible by closing all the top and bottom vents completely. Leave the beef in the covered barbecue for another 10 minutes.

Serve and enjoy. You won't believe how tender and tasty this meat is until you try it.

NOTE: If the roast does not have a fat cap, cover with beef tallow, or thinly sliced pastured butter, or strips of good natural bacon.

Roast Beef from Ancient Rome

The ancient Romans were obsessed with food. Cooking was an art to them, and the rich would spend enormous sums of money on rare ingredients and great cooks. They would often preserve meat in a large vat of honey, which would tenderize it.

We are fortunate in that some Roman recipes have survived. This includes a book written by Apicius, a famous Roman cook. The recipes assume you are familiar with Roman cooking techniques, and contain very little detail except as to the ingredients used. Often no measurements are given. Some of the recipes are very simple. For example, a recipe for roasting meat can be translated as follows:

"Roll meat in coarse salt. Roast the meat. Serve with honey."

I have used these words as the inspiration for this recipe, which is different and delicious. I have added olive oil, a very Roman ingredient, and used the honey as part of the marinade. This is a very tender roast.

Be sure to use honey that is organic, raw, and unheated, so the enzymes will still be active to tenderize the meat.

Serves 4 to 6

1 (2 to 3 pound) grassfed sirloin tip roast, with fat cap (see note below)

For the Marinade
2 tablespoons unfiltered organic extra virgin olive oil
1 tablespoon raw organic unheated honey

For Cooking
2 teaspoons coarse unrefined sea salt, crushed

1. The day before you plan to cook the roast, make the marinade. Stir the honey and olive oil together until the honey dissolves in the oil. Place the meat in a glass bowl, and coat all surfaces with the marinade. Cover, and let rest for 1 hour at room temperature, then refrigerate overnight.

2. Remove the meat from the refrigerator at least 1 hour before you plan to cook it, so it can come to room temperature.

3. Build a charcoal fire on one side of the cooker only. Bring your cooker to medium high heat, with all vents fully open.

4. When the meat is at room temperature and the cooker is ready, spread the salt out on a large plate, and roll the meat in the salt. Place the meat on the grill, in front of, but not over, the heat source. Cover, and reduce the heat to medium low by adjusting the top vents to half-closed. Cook for 1 hour at medium low heat, or until done to your taste. If you cook for more than an hour, add two handfuls of charcoal to the fire. Check for doneness at 10 minute intervals.

Serve and enjoy the exotic flavor of Ancient Rome.

NOTE: If the roast does not have a fat cap, cover with beef tallow, or thinly sliced pastured butter, or strips of good natural bacon.

Roast Beef with Italian Vegetable Marinade

Most Americans do not think of beef or barbecue when Italian cuisine is mentioned. That is a shame, because there are many fine Italian recipes for beef, and cooking with fire is an old tradition. This recipe uses some of my favorite Italian flavors to tenderize a roast. No oil is used. The flavor is wonderful.

Serves 4 to 6

1 (2 to 3 pound) grassfed sirloin tip roast

For the Marinade
1 small organic onion, coarsely chopped
1 organic carrot, peeled, and coarsely chopped
1 stalk organic celery, coarsely chopped
1 small organic tomato, coarsely chopped
2 cloves organic garlic, very finely chopped
1 teaspoon freshly ground organic black pepper
2 tablespoons fresh organic rosemary leaves, very finely chopped
¼ cup filtered water

For Cooking
1 teaspoon coarse unrefined sea salt, crushed

1. The day before you plan to cook the roast, make the marinade. Combine all marinade ingredients in a blender, and blend into a purée. Pour the marinade into a glass bowl large enough to hold the roast. Add the roast, and coat all surfaces of the roast with the marinade. Cover, and let rest at room temperature for 1 hour, then refrigerate overnight.

2. Remove the roast from the refrigerator at least 1 hour before you plan to cook it, so the meat may come to room temperature.

3. Build a charcoal fire on one side of the cooker only. Bring your cooker to medium high heat, with all vents fully open.

4. Scrape the marinade off the roast, and sprinkle the salt all over the meat. Place the roast on the grill, fat side down, in front of, but not over, the heat source. Cover, and reduce the heat to medium low by adjusting the top vents to half-closed. Cook for 30 minutes at medium low heat.

5. Turn the roast over, fat side up. Cover, and cook for another 30 minutes.

6. Check for doneness. If the roast is not done to your taste, add two handfuls of charcoal to the fire. Cover, and continue to cook until done, checking for doneness at 10 minute intervals.

7. When the roast is done, reduce the heat as low as possible by closing all the top and bottom vents completely, and let the meat rest in the covered cooker for 10 minutes.

Serve and enjoy this tender roast.

Roast Beef with Basil Chimichurri

The Pampas of South America produce some of the most tender, delicious, grassfed beef the world has ever seen. It is traditional for Argentines to eat a lot of beef, much more than Americans. The beef usually is seasoned very simply, often with nothing more than a saltwater baste. It is often served with chimichurri, a sauce that contains some hot peppers, very finely chopped parsley, and/or other fresh herbs. There are hundreds of versions. Sometimes chimichurri is used as a marinade. This marinade is particularly good for lean beef that does not have a fat cap, though it is even better if the meat has a fat cap. This version of chimichurri is my own, and is unusual in that it is based on fresh basil leaves.

Serves 4

1 (2 to 3 pound) grassfed sirloin tip roast, (or center cut shoulder roast)

For the Chimichurri

4 tablespoons unfiltered organic extra virgin olive oil

2 tablespoons dry sherry, preferably Spanish

6 cloves organic garlic, very finely chopped

¼ cup fresh organic basil leaves, very finely chopped

2 teaspoons organic dried hot red pepper flakes, (or 2 teaspoons freshly ground organic black pepper)

For Cooking

1 teaspoon coarse unrefined sea salt, crushed

1. The day before you plan to cook the roast, prepare the chimichurri marinade. Stir all ingredients for the chimichurri together until they are very well combined. Place the meat in a glass bowl, and coat all surfaces with the chimichurri. Cover, and let rest at room temperature for 1 hour, then refrigerate overnight.

2. Remove the meat from the refrigerator at least 1 hour before you plan to cook it, so it can come to room temperature.

3. Build a charcoal fire on one side of the cooker only. Bring your cooker to medium high heat, with all vents fully open.

4. When your cooker is ready, sprinkle the salt all over the roast. Place the meat on the grill, fat side down, in front of, but not over, the heat source. Cover, and reduce the heat to medium low by adjusting the top vents to half-closed. Cook for 30 minutes at medium low heat.

5. Turn the meat over, fat side up. Cover, and cook for another 30 minutes. Test for doneness. If the meat is not done to your taste, add two handfuls of charcoal to the fire. Cover, and continue to cook at medium low heat, checking for doneness at 10 minute intervals.

6. When the meat is done to your taste, reduce the heat as low as possible by closing all the top and bottom vents completely, and let rest for 10 minutes.

Sirloin Tip Roast with Oyster Sauce

Sirloin tip roast is very lean, and usually condemned to the slow cooker. What is not commonly known is that sirloin tip has very little connective tissue, and can make a wonderfully tender roast when properly marinated. Chinese oyster sauce is made from a fermented liquid that comes from fermenting oysters. Unfortunately, most brands contain a lot of MSG, but it is possible to find a version that is natural and does not contain MSG. This sauce can lend wonderful flavor to meat, and help it to become more tender. Combining it with fish sauce, as I do in this recipe, may seem too "fishy," but it is not. The flavor is deep and meaty, not at all fishy.

Serves 4

1 (2 pound) grassfed sirloin tip roast

For the Marinade

2 tablespoons MSG-free oyster sauce

2 tablespoons Thai fish sauce

3 tablespoons unfiltered organic extra virgin olive oil

1 (1 inch) piece organic ginger, crushed, and finely chopped

4 organic garlic cloves, crushed, and finely chopped

2 organic green onions, crushed, and finely chopped

1 teaspoon freshly ground organic black pepper

1. The day before you plan to cook the roast, make the marinade. Combine all the marinade ingredients, and stir well. Place the meat in a glass bowl, and pour the marinade over the meat, making sure that all surfaces of the meat are coated by the marinade. Cover, and let rest at room temperature for 1 hour, then refrigerate overnight.

2. Remove the roast from the refrigerator at least 1 hour before you plan to cook it, so it can come to room temperature.

3. Build a charcoal fire on one side of the cooker only. Bring your cooker to medium high heat, with all vents fully open. Place the roast on the grill, in front of, but not over, the heat source. Cover, and cook for 20 minutes.

4. Reduce the heat to medium low by adjusting the top vents to half-closed, and cook for another 40 minutes. If it is not done to your taste, continue cooking, and test for doneness at 5 minute intervals.

5. When the roast is done to your taste, reduce the heat as low as possible by closing all the top and bottom vents completely, and let the roast rest in the cooker for 5 minutes.

Serve and enjoy the delicious flavor of the tender meat.

Tri-Tip, Pampas Style

The Pampas of Argentina, Uruguay, and Southern Brazil are a paradise for cattle. Nourishing native grasses grow tall on the rich soil, forming a sea of grass and meadow plants that provide wonderful forage. Beef is a treasured food in all of these countries. In Brazil, beef is known as "the noble meat," a meat whose fine taste must not be touched by any but the simplest marinades and spices.

In the United States, tri-tip is a cut found mainly in California. But tri-tip is also a valued cut in the Pampas area. Tri-tip is a part of the sirloin which comes with a thick cap of its own beautiful fat. Unfortunately, this fat is often trimmed off in the United States, which takes away one of the best parts of this cut. On the Pampas, they know better, and the traditional recipes take full advantage of the flavor and tenderness provided by the natural fat cap of this delicious meat.

The meat will cook fat side down for half the cooking period. Though this is almost never done in American cooking, it is a technique that is often used in Latin America, and it works very well with this kind of meat. The meat absolutely must have a fat cap for this recipe to work. It is utterly delicious. Simple, yet so satisfying.

Serves 4 to 6

1 (2 to 2½ pound) grassfed tri-tip roast, with fat cap

3 tablespoons unfiltered organic extra virgin olive oil

1 teaspoon coarse unrefined sea salt

½ cup filtered water

1. The day before you plan to cook the tri-tip, place the meat in a glass bowl. Coat all sides of the meat with the olive oil. Cover, and let rest at room temperature for 1 hour, then refrigerate overnight.

2. Remove the meat from the refrigerator at least 1 hour before you plan to cook it, so it can come to room temperature.

3. Place the water in a small saucepan. Bring the water to a boil, then add the salt, and stir until the salt is dissolved in the water. Remove the mixture from the heat, and let cool.

4. Build a charcoal fire on one side of the cooker only. Bring your cooker to medium high heat, with all vents fully open.

5. When the meat is at room temperature and the cooker is ready, baste the meat with the saltwater mixture. Place the meat fat side down, in front of, but not over, the heat source. Cover, and reduce the heat to medium low by adjusting the top vents to half-closed. Cook at medium low heat for 20 to 30 minutes, depending on how you like it.

6. Baste the meat with the saltwater mixture. Turn the meat fat side up. Cover, and cook for another 20 to 30 minutes, depending on how you like it.

Serve and enjoy the tender meat.

San Ramon Valley Tri-Tip

California used to be cattle country. The Spanish settlers raised cattle for their hides, but also developed delicious ways of cooking beef. Huge herds of cattle roamed the immense ranchos. One such rancho covered the San Ramon Valley in Northern California. Though the rancho is long gone, a few cattle still graze in the area. My home is in the San Ramon Valley, and I am typing this recipe on land which used to be pasture.

The spices in this rub are typical of the flavorings used by the Californios. Tri-tip is a cut from the sirloin, and has some serious beef flavor, being ideal for this recipe.

Serves 4

1 (2 to 3 pound) grassfed tri-tip roast, preferably with fat cap
2 tablespoons unfiltered organic extra virgin olive oil

For the Rub
1 teaspoon organic granulated garlic powder
½ teaspoon freshly ground organic black pepper
½ teaspoon organic dried oregano, crushed between your fingers

For Cooking
1 teaspoon coarse unrefined sea salt, crushed

1. The day before you plan to cook the meat, place the meat in a glass bowl. Coat all surfaces of the meat with the olive oil. Combine the ingredients for the rub, and spread the mixture all over the meat. Cover, and let rest at room temperature for 1 hour, then refrigerate overnight.

2. Remove the meat from the refrigerator at least 1 hour before you plan to cook it, so it can come to room temperature.

3. Build a charcoal fire on one side of the cooker only. Bring your cooker to medium high heat, with all vents fully open. Sprinkle the salt all over the meat just before you plan to cook it.

4. Place the roast in front of, but not over, the heat source, fat side down. Cover, and cook for 10 minutes.

5. Turn the roast fat side up, cover, and cook for another 10 minutes.

6. Reduce the heat to medium low by adjusting the top vents to half-closed. Cook for another 10 minutes, or until done to your taste.

Serve and enjoy the tender, flavorful meat.

Shashlik Shoulder Roast

Shashlik is a Russian favorite, yet the flavors come from the Caucasus, especially the Republic of Georgia.

Pomegranate has a unique and wonderful sweet and sour flavor. It is best to use pomegranate concentrate or unsweetened pomegranate molasses rather than a bottled juice, as the juice is too diluted. Whether it is called concentrate or molasses, the only ingredient should be pomegranate. The enzymes in the onion and pomegranate do a wonderful job of making the meat tender, while adding the exotic flavor of the Caucasus.

Serves 4

1 (2 to 3 pound) grassfed center cut shoulder roast, with fat cap

For the Marinade
1 organic onion, coarsely chopped

¼ cup filtered water

2 organic garlic cloves

¼ cup pure unsweetened pomegranate concentrate

1 teaspoon freshly ground organic black pepper

3 tablespoons fresh organic cilantro, very finely chopped

1. At least 4 hours before you plan to cook the meat, make the marinade by combining all ingredients and mixing well. Place the meat in a glass bowl, and pour the marinade over the meat. Make sure all surfaces of the meat are coated with the marinade. Cover, and let rest at cool room temperature for about 4 hours, or refrigerate overnight.

2. If the meat was refrigerated, remove from it the refrigerator at least 1 hour before you plan to cook it.

3. Build a charcoal fire on one side of the cooker only. Bring your cooker to medium high heat, with all vents fully open. Scrape the onions off the meat with a spoon.

4. Place the meat in front of, but not over, the heat source, fat side down. Cover, and cook for 8 minutes.

5. Turn the meat fat side up. Cover, and cook for 8 more minutes.

6. Reduce the heat to medium low by adjusting the top vents to half-closed. Cook for 30 to 50 minutes, depending on the size of the roast and how you like it. Start checking for doneness at the 30 minute mark. Check for doneness at 10 minute intervals.

Serve and enjoy the rich, exotic flavor.

Diamond Jim Brady Roast with Garlic Baste

Diamond Jim Brady was a very wealthy and famous citizen of San Francisco around the turn of the 20th century. He was a famous gourmet, who particularly liked good beef. In fact, some San Francisco Bay Area supermarkets used to carry a "Diamond Jim" cut of roast beef until quite recently. This roast was his favorite cut of meat. It was cut from the part of the shoulder that is next to the prime rib, and is a particularly tender and flavorful piece of meat. I recently asked an experienced butcher to cut me one, and he was happy to oblige. I decided to pair this roast with a simple, but traditional baste that originated in the Basque country of Spain many years ago. Basque immigrants contributed a great deal to the food culture of San Francisco, and this Basque baste goes beautifully with this Diamond Jim roast.

Serves 4 to 6

1 (3 pound) grassfed Diamond Jim roast (shoulder roast cut from the meat next to the prime rib), or center cut shoulder roast, with fat cap (see note below)
3 tablespoons unfiltered organic extra virgin olive oil

For the Garlic Baste

½ cup organic extra virgin olive oil (does not have to be unfiltered)
4 cloves organic garlic, finely chopped

For Cooking

1 teaspoon coarse unrefined sea salt, crushed

1. The day before you plan to cook the roast, place it in a glass bowl, and coat all surfaces of the meat with the unfiltered olive oil. Cover, and let rest for 1 hour at room temperature, then refrigerate overnight.

2. While the meat is resting, make the garlic baste. Combine the ingredients in a small glass jar. Cover, and leave at room temperature overnight.

3. An hour before you plan to cook the roast, remove it from the refrigerator so it can come to room temperature. Brush all surfaces of the meat with the garlic baste.

4. Build a charcoal fire on one side of the cooker only. Bring your cooker to medium high heat, with all vents fully open. When your cooker is ready, and the meat is at room temperature, place the meat, fat side up, in front of, but not over, the heat source. Cover, and cook for 10 minutes.

5. Rotate the meat so the other side of the meat is facing the heat source. Cover, and cook for another 10 minutes.

6. Baste the meat with the garlic baste. Cover, and reduce the heat to medium low by adjusting the top vents to half-closed. Cook for 30 minutes, or until done to your taste.

Serve and enjoy Diamond Jim's favorite roast.

NOTE: If the roast does not have a fat cap, cover with beef tallow, or thinly sliced pastured butter, or strips of good natural bacon.

Superb Shoulder Roast

Beef and good wood have a tremendous affinity for each other. This recipe adds just three more ingredients to those wonderful flavors. This combination has a flavor and a tenderness that must be tasted. The small number of ingredients does not mean that the flavor is simple. It is superb. There is no salt in this recipe. Trust me, it does not need it.

Serves 4 to 6

1 (2 to 3 pound) grassfed center cut shoulder roast, with fat cap

4 tablespoons unfiltered organic extra virgin olive oil

1 teaspoon organic granulated garlic powder

1 teaspoon freshly ground organic black pepper

1. Take the roast out of the refrigerator at least 2 hours before you plan to cook it. Rub 2 tablespoons of the olive oil into the meat, covering all surfaces. Let sit at room temperature.

2. Build a charcoal fire on one side of the cooker only. Bring your cooker to medium high heat, with all vents fully open.

3. Sprinkle the roast all over with the garlic powder, coating each side lightly but thoroughly. Grind black pepper directly over each side of the roast, coating lightly but thoroughly. Place the roast, fat side down, on a plate. Pour the remaining 2 tablespoons of olive oil over the roast.

4. Place the roast on the center of the grill, fat side down. Cover, and reduce the heat to medium low by adjusting the top vents to half-closed. Cook for 30 minutes at medium low heat.

5. Turn the roast over so the fat side is up. Cover, and cook for another 30 minutes. Test for doneness. If the roast is not done to your taste, add two handfuls of charcoal to the coals, and continue to cook at medium low heat, checking for doneness at 10 minute intervals.

6. Reduce the heat as low as possible by closing all the top and bottom vents completely, and let the roast rest for 10 minutes.

Serve and enjoy some of the tastiest beef ever eaten.

Center Cut Shoulder Roast Uruguay Style

Beef raised on the Pampas of Uruguay is famous for its superb taste and tenderness. The flavor of the beef is so outstanding that it is traditionally made with very few spices and often is basted with nothing more than saltwater. It is quite common for Uruguayans to marinate beef in nothing more than olive oil before cooking. This roast is a classic example of how a few simple seasonings and a great piece of meat can unite to produce a masterpiece. The meat used in this recipe is center cut shoulder, also known as cross rib. Many meat producers suggest making this cut in a slow cooker, but it is so much better on the grill. This is a larger roast that can feed a lot of people, who will enjoy the tender, charcoal-roasted meat.

Serves 6 to 12

1 large (4½ to 6 pound) grassfed center cut shoulder roast, with fat cap

¼ cup unfiltered organic extra virgin olive oil

1 tablespoon coarse unrefined sea salt

2 cups filtered water

1. The day before you plan to cook the roast, place the meat in a glass bowl large enough to hold it, and coat all surfaces with the olive oil. Let rest at room temperature for 1 hour, covered, then refrigerate overnight.

2. Take the roast out of the refrigerator 1 hour before you plan to cook it, so it can come to room temperature.

3. Build a charcoal fire on one side of the cooker only. Bring your cooker to medium high heat, with all vents fully open. While the cooker is heating up, bring the water to a boil, add the salt, and stir well. As soon as the salt has dissolved, remove the pan from the heat.

4. When the cooker is ready, baste all sides of the meat with the saltwater mixture. Place the roast, fat side down, in front of, but not over, the heat source. Cover, and reduce the heat to medium low by adjusting the top vents to half-closed. Cook for 30 minutes at medium low heat.

5. Baste the roast with the saltwater. Cover, and cook for another 15 minutes.

6. Turn the roast over, fat side up, and baste with the saltwater. Cover, and cook for another 30 minutes.

7. Baste the roast with the saltwater once again. Add two handfuls of charcoal to the fire. Cover, and cook for another 15 minutes.

8. At this point, the roast should be rare to medium rare. If it is not done to your taste, continue cooking, checking for doneness at 10 minute intervals, and basting with the saltwater mixture each time.

9. When the roast is done to your taste, reduce the heat as low as possible by closing all the top and bottom vents completely, and let the roast remain in the cooker for 10 minutes.

Serve and enjoy the magnificent, tender meat.

Barbecued Beef Roast with Civil War Rub

This simple rub goes all the way back to the Civil War Era. The recipes I looked at were kind of vague, as "red pepper" does not specify whether the pepper was hot or mild, and "sugar" does not specify what kind of sugar was used. The word "salt" is also quite general, as there were several kinds of salt in use at this time. However, black pepper is precise. I had to use my own judgment in deciding what kind of salt, red pepper, and sugar to use. I tried to use traditional forms, and the results were absolutely delicious. Because salt can toughen grassfed meat if applied too long before cooking, I put this rub on just a couple of minutes before I placed the meat on the barbecue. This recipe shows, once again, that traditional recipes survive over time only if they are something special.

Serves 4

1 (2 to 3 pound) grassfed center cut shoulder roast, (or sirloin tip roast)

3 tablespoons unfiltered organic extra virgin olive oil

For the Rub

1 teaspoon coarse unrefined sea salt, crushed

1 teaspoon freshly ground organic black pepper

1 teaspoon unrefined natural sugar

1 teaspoon sweet paprika, organic or imported

1. The day before you plan to cook the roast, place it in a glass bowl, and coat all surfaces of the meat with the unfiltered olive oil. Cover, and let rest for 1 hour at room temperature, then refrigerate overnight.

2. An hour before you plan to cook the roast, remove it from the refrigerator so it can come to room temperature.

3. Combine the ingredients for the rub in a bowl, and mix well.

4. Build a charcoal fire on one side of the cooker only. Bring your cooker to medium high heat, with all vents fully open. When your cooker is ready, and the meat is at room temperature, sprinkle all sides of the meat with the rub. Place the meat, fat side up, in front of, but not over, the heat source. Cover, and cook for 10 minutes.

5. Rotate the meat so the other side of the meat is facing the heat source. Cover, and cook for another 10 minutes.

6. Reduce the heat to medium low by adjusting the top vents to half-closed. Cook for 30 minutes, or until done to your taste.

Serve and enjoy the Civil War flavors.

Roast Beef with the Flavors of Portugal

Portugal has a robust and fascinating cuisine. While Portugal was always a small country, it once had a huge empire that included Brazil, Angola, Mozambique, Goa, Timor, and many other territories scattered around the world. A number of exotic flavors and ingredients from Africa, Asia, and the Americas became part of Portuguese cooking.

"Roast beef" in Portuguese cooking usually means pot roast. However, I decided to create a marinade using traditional Portuguese flavors with a barbecued beef roast.

I also used smoked Spanish paprika and a piquillo pepper, as Spanish and Portuguese cuisines are closely related. Piquillo peppers are grown in the Lodosa Valley in Spain, smoked over wood fires, and placed in jars with olive oil and garlic. They are not hot, but have a unique and wonderful flavor. If you can't find them, the roast will still be delicious, but it will be even better with them. This roast is both different and delicious.

Serves 6 to 10

> 1 (3 to 5 pound) grassfed center cut shoulder roast

For the Marinade

> 3 tablespoons unfiltered organic extra virgin olive oil
> 1 tablespoon organic tomato paste
> 2 tablespoons organic Italian parsley leaves, finely chopped
> 2 teaspoons smoked sweet paprika, preferably Spanish
> ½ teaspoon hot smoked paprika, preferably Spanish
> 2 imported bay leaves, crumbled
> 4 cloves organic garlic, crushed, and chopped
> 1 piquillo pepper, very finely chopped, (optional)

For Cooking

> 1 teaspoon coarse unrefined sea salt, crushed

1. The day before you plan to cook the roast, make the marinade. Combine all ingredients and stir well. Place the roast in a glass bowl, and pour the marinade over the roast, making sure all surfaces are coated by the marinade. Cover, and let rest at room temperature for 1 hour, then refrigerate overnight.

2. Take the roast out of the refrigerator at least 1 hour before you plan to cook it, so it can come to room temperature.

3. Build a charcoal fire on one side of the cooker only. Bring your cooker to medium high heat, with all vents fully open. When the roast is at room temperature and the cooker is ready, sprinkle the salt over the meat. Place the meat on the grill, in front of, but not over, the heat source, fat side up.

4. Cover, and reduce the heat to medium low by adjusting the top vents to half-closed. Cook for 1 to 2 hours, depending on the size of the roast and how you like it. Start checking for doneness after 1 hour. If the roast is not done to your taste, add two handfuls of charcoal to the fire. Check for doneness at 10 minute intervals.

Roman Round Roast

Eye of round is one of the most flavorful cuts of beef. It is also one of the toughest, with very little fat. I have to confess that I was intimidated by the very thought of getting grassfed round roast tender. Even the grain-fed round roasts I made in the distant past had been tough. But I really wanted to unlock the flavor of this cut of meat. I knew that my Roman-style marinade had enormous tenderizing power, as well as great flavor. I decided to get some expert help. My friend Brian is a master butcher, who is also a classically trained chef. Brian suggested cooking the roast to 120 to 125 degrees, and slicing it very thin, against the grain. The combination of smoldering charcoal, Roman marinade, and Brian's excellent advice, resulted in one of the most tender, delicious roasts that I have ever had.

Serves 4

1 (2 to 3 pound) grassfed eye of round roast, with fat cap if possible

For the Marinade

1 tablespoon raw organic unheated honey

1½ tablespoons white wine, preferably Spanish sherry

3 tablespoons unfiltered organic extra virgin olive oil

2 teaspoons Thai fish sauce

1 teaspoon organic dried thyme

½ teaspoon dry coriander seeds, in powder form

1 teaspoon freshly ground organic black pepper

For Cooking

1 teaspoon coarse unrefined sea salt, crushed

1. The day before you plan to cook the meat, prepare the marinade by mixing all ingredients together. Keep stirring until the honey has completely dissolved into the other ingredients. Place the meat in a glass bowl, and cover all surfaces of the meat with the marinade. Cover, and let rest at room temperature for 1 hour, then refrigerate overnight.

2. Remove the meat from the refrigerator at least 1 hour before you plan to cook it, so it can come to room temperature.

3. Build a charcoal fire on one side of the cooker only. Bring your cooker to medium high heat, with all vents fully open. Sprinkle all sides of the meat with the salt. Place the roast in front of, but not over, the heat source.

4. Cover, and reduce the heat to medium low by adjusting the top vents to half-closed. Cook the roast for 30 minutes at medium low heat. Check the temperature with the meat thermometer. The roast is ready if the temperature is between 120 to 125 degrees Fahrenheit. Check for doneness at 10 minute intervals (or 5 minute intervals when the temperature is close to 120 degrees).

5. When you have reached the proper temperature, reduce the heat as low as possible by closing all the top and bottom vents completely, and let the roast remain in the cooker for another 5 to 10 minutes.

6. Serve the roast, slicing it very thinly across the grain with a sharp knife.

Barbecued Grassfed Brisket

Grassfed meat does not get much respect from the masters of American barbecue who compete in barbecue contests and are experts in the art of cooking low and slow. These folks have enormous skill and expertise, but the beef they cook is not grassfed. Part of the reason for this is that meat at the big-time barbecue competitions is always provided by the organizers of the event, and is always grain-finished.

The meat of choice at these barbecue contests is brisket, which has a reputation of being the most difficult meat to barbecue. Brisket is a very tough piece of meat, but it can be tender and unbelievably flavorful when properly cooked. The barbecue masters will usually marinate the brisket in a dry rub containing salt, sugar, and often MSG, and many other ingredients. They will cook the brisket at very low temperatures for a very long time, sometimes as long as 24 hours. Many of them have the brisket wrapped in aluminum foil for a large part of the cooking time.

I have read comments by several barbecue masters that expressed the opinion that grassfed brisket just cannot be tender when barbecued, no matter how long they cook it. So I was somewhat intimidated when I decided that I would barbecue brisket, and that it would be tender. The barbecue masters were wrong. This grassfed brisket is tender, delicious, and takes much less time to cook than conventional barbecued brisket. The total cooking time is about three and a half hours. And I did not use salt, sugar, or MSG, which are commonly used in conventional barbecue rubs. This recipe shows that barbecued grassfed brisket can be tender and flavorful. In fact, grassfed meat works beautifully with the flavors of the barbecue.

Serves 4

½ grassfed brisket, approximately 4 pounds
4 tablespoons unfiltered organic extra virgin olive oil
1 (2 inch) piece fresh organic ginger, crushed and very finely chopped
4 organic garlic cloves, crushed and very finely chopped

For the Dry Rub

2 teaspoons organic granulated garlic powder
1 teaspoon organic granulated onion powder
1 teaspoon freshly ground organic black pepper

For Basting

½ cup melted grassfed beef fat

1. The night before you plan to cook the meat, coat all surfaces of the brisket with the olive oil. Press the crushed ginger and garlic into the meat. Place in a glass bowl, cover, and let rest at room temperature for 1 hour, then refrigerate overnight.

2. Take the meat out of the refrigerator at least 1 hour before you plan to cook it, so it can come to room temperature.

3. Use a spoon to remove the pieces of ginger and garlic from the meat. Mix the ingredients for the dry rub together, then sprinkle it all over the meat.

4. Build a charcoal fire on one side of the cooker only. Bring your cooker to medium high heat, with all vents fully open.

5. When the meat has rested for 1 hour and your cooker is ready, place the meat fat side down, in front of, but not over, the heat source. Baste the meat with the melted beef fat. Cover, and reduce the heat to medium low by adjusting the top vents to half-closed. Cook for 30 minutes at medium low heat.

6. Add two handfuls of charcoal to the fire. Turn the meat fat side up. Baste with the beef fat. Cover, and cook for 1 hour.

7. Add two handfuls of charcoal to the fire. Baste the meat with the beef fat. Cover, and reduce the heat to low by closing all the top and bottom vents to only one-quarter inch open. Cook for 1 hour at low heat.

8. Add two handfuls of charcoal to the fire. Baste the meat again with the beef fat. Cover, and cook for 1 final hour.

Slice the brisket thinly across the grain and enjoy the wonderful barbecued meat.

Barbecued Beef Ribs with Pampas Seasoning

The seasoning used for beef ribs on the Argentine Pampas is very simple. It is either salt or a salt brine. This cut of beef, which consists of the same bones that are part of the prime rib, does not have much meat on it. However, the meat that is there has a deep, rich flavor, which is enhanced by its being literally next to the bone, and is very satisfying. The slow cooking process really brings out the rich beefy flavors of the ribs. Some believe that this is the most flavorful part of the entire steer. Since most grassfed prime rib is cut into boneless steaks, the producers are left with a lot of leftover prime rib bones, which are perfect for this recipe.

Serves 4

2 racks of grassfed prime rib bones

2 tablespoons unfiltered organic extra virgin olive oil

2 teaspoons coarse unrefined sea salt, crushed

1. An hour before you plan to barbecue the ribs, rub the unfiltered olive oil all over the meat part of the bones. Let rest for 1 hour at room temperature.

2. Build a charcoal fire on one side of the cooker only. Bring your cooker to medium high heat, with all vents fully open.

3. Rub the salt all over the ribs just before you place the meat in the cooker.

4. Place the ribs in front of, but not over, the heat source. Immediately reduce the heat to low by closing all the top and bottom vents to only one-quarter inch open. Cook for 12 hours, or until the ribs are tender when pierced with a fork.

5. Add more fuel to the fire as needed. Two handfuls of charcoal every 45 minutes or so, should be sufficient.

Serve and enjoy the rich flavor of this tender meat.

Grassfed Bul Kalbi

Beef has been popular in Korea since ancient times. The traditional cuisine in Korea is one of the healthiest ever devised by humankind, and beef was a treasured and valued food. Korean-style barbecue has become popular in the United States, but the ingredients used here are not particularly traditional, consisting of grain-finished meat, industrial soy sauce, and factory vegetables.

In old Korea, the beef was always grassfed, the vegetables were organic, and the seasonings were traditionally made. Bul kalbi is the name of a traditional short rib dish. This dish is made with short ribs that have been thinly cut with some bone, and are grilled with hardwood charcoal. This bul kalbi uses traditional ingredients and has a nice, exotic flavor.

Serves 4

2 pounds grassfed beef short ribs, thinly cut for grilling in the Korean style

For the Marinade

1½ teaspoons raw organic unheated honey

3 tablespoons unrefined organic toasted sesame oil

2 tablespoons Thai fish sauce

1 organic sweet pear, peeled, and puréed, with its juice

1 (2 inch) piece organic ginger, crushed, and very finely chopped

4 cloves organic garlic, crushed, and very finely chopped

2 organic green onions, very finely chopped

1. The day before you plan to cook the ribs, make the marinade. Combine all ingredients for the marinade in a bowl, and mix well, stirring until the honey has dissolved.

2. Place the meat in a glass bowl. Pour the marinade over the meat, making sure that all surfaces of the meat are coated with the marinade. Cover the bowl, and refrigerate overnight.

3. Remove the meat from the refrigerator at least 1 hour before you plan to cook it, so it can come to room temperature.

4. Build a charcoal fire on one side of the cooker only. Bring your cooker to medium high heat, with all vents fully open.

5. When the ribs are at room temperature and the cooker is ready, place the short ribs on the grill, in front of, but not over, the heat source. Cover, and cook for 3 to 4 minutes on each side.

Serve and enjoy this Korean masterpiece.

Grilled German Hamburger

The very word "hamburger" comes from the city of Hamburg, in Germany. This dish reflects the fondness that Germans have traditionally had for ground meat, which was usually made into sausages.

The spices in this mixture were probably not used with the original hamburger, but are widely used in German cooking. This hamburger has an absolutely wonderful flavor.

Serves 4

1 pound grassfed ground beef
1 teaspoon organic mustard powder
1 teaspoon organic granulated onion powder
½ teaspoon organic dried parsley
1 teaspoon freshly ground organic black pepper
½ teaspoon coarse unrefined sea salt, crushed

1. Combine all ingredients, and mix well. Form the mixture into 4 equally sized hamburger patties, approximately 1 inch thick.

2. Build a charcoal fire on one side of the cooker only. Bring your cooker to medium high heat, with all vents fully open. When the cooker is ready, place the burgers in front of, but not over, the heat source. Cover, and cook over medium high heat for 5 minutes.

3. Turn the burgers over. Cover, and cook for 5 more minutes.

Serve and enjoy.

Delicious Liver Burger

Many people think the words "delicious" and "liver" never go together, but they are mistaken. Liver from grassfed animals is one of the healthiest and most nutrient-dense foods you can get. The combination of liver sausage with a few carefully chosen ingredients results in a burger that is just as delicious as it is nutritious. This recipe was made with U.S. Wellness Meats Raw Uncooked Braunschweiger, but would work well with any good grassfed liver sausage.

The hot spices give a wonderful flavor to the meat, so you don't even know that you are eating liver. You may wish to tone the spices down if you are cooking for children.

Serves 4

1 pound U.S. Wellness Meats Raw Uncooked Braunschweiger, (or other grassfed meat sausage)

2 organic eggs, preferably pastured

¼ cup breadcrumbs, preferably made from sprouted or sourdough bread

1 teaspoon imported hot paprika, (or ½ teaspoon organic cayenne pepper, or 1 teaspoon freshly ground organic black pepper)

½ teaspoon organic white pepper

½ teaspoon organic mustard powder

4 thin slices natural cheese of your choice

1. Place the Braunschweiger in a large glass bowl. Crumble the Braunschweiger into tiny pieces. Add the eggs, breadcrumbs, and spices. Mix very well. Divide the mixture into 4 equally sized hamburger patties, approximately 1 inch thick.

2. Build a charcoal fire on one side of the cooker only. Bring your cooker to medium high heat, with all vents fully open. When the cooker is ready, place the hamburger patties in front of, but not over, the heat source. Cover, and cook for 5 minutes.

3. Turn the patties over. Cover, and cook for another 4 minutes.

4. Place 1 slice of cheese on each of the patties. Cover, and cook for 1 more minute.

Serve and enjoy the wonderful spicy flavors.

Pizzaburger

I used to love commercial pizza. Of course, I had to give that up, once I learned what was in it, but I still miss the old flavors. This led me to wondering if the pizza flavors that I missed would go well in a grassfed hamburger. The result is this recipe. It does not taste like pizza, but it has a wonderful flavor of its own.

Serves 4

1 pound grassfed ground beef

2 tablespoons organic tomato purée

2 tablespoons grated parmesan cheese

1 tablespoon fresh organic basil, finely chopped

1 clove organic garlic, finely chopped

1 tablespoon unfiltered organic extra virgin olive oil

For the Topping

4 slices mozzarella cheese

1. Mix all the ingredients (except the mozzarella cheese) together. When well mixed, form into 4 equally sized hamburger patties, about 1 inch thick.

2. Build a charcoal fire on one side of the cooker only. Bring your cooker to medium high heat, with all vents fully open. When the cooker is ready, place the burgers in front of, but not over, the heat source. Cover, and cook for 5 minutes.

3. Turn the burgers over. Cover, and cook for 4 more minutes.

4. Place a slice of mozzarella cheese on each burger. Cover, and cook for 1 more minute.

Serve and enjoy.

Transylvanian Garlic Burger

Grilled ground meat is very traditional in Transylvania, indeed in all of Romania. Transylvania is a region that is home to several very diverse peoples, primarily Romanian, but with large German, Armenian, and Gypsy minorities. This has led to the creation of a unique and delicious cuisine. Garlic has been associated with Transylvania, largely as a result of the popularity of vampire novels and movies. The most famous vampire of them all, Count Dracula, came from Transylvania and could be repelled by garlic. Garlic is actually a valued part of Transylvanian cooking.

The spices in these burgers recreate the great taste of Transylvanian cooking, and the garlic might actually protect against vampires.

Serves 4

1 pound grassfed ground beef

2 cloves organic garlic, very finely chopped

¼ teaspoon organic cloves, ground

½ teaspoon organic dried oregano, crushed between your fingers

½ teaspoon freshly ground organic black pepper

1 teaspoon sweet paprika, preferably Hungarian

½ teaspoon coarse unrefined sea salt, crushed

1. Mix all ingredients together, and divide the mixture into 4 equally sized hamburger patties approximately 1 inch thick.

2. Build a charcoal fire on one side of the cooker only. Bring your cooker to medium high heat, with all vents fully open. Place the burgers in the cooker in front of, but not over, the heat source. Cover, and cook for 5 minutes.

3. Turn the burgers over. Cover, and cook for 5 more minutes.

Serve and enjoy.

Balkan Burger

Many of the Balkan countries, such as Bulgaria, Serbia, Greece, Romania, and Montenegro, were ruled for hundreds of years by the Ottoman Turks. The Ottomans had a very sophisticated cuisine, and the cooking of all of these countries demonstrates that influence. This recipe could have come from any one of these countries, as it contains cooking themes common to all of them. This is an exotic and delicious hamburger.

Serves 4

1 pound grassfed ground beef
1 slice natural bread, sprouted or sourdough
¼ cup filtered water
1 organic egg, preferably pastured
1 small organic yellow onion, finely chopped
2 more tablespoons filtered water
2 tablespoons fresh organic Italian parsley, finely chopped
½ teaspoon coarse unrefined sea salt, crushed
½ teaspoon freshly ground organic black pepper
¼ teaspoon organic cumin
¼ teaspoon organic granulated garlic powder
4 thin slices full-fat cheese of your choice

1. At least 1 hour before you plan to cook the burgers, soak the bread in ¼ cup filtered water for 5 minutes. Squeeze the water out of the bread, crumble in your hands, and place in a glass bowl. Add the rest of the ingredients (except for the cheese slices) to the bowl. Mix well with a spoon until the ingredients are well combined. Form into a compact mass with your hands. Cover the bowl, and refrigerate for 1 hour.

2. Remove the mixture from the refrigerator, and form into 4 equally sized hamburger patties approximately 1 inch thick.

3. Build a charcoal fire on one side of the cooker only. Bring your cooker to medium high heat, with all vents fully open. When the cooker is ready, place the burgers in front of, but not over, the heat source. Cover, and cook for 5 minutes on each side.

4. Place a cheese slice on top of each burger. Cover, and cook for 30 seconds.

Serve and enjoy.

Cinnamon Burger

Cinnamon is one of the oldest and most valued spices. It has been reported to have a number of health benefits, including normalizing insulin resistance and helping the body manage blood sugar better. This may be why cinnamon has been traditionally used only with desserts in Europe. However, cinnamon has a long tradition of flavoring meats in India and the Middle East. This recipe combines cinnamon with another one of the world's oldest spices, black pepper, to create an unusual and absolutely delicious burger. The addition of butter and the wood flavor of the grill set off the spices perfectly.

Serves 4

1 pound grassfed ground beef

½ teaspoon organic ground cinnamon

1 teaspoon freshly ground black pepper

½ teaspoon coarse unrefined sea salt, crushed

1 tablespoon pastured butter, cut into tiny pieces

1 organic egg, preferably pastured

1. Combine the cinnamon, black pepper, salt, and butter. Add the meat and the egg, and mix well. Form into 4 equally sized hamburger patties about 1 inch thick.

2. Build a charcoal fire on one side of the cooker only. Bring your cooker to medium high heat, with all vents fully open. When the cooker is ready, place the burgers in front of, but not over, the heat source. Cover, and cook for 5 minutes.

3. Turn the burgers over. Cover, and cook for 5 more minutes.

Serve and enjoy the remarkable flavor of these cinnamon burgers.

Curry Burger

Most Indian cookbooks will tell you that there is no such thing as curry powder, and that the word curry just refers to a mixture of spices. It was traditional for Indian families to make their own seasoning mixes, and there are hundreds of varieties. Often the spices were freshly ground and then toasted in a hot frying pan. But while I have great respect for Indian culinary traditions, it is much easier and faster to use a good, organic, pre-made curry powder.

This burger has incredible flavor. While the taste is unusual, it makes a nice change from the usual burger.

Serves 4

1 pound grassfed ground beef

1 slice natural bread, preferably sprouted or sourdough

1 organic egg, preferably pastured

1 tablespoon unfiltered raw organic apple cider vinegar

2 tablespoons full-fat organic unhomogenized milk

2 teaspoons organic curry powder

½ teaspoon organic onion powder

½ teaspoon organic granulated garlic powder

½ teaspoon coarse unrefined sea salt, crushed

¼ teaspoon thick organic hot sauce

1. Turn the bread into breadcrumbs, using a blender or food processor. Break the egg into a large bowl, and beat lightly with a fork. Add the rest of the ingredients to a bowl, and mix well. Divide the mixture into 4 equally sized hamburger patties approximately 1 inch thick.

2. Build a charcoal fire on one side of the cooker only. Bring your cooker to medium high heat, with all vents fully open. Place the burgers in the cooker in front of, but not over, the heat source. Cover, and cook for 5 minutes.

3. Turn the burgers over. Cover, and cook for 5 more minutes.

Serve and enjoy.

Cajun Burger

The Cajun people of Louisiana have one of the most interesting backgrounds and fascinating cuisines of any people in the United States. Their ancestors came from France and lived in an area of Canada known as Acadia. They were driven from their homeland during one of the colonial wars between France and England. The French government resettled them in Louisiana, which was under French rule at the time. The transition from the cold north to the sweltering, semi-tropical south caused them to create a truly unique and delicious cuisine. This cuisine is known for its use of hot spices. This burger does justice to its name, being full of flavor and spicy heat.

Serves 4

1 pound grassfed ground beef

½ teaspoon organic cayenne pepper

½ teaspoon freshly ground organic black pepper

½ teaspoon organic white pepper

1 teaspoon organic granulated garlic powder

1 teaspoon organic granulated onion powder

1 teaspoon coarse unrefined sea salt, crushed

¼ teaspoon organic dried thyme, crushed between your fingers

1. Mix all ingredients together, and divide the mixture into 4 equally sized hamburger patties approximately 1 inch thick.

2. Build a charcoal fire on one side of the cooker only. Bring your cooker to medium high heat, with all vents fully open. Place the burgers in the cooker in front of, but not over, the heat source. Cover, and cook for 5 minutes.

3. Turn the burgers over. Cover, and cook for 5 more minutes.

Serve and enjoy.

Skinless Sausage — Romanian Style

This dish is known by the name of mititei in Romania. It is perhaps the favorite meat dish in that nation and it is the result of an accident. It is said that a famous restaurant ran out of sausage one night. The resourceful cook seasoned some ground meat with a spice mixture used for the sausage, shaped the meat to resemble sausages, and cooked them over charcoal. There are many different versions. This is mine, and my family loves it.

Serves 4

1 pound grassfed ground beef
½ teaspoon organic granulated garlic powder
½ teaspoon freshly ground organic black pepper
½ teaspoon hot paprika, preferably Hungarian
½ teaspoon sweet paprika, preferably Hungarian
½ teaspoon organic onion powder
½ teaspoon organic dried marjoram, (or thyme)
1 teaspoon coarse unrefined sea salt, crushed
1 tablespoon unfiltered organic extra virgin olive oil
2 tablespoons filtered water

1. Place all ingredients in a bowl. Mix well for about 2 to 3 minutes, using a large spoon or your own well-washed hands. Cover the bowl, and refrigerate for 30 minutes.

2. Remove the mixture from the refrigerator, wet your hands, and form the mixture into 8 equally sized sausage-shaped pieces, about 1 inch thick.

3. Build a charcoal fire on one side of the cooker only. Bring your cooker to medium high heat, with all vents fully open. Place the skinless sausages in front of, but not over, the heat source. Cover, and cook for 5 minutes.

4. Turn the sausages over. Cover, and cook for 5 more minutes.

Serve hot.

Grassfed
Bison

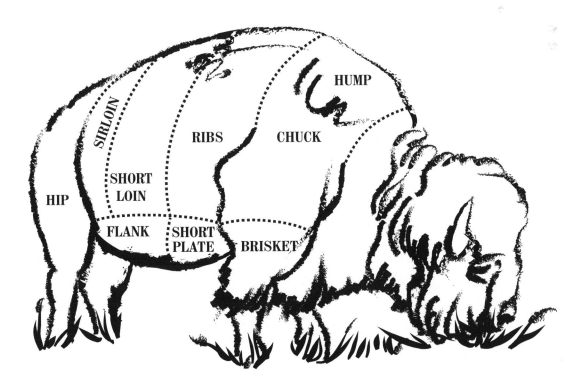

Judging Doneness in Grassfed Bison

Bison is ready at a lower temperature than beef. The cooking times given in this book are an estimate, based on experience. This is why variable times are given for so many recipes. These times should give excellent results for most grassfed bison. Do not be afraid to change the cooking times based on your experience. In time, you will get a feel for your barbecue cooker, and the particular kind of bison you are cooking.

Judging Doneness

If you are cooking a roast, or a thick steak, a good quality instant-read meat thermometer can really help you judge the doneness of the meat, and how fast it is cooking. The ease with which the thermometer goes into the meat can also give you a good idea of how tender the meat is.

Doneness for Grassfed Bison	
Rare	110 – 120 degrees
Medium Rare	121 – 125 degrees
Medium	126 – 130 degrees
Bison is at its best when rare, or medium rare.	

A meat thermometer does not work for steaks, because the meat is not thick enough.

Another way of judging temperature is to stick a metal skewer or roasting fork into the meat, withdraw it, and test the temperature of the metal with your finger. If it is cool, the meat is not ready. If it is somewhat warm, it is rare. If it is slightly hot, it is medium rare. If it is hot, it is medium. Once you have enough experience at comparing the temperature of the metal with the doneness of the meat, you will know how done the meat is, according to your standards.

The ease with which the skewer or fork goes into the meat will give you a good idea of its tenderness. Steaks can toughen if they are cooked too long.

Many cooking authorities will tell you to never pierce the meat while cooking, or you will "lose valuable juices." I have never found this to be true for grassfed meat. Yes, sometimes some juice comes out, but it does not hurt the taste or juiciness of the meat.

Basic Grilled Bison Steak

This recipe demonstrates how absolutely delicious grassfed bison can be, when its own natural flavor is brought out. This recipe has only two ingredients. It uses the Native American practice of NOT salting grilled bison. The flavors of the wood and the bison complement each other perfectly.

This recipe is great not only with strip loin, but also with tenderloin, ribeye, and sirloin steak.

Serves 4

2 pounds grassfed bison strip steaks, (or tenderloin, rib, or sirloin steaks), from ¾ to 1½ inches thick

3 tablespoons unfiltered organic extra virgin olive oil

1. The day before you plan to cook the steaks, rub the olive oil over all surfaces of the steaks, coating them evenly. Place in a covered glass or ceramic container. Let rest for 1 hour at room temperature, then refrigerate overnight.

2. An hour before you plan to cook the steaks, remove the meat from the refrigerator, so the steaks can come to room temperature.

3. Build a charcoal fire on one side of the cooker only. Bring your cooker to medium high heat, with all vents fully open. Place the steaks on the grill, in front of, but not over, the heat source. Cover the grill, and cook for 4 minutes.

4. Turn the steaks over, and cook for another 4 minutes. The thicker steaks will be rare, the medium-thickness steaks will be medium rare, and the thinner steaks will be medium. Depending on the thickness of your steak, you can cook them for a shorter or a longer time to get them the way you want.

Serve and enjoy.

Bison Porterhouse Steak

The Porterhouse has often been called the king of steaks. People usually think of beef when they think of Porterhouse, but a bison Porterhouse is also magnificent. This wonderful cut contains a large portion of strip loin and tenderloin, attached to a huge bone. Part of the bone is very flat, and you can actually cook the steak while it's resting on the bone, which is crucial for this recipe.

Grassfed bison has a wonderful, slightly sweet taste of its own, which is enhanced by a coating of its own delicious fat. I invented this recipe for a special wedding anniversary, and we loved it.

Serves 2 to 4

1 grassfed bison Porterhouse steak, 2 to 2½ inches thick, approximately 3 pounds
2 tablespoons unfiltered organic extra virgin olive oil
2 tablespoons melted grassfed bison fat, (or melted grassfed bison suet)
1 clove organic garlic, crushed

1. The day before you plan to cook the steak, place it in a glass bowl and cover all surfaces with the olive oil. Cut the garlic clove in half, and place a half on each side of the meat. Cover, and let rest at room temperature for 1 hour, then refrigerate overnight.

2. Remove the steak from the refrigerator at least 1 hour before you plan to cook it, so it can come to room temperature. Put the steak on a plate.

3. Melt the bison fat (or suet) over low heat in a small pan. As soon as the fat has melted, pour half of it over one side of the bison steak. Turn the steak over, and pour the remaining fat over the other side of the steak. Try to coat each side with the fat as you pour it. The fat may turn solid after it is poured on the cool meat, which is fine.

4. Build a charcoal fire on one side of the cooker only. Bring your cooker to medium high heat, with all vents fully open. Place the steak on the grill, in front of, but not over, the heat source. Cover, and cook for 8 minutes.

5. Turn the steak over. Cover, and cook for another 7 minutes.

6. Reduce the heat of your cooker to medium low by adjusting the top vents to half-closed. Place the steak directly on the wide, flat bone that covers the top of the steak. The steak will actually rest on this bone while it finishes cooking. Cover, and cook for 10 to 18 minutes, depending on how you like it. 10 minutes will give you a very rare steak.

Serve and enjoy this wonderful bison.

Bison Steak with the Flavors of Old America

The flavor of grassfed bison is exquisite, and should not be masked by too much seasoning. The Native Americans knew this, and found ways of seasoning bison that really enhanced its flavor.

A combination of wild sage and wild onions was often used to flavor bison. I believe that fresh American sage is closely related to the wild sage that was used by the Native Americans. Green onions will do as a substitute for wild onions. While the Native Americans did not use olive oil, I have found that it draws the traditional flavors into the meat.

This recipe is yet another demonstration of the fact that traditional flavor combinations taste great. As usual, no salt is used, as the Native Americans usually did not use salt when cooking bison.

Serves 4

4 grassfed bison ribeye steaks, about 8 ounces each, about 1 inch thick

For the Marinade
2 tablespoons unfiltered organic extra virgin olive oil
Leaves from 4 large sprigs of fresh organic sage, coarsely chopped
4 organic green onions, both white and green parts, coarsely chopped

1. The day before you plan to cook the steaks, rub the olive oil all over the steaks, covering all surfaces of the meat. Crush the sage and green onions together. Rub the sage/onion mixture all over the steaks. Place the steaks in a glass bowl, cover, and let sit for 1 hour at room temperature, then refrigerate overnight.

2. Remove the steaks from the refrigerator 1 hour before you plan to cook them, so they can come to room temperature.

3. Build a charcoal fire on one side of the cooker only. Bring your cooker to medium high heat, with all vents fully open. When the steaks are at room temperature, scrape the marinade off the steaks.

4. Place the steaks in front of, but not over, the heat source. Cover the grill. Cook for 3 minutes on each side for rare; 4 minutes on each side for medium rare; or 5 minutes on each side for medium.

Serve and enjoy the great flavors of Old America.

Bison Ribeye with Classic European Marinade

Bison was not usually eaten in Europe, with the exception of Poland. Venison, however, was a European favorite. The traditional European marinades for venison all included a large amount of wine. The problem is that wine tends to toughen grassfed meat. I believe the wine was put there to preserve the meat when there was no refrigeration. I decided to leave out the wine and combine various traditional ingredients in an oil-based marinade. The result? Extremely tender, flavorful, and delicious bison.

Serves 4

2 pounds grassfed bison ribeye steaks, about 1 inch thick

For the Marinade

3 organic green onions, finely chopped

1 tablespoon organic parsley, finely chopped

1 medium organic carrot, finely chopped

2 teaspoons fresh organic thyme leaves, finely chopped

½ teaspoon freshly ground organic black pepper

2 small dried bay leaves, organic or imported, crushed

¼ cup unfiltered organic extra virgin olive oil

1. At least 2 hours before you plan to cook the meat, prepare the marinade by combining all ingredients and mixing well. Place the steaks in a glass bowl, and cover all surfaces of the meat with the marinade. Cover the bowl, and let rest at room temperature for 2 hours. (Alternatively, you can let the meat rest at room temperature for 1 hour, then refrigerate overnight.)

2. If your meat was refrigerated, be sure to take the meat out of the refrigerator at least 1 hour before you plan to cook it, so it can come to room temperature.

3. When you are ready to cook the meat, scrape the marinade off the steaks with a spoon. It is okay if a few small bits of the marinade cling to the steaks.

4. Build a charcoal fire on one side of the cooker only. Bring your cooker to medium high heat, with all vents fully open. Place the meat in front of, but not over, the heat source. Cover, and cook for 3 to 5 minutes on each side, depending on how you like the meat.

Serve and enjoy the wonderful flavors of this tender meat.

Grilled Bison with Wild Onion Marinade

The natural flavor of bison is so good that it needs little or no help. Nevertheless, the Native Americans were reported to flavor their bison with wild onions. As I have great respect for traditional cooking, I tried basing a marinade on wild onions. The results? Delicious. The onion somehow heightened the taste of the tender bison, without overwhelming it. While this marinade has only two ingredients, they combine perfectly to create a delicious flavor.

Wild onions look a lot like green onions, except that they are bigger and thicker. If you can't find wild onions, green onions also work well with this recipe.

Serves 4

4 grassfed bison ribeye (or strip) steaks, approximately 1 inch thick
1 to 2 wild onions (or 2 to 4 green onions), both white and green parts
2 tablespoons unfiltered organic extra virgin olive oil

1. At least 2 hours before you plan to cook the meat, rub the olive oil into all sides of the steaks. Crush the onions and chop finely. Press the crushed onions and their juices into all sides of the meat. Let marinate at least 2 hours at room temperature. (Alternatively, you can let the meat rest at room temperature for 1 hour, then refrigerate overnight.)

2. If you have refrigerated the steaks, remove them from the refrigerator 1 hour before cooking, so they can come to room temperature.

3. Build a charcoal fire on one side of the cooker only. Bring your cooker to medium high heat, with all vents fully open.

4. Brush the onions off the meat. Don't worry if a few small pieces stick to the meat.

5. Place the steaks in front of, but not over, the heat source. Cover, and cook for 4 minutes on each side.

Serve immediately, and enjoy the great flavor.

Grilled Bison Strip Steak
Marinated in German Soup Greens

Grassfed bison strip steak, when cooked right, is one of the most tender, richly textured, absolutely delicious pieces of meat you will ever bite into. When barbecued, it's even better.

This recipe uses a marinade based on a traditional German vegetable combination, known as "soup greens." It really tenderizes the bison, bringing out its wonderful natural flavor.

Serves 4

2 pounds grassfed bison strip steaks, from ¾ to 1½ inches thick, (I use steaks of varying thicknesses for my family, since some people prefer it more done than others)

For the Marinade

Green leaves from 1 small organic leek, carefully washed

2 small leafy stalks of organic celery from the inside of the bunch (the celery leaves are very important to this dish)

1 small organic carrot

¼ bunch organic Italian parsley, with stems

¼ cup unfiltered organic extra virgin olive oil

1. The day before you plan to cook the steaks, finely chop the vegetables. I like to chop them all together on a large wooden cutting board. When all the vegetables are finely chopped, combine well with the olive oil. Place the meat in a glass bowl. Coat the meat with the marinade, making sure that all surfaces are well coated. Cover, and let rest at room temperature for 1 hour, then refrigerate overnight.

2. About 1 hour before you plan to cook the steaks, remove the steaks from the refrigerator so they can come to room temperature. Scrape off the marinade with a spoon. It's okay if some stray vegetable pieces cling to the meat.

3. Build a charcoal fire on one side of the cooker only. Bring your cooker to medium high heat, with all vents fully open. Place the steaks in front of, but not over, the heat source. Cover, and cook for 3 to 5 minutes on each side, depending on the thickness of the steaks and how you like them.

4. Reduce the heat as low as possible by closing all the top and bottom vents completely, and let the steaks rest for 5 minutes in the covered cooker.

Serve and enjoy — you are in for a treat!

Blueberry Bison Steak

Blueberries are a nutritional powerhouse, being full of bioflavonoids and many other beneficial nutrients. The Native Americans often used blueberries to flavor bison. It is often possible to find wild organic blueberries, though they are usually frozen. These wild blueberries have incredible flavor. While the Native Americans did not use olive oil, the flavor combination of unfiltered extra virgin olive oil and wild blueberries gives an absolutely wonderful taste to these steaks.

Serves 4

4 grassfed bison strip steaks, totaling 1¼ to 2 pounds
¼ cup organic blueberries, preferably wild, fresh or thawed
3 tablespoons unfiltered organic extra virgin olive oil

1. The day before you plan to cook the steaks, combine the olive oil and blueberries, and mix well. Place the steaks in a glass bowl, and pour the mixture over the steaks, stirring to make sure that all surfaces of the meat are coated. Cover, and let rest at room temperature for 1 hour, then refrigerate overnight.

2. Remove the steaks from the refrigerator at least 1 hour before you plan to cook them, so they can come to room temperature.

3. Build a charcoal fire on one side of the cooker only. Bring your cooker to medium high heat, with all vents fully open. Remove any blueberry pulp from the surface of the steaks with a spoon. It's okay if a few bits cling to the meat. Place the steaks in front of, but not over, the heat source. Cover, and cook for 3 to 4 minutes on each side, depending on how you like them.

Serve and enjoy this unique and wonderful flavor.

Barbecued Bison Tenderloin Steak

The tenderloin, whether it comes from cattle, wild game, or bison, is always the most tender cut on the animal. It is also very lean. Why is it so tender? The muscle from which tenderloin is cut, also known as the backstrap, is seldom used and remains soft. The lack of use and fat usually means that the tenderloin does not have as strong a flavor as most of the other meat cuts. This means that tenderloin is very receptive to traditional flavors. Tenderloin is usually very expensive, but can be a wonderful treat for a special occasion, especially if care is taken to enhance its flavor.

I mean only natural enhancements, of course, and this recipe uses two of the very best — melted bison fat, and traditional charcoal. This tenderloin steak is so tender, and so delicious.

Serves 4

2 pounds grassfed bison tenderloin steaks, cut about 1 to 1¼ inches thick

2 tablespoons unfiltered organic extra virgin olive oil

3 tablespoons melted grassfed bison fat, (or melted grassfed bison suet)

1. At least 1 hour before you plan to cook the meat, place the steaks in a glass bowl, and rub all sides with the olive oil. Cover, and let rest at room temperature for 1 hour.

2. Build a charcoal fire on one side of the cooker only. Bring your cooker to medium high heat, with all vents fully open.

3. Melt the bison fat (or suet) over low heat. Place the steaks on a plate. Brush the melted fat all over the steaks. The fat may solidify on the steaks, but that is to be expected.

4. Place the steaks on the grill, in front of, but not over, the heat source. Cover, and cook for 3 to 5 minutes on each side, or until done to your taste.

Serve and enjoy the rich flavor of the tender meat.

Buttered Bison Steak

Bison sirloin steak is even leaner than other bison steaks. Because of this leanness, I enhanced it with good animal fat, in one of its most delicious forms — pastured butter. The meat came out very tender with an absolutely wonderful flavor.

Serves 2 to 4

2 grassfed bison top sirloin steaks, approximately ½ to 1 pound each
3 tablespoons unfiltered organic extra virgin olive oil
2 tablespoons pastured butter, cut into 8 thin slices

1. At least 2 hours before you plan to cook the steaks, place them in a glass bowl, and coat all surfaces with the olive oil. Cover, and let rest at room temperature for 2 hours.

2. Build a charcoal fire on one side of the cooker only. Bring your cooker to medium high heat, with all vents fully open. Place the steaks on a plate. Place 2 of the 8 butter slices on each steak. (You will use a total of 4 butter slices, and you will have 4 butter slices remaining.)

3. Using a spatula, carefully place the steaks in front of, but not over, the heat source, butter side up. Cover, and cook for 4 to 5 minutes.

4. Turn the steaks over. Carefully place the remaining butter slices on the steaks (2 to each steak). Cover, and cook for another 4 to 5 minutes, or until done to your taste.

Serve and enjoy this wonderful, tender bison.

Bison Sirloin Steak with Traditional Flavors

Bison sirloin steak is one of the leanest cuts of steak. Traditional peoples always made sure that lean meat was cooked with or served with fat. I follow this tradition by using more fat in the marinade. I also added some traditional Native American flavors. The combination is both tender and delicious.

Serves 4

2 pounds grassfed bison sirloin steaks, cut about 1 inch thick

For the Marinade

4 tablespoons unfiltered organic extra virgin olive oil

2 organic green onions, finely chopped

2 cloves organic garlic, finely chopped

1 teaspoon fresh organic sage leaves, finely chopped

1. The day before you plan to cook the steaks, make the marinade. Combine all marinade ingredients and mix well. Place the steaks in a glass bowl and pour the marinade over the steaks, making sure all surfaces of the meat are coated with the marinade. Let rest at room temperature for 1 hour, then refrigerate overnight.

2. At least an hour before you plan to cook the steaks, remove them from the refrigerator so they can come to room temperature.

3. Build a charcoal fire on one side of the cooker only. Bring your cooker to medium high heat, with all vents fully open. Brush the marinade off the steaks. It's okay if a few bits cling to the meat. Place the steaks in front of, but not over, the heat source. Cover, and cook for 3 to 4 minutes on each side.

Serve and enjoy the tender, delicious meat.

Traditional Bison Prime Rib

The prime rib of a bison is a magnificent cut of meat. I follow the custom of some Native Americans by using nothing to flavor the bison except the fuel of the fire and the bison's own natural bone and fat. I do depart from tradition by marinating the meat in unfiltered extra virgin olive oil. The combination of these methods results in a tender roast with the unique, natural, sweet flavor of charcoal-roasted bison. Very simple and absolutely delicious.

Serves 4 to 6

1 grassfed bison bone in prime rib roast, about 4 pounds, with fat cap
¼ cup unfiltered organic extra virgin olive oil

1. The day before you plan to cook the meat, place it in a glass bowl. Rub the olive oil over all surfaces of the meat. Cover, and let sit at room temperature for 1 hour, then refrigerate overnight.

2. At least 1 hour before you plan to cook the meat, remove the roast from the refrigerator so it can come to room temperature.

3. Build a charcoal fire on one side of the cooker only. Bring your cooker to medium high heat, with all vents fully open.

4. Place the roast on its side, as if you were cooking a giant steak. Place it in front of, but not over, the heat source. Cover, and cook for 7 minutes.

5. Turn the roast over. Cover, and cook for another 7 minutes.

6. Place the roast in the center of the grill, bone side down, fat side up. Cover, and reduce the heat to medium low by adjusting the top vents to half-closed. Cook for 30 minutes at medium low heat.

7. Check the roast for doneness. If the roast is not done, continue cooking, checking for doneness at 5 minute intervals.

8. When the roast is ready, reduce the heat as low as possible by closing all the top and bottom vents completely, and let it rest for 5 minutes.

The roast should have a beautiful color, be tender and juicy, and have the sweet, wonderful taste of grassfed bison.

Double Bison Chop with Native American Bison Baste

The Native Americans were wonderful cooks and their traditional diet produced strong, robust people whose health and physical prowess astonished the first European visitors. Bison meat and fat were a huge part of their diet, especially on the Great Plains.

Some of the best barbecue I ever had in my life came from a restaurant that used a secret baste. The baste came from a member of the Kiowa tribe. The ingredients of the baste remained a secret, and the secret was lost when the restaurant changed ownership.

I had been searching for the secret of that baste for many years until I finally researched the cooking customs of the Native Americans. This enabled me to find the secret ingredient — animal fat. This baste could not be simpler. This recipe has resulted in the very best bison I have ever tasted. The combination of the thick bison rib roast cooked in front of smoldering charcoal, with the baste bringing out the natural sweetness of the bison meat, and the incredible tenderness when you bite into the flavorful bison — it doesn't get any better than this.

Serves 4

1 (2-rib) grassfed bison bone in prime rib roast, with fat cap and chine bone if possible

3 tablespoons unfiltered organic extra virgin olive oil

For the Baste

½ cup homemade bone broth, preferably *Bison* or *Beef Bone Broth* (pages 50 – 51)

¼ cup melted grassfed bison fat, (or melted grassfed bison suet)

1. At least 2 hours before you plan to cook the meat, place it in a glass container large enough to hold it. Rub all surfaces of the meat with the olive oil. Let rest at room temperature for 1 hour. At this point, you can either refrigerate it overnight, or let it marinate at room temperature for 1 more hour.

2. If you have refrigerated the meat overnight, remove it from the refrigerator at least 1 hour before cooking, so it can come to room temperature.

3. Prepare the baste by combining the broth and bison fat (or suet) in a small pan. Heat over low heat until the fat melts into the broth.

4. Using a basting brush, brush the baste on all sides of the meat and let sit for at least 30 minutes at room temperature. The fat may solidify on the meat surface, which is fine.

5. Build a charcoal fire on one side of the cooker only. Bring your cooker to medium high heat, with all vents fully open. Place the bison in front of, but not over, the heat source, with the bone side facing the heat source. Cover, and cook for 8 minutes.

6. Turn the meat over, this time with the fat side facing the heat source. Baste the meat. Cover, and cook for another 8 minutes.

7. Turn the meat over and baste it again. Cover, and reduce the heat on the cooker to medium low by adjusting the top vents to half-closed. Cook for 10 minutes at medium low heat.

8. Turn the meat over and baste one more time. Cover, and cook for another 10 minutes.

9. This should give you a wonderful, rare bison roast. Or you can continue cooking at medium low heat for a few more minutes, until it is done to your taste.

Serve and enjoy the sweet, tender meat.

Buttered Bison Ribeye Roast

Bison had a wonderful flavor all its own, but needs fat to stay tender. I decided to try one of the oldest and most traditional bastes in European cooking with a bison ribeye roast. The baste is melted butter. It does not get more simple than that. The taste was not simple, it was rich and sweet, redolent with the unique sweet taste of bison. The roast came out beautifully browned, meltingly tender, as the sweet natural taste of the bison was enhanced by this most traditional baste.

Serves 4

1 (2 pound) grassfed bison ribeye roast
3 tablespoons unfiltered organic extra virgin olive oil
3 tablespoons pastured butter, melted

1. The day before you plan to cook the roast, place the meat in a glass bowl. Coat all surfaces of the meat with the olive oil. Cover, and let rest for 1 hour, then refrigerate overnight.

2. Remove the roast from the refrigerator at least 1 hour before you plan to cook it, so it can come to room temperature.

3. Build a charcoal fire on one side of the cooker only. Bring your cooker to medium high heat, with all vents fully open.

4. Brush all surfaces of the meat with some of the butter.

5. Place the roast in front of, but not over, the heat source, fat side up. Cover, and cook for 15 minutes.

6. Baste the roast with butter, and rotate the roast so the other side faces the heat source. Cover, and cook for 15 more minutes.

7. Baste with the remaining butter. Cover, and reduce the heat to medium low by adjusting the top vents to half-closed. Cook for 10 minutes at medium low heat.

8. Reduce the heat as low as possible by closing all the top and bottom vents completely, and let rest for 5 minutes.

Serve and enjoy the sweet bison flavor.

Roast Bison with Native American Baste

The Native Americans of the Great Plains obtained most of their food from the great herds of bison that used to live there. The bison herds were so huge that it would take days for them to pass a particular area. Bison meat, bison fat, and the organs of bison were the most important part of their diet. One of the many ways that bison was prepared was by roasting it in front of a fire that had burned down to embers. While definitive information is hard to come by, I did come across some old reports that talked about the use of melted bison fat for basting. The meat in this recipe is brushed with a simple baste containing just three ingredients. The flavor and tenderness of this bison is astonishing.

Serves 4

1 grassfed bison sirloin tip roast, approximately 2 pounds
2 tablespoons unfiltered organic extra virgin olive oil

For the Baste

¼ cup homemade bone broth, preferably *Bison* or *Beef Bone Broth* (pages 50 – 51)
2 tablespoons melted grassfed bison fat
1 organic green onion, finely chopped

1. The day before you plan to cook the meat, place the meat in a glass bowl, coating all sides with the olive oil. Cover, and let rest at room temperature for 1 hour, then refrigerate overnight.

2. Take the meat out of the refrigerator at least 1 hour before you plan to cook it, so it can come to room temperature.

3. Combine the ingredients for the baste in a small saucepan, and heat over low heat until all ingredients are warm. Remove from the heat, and stir well. Coat all sides of the meat with the baste, and let it rest at room temperature until the hour is up.

4. Build a charcoal fire on one side of the cooker only. Bring your cooker to medium high heat, with all vents fully open. When the meat is ready to be cooked, place the meat in front of, but not over, the heat source. Cover, and cook for 15 minutes.

5. Reduce the heat to medium low by adjusting the top vents to half-closed, and cook for another 25 minutes, or until done to your taste.

Enjoy the rich, sweet flavor of the bison.

Roast Bison Tri-Tip

Grassfed bison is one of my favorite meats. It has a fantastic flavor of its own, slightly sweet, and can be meltingly tender if properly cooked. Yet bison is very lean. Grassfed bison tri-tip is a lean piece of meat, but has a rich flavor. Our ancestors dealt with lean meat by cooking it with lots of fat, and that is exactly what I do here. I use the ancient Chinese technique of using the fat of another animal to flavor the meat, in this case pork lard. The pork lard helps keep the meat tender, enhancing the taste without overwhelming the superb natural flavor.

Serves 4

1 (1½ to 2½ pound) grassfed bison tri-tip roast, any silverskin removed

3 tablespoons unfiltered organic extra virgin olive oil

4 tablespoons unhydrogenated natural pork lard, melted, (or melted grassfed beef tallow)

1. The day before you plan to cook the roast, place the bison in a glass bowl. Coat all surfaces of the meat with the olive oil. Cover, and let rest at room temperature for 1 hour, then refrigerate overnight.

2. An hour before you plan to cook the meat, remove it from the refrigerator so the meat can come to room temperature.

3. Build a charcoal fire on one side of the cooker only. Bring your cooker to medium high heat, with all vents fully open.

4. When the cooker is ready, remove the meat from the bowl. Place on a plate and baste all surfaces with the melted lard.

5. Place the meat on the grill, in front of, but not over, the heat source. Cover, and cook at medium high heat for 10 minutes.

6. Reduce the heat to medium low by adjusting the top vents to half-closed, and cook for 20 minutes at medium low heat.

7. Baste the meat with the lard, turn it over, and baste the other side of the meat with the lard. Cover the cooker, and cook for another 20 minutes.

Serve and enjoy the wonderfully flavorful, tender meat.

Roast Bison Hump

The hump was the part of the bison that was most valued by the Native Americans who lived on the Great Plains. The hump was full of a very high quality fat that was a crucial ingredient in pemmican. Pemmican, a mixture of bison meat, bison fat, and berries, lasted a very long time without spoiling and was a basic food. The meat of the hump was roasted as a special treat. A number of American explorers, trappers, and other pioneers wrote of how roast bison hump was some of the best meat they ever tasted.

The meat of the hump is unique to bison with a deep, yet mild flavor. The meat is quite dense, containing a fair amount of fat and membranes, and has a texture of its own. The texture is tender, a bit gelatinous, and slightly chewy without being tough. Each bite releases great flavor, and is very filling.

Hump roasts come in different sizes, with differing amounts of fat, depending on the producer. I usually get a roast about 4 pounds, with a fair amount of fat on top. Because the meat is so filling, I cut this into two roasts of 2 pounds each.

The natural flavor of this roast is so magnificent that very little seasoning should be used.

Serves 4 to 8

1 (2 to 4 pound) grassfed bison hump roast, with fat cap
2 to 4 tablespoons unfiltered organic extra virgin olive oil

1. The day before you plan to cook the roast, place the meat in a glass bowl, and coat all surfaces with the olive oil. Cover, and let rest at room temperature for 1 hour, then refrigerate overnight.

2. Take the roast out of the refrigerator at least 1 hour before you plan to cook it, so it can come to room temperature.

3. Build a charcoal fire on one side of the cooker only. Bring your cooker to medium high heat, with all vents fully open.

4. When the meat is at room temperature and the cooker is ready, place the meat in front of, but not over, the heat source, fat side down. Cover, and reduce the heat to medium low by adjusting the top vents to half-closed. Cook for 30 minutes at medium low heat.

5. Turn the meat fat side up, and continue to cook until done to your taste. This will take another 20 to 50 minutes, depending on the size and shape of your roast. Bison hump should be served rare to medium rare. You may come across various thin membranes when you slice the roast. Don't worry, the meat between the membranes should be very tender.

Serve and enjoy the rich flavor of bison hump.

Blueberry Bison Hump

While bison hump tastes great with minimum seasoning, this blueberry marinade sets off the bison hump perfectly, giving it a slightly exotic and absolutely delicious flavor. The Native Americans often cooked bison with wild blueberries. While this combination may seem unusual, the flavors of bison and blueberry blend beautifully into a wonderful taste experience.

Serves 4 to 8

1 (2 to 4 pound) grassfed bison hump roast, with fat cap
3 tablespoons unfiltered organic extra virgin olive oil
¼ cup organic blueberries, preferably wild, puréed in a blender

1. The day before you plan to cook the roast, place the meat in a glass bowl. Mix the olive oil and blueberry purée thoroughly. Coat all surfaces of the meat with the olive oil and blueberry mixture. Press the mixture into the meat. Cover, and let rest at room temperature for 1 hour, then refrigerate overnight.

2. Take the roast out of the refrigerator at least 1 hour before you plan to cook it, so it can come to room temperature.

3. Build a charcoal fire on one side of the cooker only. Bring your cooker to medium high heat, with all vents fully open.

4. When the meat is at room temperature and the cooker is ready, scrape the purée off the meat with a spoon. Place the meat in front of, but not over, the heat source, fat side down. Cover, and reduce the heat to medium low by adjusting the top vents to half-closed. Cook for 30 minutes at medium low heat.

5. Turn the meat fat side up, and continue to cook until done to your taste. This will take another 20 to 50 minutes, depending on the size and shape of your roast. Bison hump should be served rare to medium rare. You may come across various thin membranes when you slice the roast. Don't worry, the meat between the membranes should be very tender.

Serve and enjoy the exotic flavor.

Great Plains Bison Burger

The Native Americans of the Great Plains lived by hunting the great herds of bison that used to roam this vast area. One of their favorite seasonings was wild onions. Wild onions are rather hard to come by, so I usually use organic green onions as a substitute. This recipe, with only two ingredients, is so simple that it is hard to believe how wonderful it tastes. Not to worry, you'll understand what I mean once you taste it.

Serves 4

1 pound grassfed ground bison
2 organic green onions, very finely chopped

1. Mix the green onions with the bison and form into 4 equally sized hamburger patties, approximately 1 inch thick.

2. Build a charcoal fire on one side of the cooker only. Bring your cooker to medium high heat, with all vents fully open.

3. When your cooker is ready, place the hamburger patties in front of, but not over, the heat source. Cover, and cook the bison burgers for 4 to 5 minutes on each side, depending on how you like them.

Serve and enjoy the wonderful flavors.

Bison Burger with Native American Flavors

Grassfed bison has a clean, slightly sweet flavor that is just wonderful. I think the Native Americans who hunted the bison must have known this, because their traditional seasonings brought out the natural flavor of the meat, rather than overwhelming it. Salt was almost never used in the cooking of fresh bison, and no salt is needed. This recipe combines three ingredients that Native Americans often used with bison, and has the terrific flavor of bison. The olive oil was not used by Native Americans, but it helps unite the flavors.

Serves 4

1 pound grassfed ground bison
1 teaspoon unfiltered organic extra virgin olive oil
1 organic green onion, very finely chopped
2 medium-sized organic garlic cloves, very finely chopped
2 teaspoons fresh organic sage leaves, very finely chopped, (or 1 teaspoon dried sage leaves, crumbled)

1. Mix all ingredients together. When the ingredients are well mixed, leave in a covered glass bowl while you start your cooker.

2. Build a charcoal fire on one side of the cooker only. Bring your cooker to medium high heat, with all vents fully open. When the cooker is ready, form the mixture into 4 equally sized hamburger patties about 1 inch thick.

1. Place the hamburger patties in front of, but not over, the heat source. Cover, and cook the bison burgers for 4 to 5 minutes on each side, depending on how you like them.

Serve and enjoy the clean, pure flavors of bison.

Bison Burger with Great Plains Rub

Bison has a wonderful flavor of its own. The Native Americans of the Great Plains did not, as far as I know, have access to powdered spices. But they did like to flavor bison with wild onions, garlic, and sage.

I decided to make a rub using the dried form of these three ingredients and see how it worked. Fortunately, it turned out to be delicious. The Native Americans did not use salt when cooking bison over a fire, and neither do I. The olive oil helps disperse the flavor of the spices into the meat.

Serves 4

1 pound grassfed ground bison

For the Rub

½ teaspoon organic granulated garlic powder

½ teaspoon organic onion powder

½ teaspoon dried organic sage, crumbled with your fingers

1 teaspoon unfiltered organic extra virgin olive oil

1. Combine the ingredients for the rub and mix well.

2. Add the rub to the meat, mixing well.

3. Build a charcoal fire on one side of the cooker only. Bring your cooker to medium high heat, with all vents fully open.

4. Form the meat into 4 equally sized hamburger patties, approximately 1 inch thick.

5. When your cooker is ready, place the hamburger patties in front of, but not over, the heat source. Cover, and cook the bison burgers for 4 to 5 minutes on each side, depending on how you like them.

Serve and enjoy the flavorful meat.

Great Plains Cherry Bison Burger

The Native Americans, who used the bison as their main food source, often combined the meat with berries or fruits. Much of the meat was made into pemmican, a mixture of dried bison meat, bison tallow, ground cherries, and sometimes honey.

Pemmican was a form of concentrated, nutrient-dense food that was designed to last, and helped the people survive the winter. But it was not known for its good taste. The cherries usually used in pemmican were a variety called "chokecherries." These fruits earned the name, according to the early settlers, because their juice was so bitter that people would choke on it.

Despite this information, I decided to see if I could make a delicious burger based on the ingredients in pemmican. For obvious reasons, I decided to use sweet, delicious cherries as a substitute for the other kind. The result is this burger which is absolutely delicious — though it will not last the winter.

Serves 4

1 pound grassfed ground bison
¼ cup organic cherries, pits removed, and very finely chopped
1 teaspoon raw organic unheated honey

1. Place all ingredients in a large bowl, and mix well. Form the mixture into 4 equally sized hamburger patties, approximately 1 inch thick.

2. Build a charcoal fire on one side of the cooker only. Bring your cooker to medium high heat, with all vents fully open.

3. When your cooker is ready, place the hamburger patties in front of, but not over, the heat source. Cover, and cook the bison burgers for 4 to 5 minutes on each side, depending on how you like them.

Serve and enjoy this delicious combination of flavors.

Blueberry Bison Burger

Blueberries were often used by the Native Americans to flavor bison, as were wild onions. While the Native Americans did not eat hamburgers, their traditional flavorings are great in this bison burger, which is both unusual and delicious.

Serves 4

1 pound grassfed ground bison
¼ cup organic (or wild) blueberries, very finely chopped or puréed in a blender
1 organic green onion, very finely chopped

1. Place all ingredients in a large bowl, and mix well. Form the mixture into 4 equally sized hamburger patties, approximately 1 inch thick.

2. Build a charcoal fire on one side of the cooker only. Bring your cooker to medium high heat, with all vents fully open.

3. When your cooker is ready, place the hamburger patties in front of, but not over, the heat source. Cover, and cook the bison burgers for 4 to 5 minutes on each side, depending on how you like them.

Serve and enjoy.

Spicy Bison Cheeseburger

Bison has a wonderful flavor of its own, and needs minimal seasoning. But bison is also wonderful when combined with traditional European seasonings, which makes for an interesting flavor variation.

This mix of traditional European flavors is very good with any meat. Adding the Havarti cheese makes it even better.

Serves 4

1 pound grassfed ground bison

For the Spice Mix

1 teaspoon organic dried mustard

1 teaspoon organic onion powder

½ teaspoon organic garlic powder

½ teaspoon freshly ground organic black pepper

¼ teaspoon organic dried thyme leaves, crushed between your fingers

½ teaspoon sweet paprika, preferably from Hungary or Spain

¼ teaspoon hot paprika, preferably from Hungary or Spain

For Cooking

4 thin slices Havarti cheese, preferably Danish, (or other full-fat natural cheese of your choice)

1. Mix all ingredients for the spice mix together, making sure they are well combined. Combine the spice mix and the meat, mixing well. Leave in a covered glass bowl.

2. Build a charcoal fire on one side of the cooker only. Bring your cooker to medium high heat, with all vents fully open. When the cooker is ready, form the mixture into 4 equally sized hamburger patties about 1 inch thick.

3. Place the hamburger patties in front of, but not over, the heat source. Cover, and cook for 5 minutes.

4. Turn the patties over. Cover, and cook for another 4 minutes.

5. Place one slice of cheese on each burger. Cover, and cook for 1 more minute.

Serve and enjoy the wonderful traditional European flavors.

Grassfed
Lamb

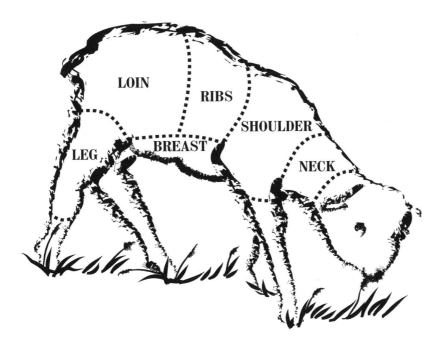

Judging Doneness in Grassfed Lamb

Grassfed lamb should be cooked to a somewhat higher temperature than grassfed beef or grassfed bison. Grassfed lamb that is too rare will be tough and chewy. Grassfed lamb that has been cooked too long may develop an unpleasant taste.

Not all grassfed lamb is the same. The different breeds vary greatly in size and tenderness. Lamb that was bred for meat will be more tender and taste much better than lamb that was bred for wool. Grassfed lamb, perhaps more than any other meat, tastes like what it eats. That is why the same breed of lamb from two different regions can have a completely different taste. The grasses, herbs, and meadow plants eaten by the lamb have a powerful impact on its flavor.

The cooking times given in this book are an estimate based on experience. These times should give excellent results for most grassfed lamb. Do not be afraid to change the cooking times based on your own experience.

Judging Doneness

If you are cooking a roast, or thick chops, a good quality instant-read thermometer can really help you judge the doneness of the meat, and how fast it is cooking. The ease with which the thermometer goes into the meat can also give you a good idea of how tender the meat is.

Doneness for Grassfed Lamb	
Rare	125 – 130 degrees
Medium Rare	131 – 140 degrees
Medium	141 – 150 degrees
Well Done	151 degrees and up

A meat thermometer does not work for thin chops, because the meat is not thick enough.

Another way of judging temperature is to stick a metal skewer or roasting fork into the meat, withdraw it, and test the temperature of the metal with your finger. If it is cool, the meat is not ready. If it is somewhat warm, it is rare. If it is slightly hot, it is medium rare. If it is hot, it is medium. Once you have enough experience at comparing the temperature of the metal with the doneness of the meat, you will know how done the meat is, according to your standards.

The ease with which the skewer or fork goes into the meat will give you a good idea of its tenderness. Chops can toughen if they are cooked too long.

Cretan Lamb Chops

The island of Crete is home to one of the oldest civilizations, the Minoans. Very little is known about Minoan cuisine, except that the most prized foods were pastured meats such as lamb, pork, and goat. As with all traditional peoples, the fattiest meat was prized the most. The modern Cretans continue this tradition, and they have a unique and wonderful way of flavoring lamb.

The use of thyme to flavor lamb is traditional in much of Europe, usually the leaves are the only part used. The Cretans use the whole sprig, including the woody stem, which gives a rare depth of flavor. Be sure to wipe the thyme off the chops before eating, or you could wind up with twigs between your teeth. It is much better just to eat the flavorful, delicious lamb.

Serves 4

8 medium grassfed loin (or rib) lamb chops, ½ to ¾ inch thick
3 tablespoons unfiltered organic extra virgin olive oil
1 bunch organic thyme, including the whole stem, washed with filtered water
1 teaspoon coarse unrefined sea salt, crushed

1. At least 1 hour before you plan to cook the chops, place the meat in a glass bowl. Coat all surfaces of the meat with the olive oil. Using a heavy cleaver, or the back of a sturdy knife, lightly crush the thyme stems. This will help to release their flavor into the meat. Press the thyme stems into all surfaces of the meat. Cover, and let rest at room temperature for about 1 hour.

2. Build a charcoal fire on one side of the cooker only. Bring your cooker to medium high heat, with all vents fully open. When the chops have marinated for 1 hour, sprinkle them with the salt, then place them in front of, but not over, the heat source. Don't worry if some of the thyme stems fall off. Cover, and cook for about 4 minutes on each side.

3. Brush all the thyme sprigs off the roast.

Serve hot and enjoy these flavorful chops.

Lamb Chops with the Flavors of Spain

Spain has long been known for the excellence of its grassfed lamb. The sheep often graze on pastures rich with herbs like rosemary and thyme, which give an exquisite flavor to the meat. We do not have such pastures in the United States, but a similar effect can be achieved with the use of rosemary and thyme. Garlic and parsley are traditionally used for cooking lamb in Spain, and the combination of all these flavors is superb. The olive oil brings all these flavors together and brings them into the meat. The taste is even better when the herb-infused meat is touched with the ancient magic of burning charcoal. These chops are delicious.

Serves 4

8 medium grassfed loin (or rib) lamb chops, about 1 inch thick

For the Marinade

Leaves from 8 sprigs fresh organic thyme, finely chopped

Leaves from 1 large sprig organic rosemary, finely chopped

2 cloves organic garlic, finely chopped

2 teaspoons organic Italian parsley leaves, finely chopped

3 tablespoons unfiltered organic extra virgin olive oil

For Cooking

1 teaspoon coarse unrefined sea salt, crushed

1. The night before you plan to cook the meat, place the chops in a glass bowl. Prepare the marinade by combining all the ingredients and mixing well. Pour the marinade over the chops, making sure that all surfaces of the chops are covered by the marinade. Cover, and let rest at room temperature for 1 hour, then refrigerate overnight.

2. Remove the chops from the refrigerator at least 1 hour before you plan to cook them, so they can come to room temperature.

3. Build a charcoal fire on one side of the cooker only. Bring your cooker to medium high heat, with all vents fully open. When the chops have been out of the refrigerator for an hour, sprinkle them with the salt, then place them in front of, but not over, the heat source.

4. Cover, and cook for 5 to 7 minutes on each side, depending on how you like your chops.

Serve hot and enjoy the terrific flavors of this tasty lamb.

French Lamb Chops with Classic Flavors

Traditional French cuisine is huge in scope, and there are many classic flavor combinations. It is common for the French to cook lamb with parsley, often as part of a breadcrumb coating spread over the lamb. I decided to try some of the flavors without the breadcrumbs.

The result? Tender chops with a classic flavor. The mustard adds just the right touch. The unique flavor of barbecue really makes these chops special.

Serves 4

8 medium grassfed loin (or rib) lamb chops, about 1 inch thick

For the Marinade

2 tablespoons fresh organic Italian parsley, finely chopped

Leaves from 2 sprigs fresh organic thyme, finely chopped

1 clove organic garlic, finely chopped

1 tablespoon whole grain Dijon mustard, preferably French, organic if possible

2 tablespoons unfiltered organic extra virgin olive oil

1. At least 1 hour before you plan to cook the chops, make the marinade by combining all ingredients and mixing well. Place the chops in a glass bowl, and coat all surfaces with the marinade. Cover, and let rest at room temperature for 1 hour.

2. Build a charcoal fire on one side of the cooker only. Bring your cooker to medium high heat, with all vents fully open. When the chops have marinated for 1 hour, place them on the grill, in front of, but not over, the heat source. Cover, and cook for 5 to 7 minutes on each side, depending on how you like your chops.

Serve hot off the grill and enjoy the classic flavors.

Lamb Chops in the Style of Ancient Rome

The ancient Romans put enormous efforts into having exciting, delicious food. Their cuisine was the basis of Italian cuisine, and Italian cuisine was the first fine cuisine in Europe, the mother of all others. We are fortunate that an ancient Roman cookbook has survived, written by a famous Roman cook, Apicius. Many of the recipes use ingredients that are no longer available, such as silphium root. Silphium root could not be cultivated. It came from a plant that grew only in the Libyan Desert. The Romans harvested so much of this root that the plant became extinct. We think that the root tasted somewhat like garlic, though we do not really know. Nevertheless, the Romans used many ingredients that we still use today. The marinade in the following recipe was inspired by a recipe Apicius developed for roasting meat. Almost half of the ingredients are no longer available, so I did some experimenting. The result is one of the most delicious marinades for lamb chops that I have ever had.

Serves 4

8 grassfed loin (or rib) lamb chops, about 1 inch thick

For the Marinade

2 imported bay leaves, crushed between your fingers

3 tablespoons fresh organic Italian parsley leaves, very finely chopped

4 cloves organic garlic, crushed, and very finely chopped

1 (1 inch) piece fresh organic ginger, crushed and very finely chopped

¼ teaspoon dried organic oregano, crushed between your fingers

2 teaspoons fresh organic celery leaves, very finely chopped

1 teaspoon freshly ground organic black pepper

3 tablespoons unfiltered organic extra virgin olive oil

1½ tablespoons Thai fish sauce

1. At least 1 hour before you plan to cook the chops, prepare the marinade. Combine all ingredients in a bowl, and mix well. Place the lamb chops in a glass bowl, and pour the marinade over the chops, making sure that all surfaces of the meat are covered by the marinade. Cover the bowl, and let rest at room temperature for 1 hour.

2. Build a charcoal fire on one side of the cooker only. Bring your cooker to medium high heat, with all vents fully open.

3. When your cooker is ready and the meat has marinated for 1 hour, place the meat in front of, but not over, the heat source. Cover, and cook for 5 minutes on each side, or until done to your taste.

Serve hot and enjoy the flavors of ancient Rome.

Lamb Chops Diana

The combination of garlic and fresh basil has been very popular in Italy for centuries. Perhaps the most famous dish using this combination is pesto, a seasoning paste that is usually eaten with pasta. I thought the combination might be good on lamb as well — and I was right.

Fresh organic basil has a wonderful aroma and flavor that is unique and magnificent. There is no substitute. Dried basil will not work in this recipe. My local farmers' market has some wonderful fresh basil, in season, and that is when I make this dish.

I was introduced to the joy of fresh basil by my dear, departed friend, Diana DeBardeleben. Diana was one of the nicest, kindest, and most loving people I ever met. She did have an appreciation for fine food, and she would have enjoyed this dish, as she truly did love fresh basil.

Serves 4

8 grassfed loin (or rib) lamb chops, approximately ½ pound each

For the Marinade

¼ cup fresh organic basil leaves, very finely chopped

4 large cloves organic garlic, very finely chopped

1 teaspoon coarse unrefined sea salt, crushed

½ teaspoon freshly ground organic black pepper

2 tablespoons dry white wine, preferably Spanish sherry

4 tablespoons unfiltered organic extra virgin olive oil

1. The day before you plan to cook the chops, make the marinade. Combine all the ingredients, and mix well. Place the chops in a glass bowl, and cover with the marinade, making sure all surfaces have been coated. Cover, and let rest at room temperature for 1 hour, then refrigerate overnight.

1. Take the chops out of the refrigerator at least 1 hour before you plan to cook them, so they can come to room temperature.

2. Build a charcoal fire on one side of the cooker only. Bring your cooker to medium high heat, with all vents fully open. When the chops have been out of the refrigerator for an hour, place them in front of, but not over, the heat source. Cover, and cook for 5 minutes on each side, or until done to your taste.

Serve and enjoy the wonderful flavors of this basil-infused lamb.

Barbecued Shoulder Lamb Chops with a Classic Marinade

Not many people realize that chops cut from the lamb shoulder can be successfully made to be tender and delicious. Shoulder lamb chops also have the advantage of being much less expensive than other chops. The combination of olive oil and lemon juice to marinate lamb is thousands of years old, and is used as a marinade base in dozens of lamb-loving countries. I have seen marinades for lamb that feature this combination in Greek, Italian, Portuguese, Spanish, Bulgarian, Turkish, Egyptian, Russian, Georgian, Serbian, Romanian, and French versions. Just about all of these versions also include garlic, as does this one.

There is a reason why so many cuisines use this flavor combination — it is a wonderful marinade for lamb.

Serves 4

4 grassfed shoulder lamb chops

For the Marinade
¼ **cup unfiltered organic extra virgin olive oil**

2 tablespoons freshly squeezed organic lemon juice

1 organic green onion, finely chopped

4 cloves organic garlic, finely chopped

1 tablespoon organic parsley, finely chopped

1 teaspoon coarse unrefined sea salt, crushed

1 teaspoon freshly ground organic black pepper

1. At least 1 hour before you plan to cook the meat, make the marinade by combining all ingredients and stirring well. Place the chops in a glass bowl, and cover all surfaces of the meat with the marinade. Cover, and let rest at room temperature.

2. Build a charcoal fire on one side of the cooker only. Bring your cooker to medium high heat, with all vents fully open. Place the chops in front of, but not over, the heat source. Cover the cooker, and cook for 7 minutes.

3. Turn the chops over. Cover, and cook for another 7 minutes. This should give you a medium done chop. (See **note** below.)

Serve and enjoy while the lamb is hot.

NOTE: Because of its unique texture, lamb shoulder should be served when it is pink or medium, never rare.

Rack of Lamb with French Flavors

Grassfed lamb has a wonderful flavor of its own and requires little in the way of seasoning. France is renowned for its fine and complex cuisine, yet many of the very best dishes are very simple. Salt, garlic, thyme, and pepper are often combined in France as a seasoning for lamb, and the flavor is just wonderful. Rubbing duck fat on the lamb may seem unusual, but duck fat is often used to flavor red meat in France. The duck fat combines perfectly with the other ingredients and the smoldering charcoal to create a truly wonderful taste experience. I recommend using the best French sea salt you can find, as it will make a huge difference in this recipe.

Serves 2 to 4

1 (1½ to 3 pound) grassfed rack of lamb, (or bone in grassfed lamb loin)

For the Marinade

2 tablespoons rendered duck fat, (or pork lard, or olive oil)

1 tablespoon fresh organic thyme leaves, finely chopped

4 cloves organic garlic, very finely chopped

1 teaspoon coarse unrefined sea salt, crushed

½ teaspoon freshly ground organic black pepper

1. At least 1 hour before you plan to cook the meat, make the marinade. Combine all ingredients and mix well. Rub the marinade all over the rack of lamb, being sure to cover all surfaces. Cover, and let rest at room temperature for 1 hour.

2. Build a charcoal fire on one side of the cooker only. Bring your cooker to medium high heat, with all vents fully open. Place the lamb on the grill, with the long side in front of, but not over, the heat source, fat side up. Cover, and cook for 25 to 40 minutes, depending on the size of the lamb and how you like it cooked.

Serve and enjoy the wonderful flavors. Lamb is best served hot, not warm.

Sardinian Rack of Lamb

Sardinia is a large island in the middle of the Mediterranean Sea, with a long history, and a cuisine that goes back to antiquity. Like just about every other Mediterranean people, the Sardinians valued meat over all other foods. The Sardinians developed a rather unique way of roasting meat. The ultimate example of this method would be to roast a whole lamb or goat in front of a smoldering fire of aromatic wood, with a few carefully chosen seasonings. When the roast was ready, the entire roasted animal would be placed on a huge bed of myrtle leaves, and covered with yet more leaves. The meat would be left in this covering of leaves for about 30 minutes, which would give it incredible flavor.

Roasting a whole animal and finding whole beds of unsprayed myrtle leaves is not practical for the average home cook, so I have devised a much easier and smaller-scale method. A rack of lamb is soaked in a fragrant marinade full of ingredients traditionally used in Sardinian cooking, with bay leaves and sage leaves substituting for the myrtle. After I developed this recipe, I found a source of myrtle, but this recipe is delicious just the way it is.

Serves 4

1 large (3 to 4 pound) grassfed rack of lamb, (or 2 small racks of equivalent weight)

For the Marinade

2 tablespoons unfiltered organic extra virgin olive oil

2 tablespoons dry white wine, preferably imported

4 imported bay leaves, crushed between your fingers

1 teaspoon dried organic sage leaves, preferably imported, crushed between your fingers

2 cloves organic garlic, very finely chopped

1 tablespoon raw organic unheated honey, (optional)

1 teaspoon coarse unrefined sea salt, crushed

1. The day before you plan to cook the meat, prepare the marinade. Combine all ingredients, and mix well. If you are using the honey, keep stirring the mixture until the honey dissolves. Place the meat in a glass bowl, and pour the marinade over the meat, making sure that all surfaces are covered by the marinade. Cover the bowl, and let rest at room temperature for 1 hour, then refrigerate overnight.

2. Remove the meat from the refrigerator at least 1 hour before you plan to cook it, so it can come to room temperature.

3. Build a charcoal fire on one side of the cooker only. Bring your cooker to medium high heat, with all vents fully open. Place the meat in front of, but not over, the heat source, with the long side of the roast facing the heat source (fat side up). Cover, and cook for 30 to 40 minutes, depending on the size of the lamb rack and how you like it done.

4. Reduce the heat to low by closing all the top and bottom vents to only one-quarter inch open. Let rest for 5 minutes.

The Champion's Portion

In modern times, we can buy any meat we can afford, and eat it. However, this was not always the case. Ancient peoples would often share a whole barbecued animal. The cut of meat served often depended on social status, with the most respected people getting the best cuts of meat. The best cut of meat in Homeric times, and in ancient Ireland, was the "Champion's Portion." This consisted of the meat along the chine bone of the animal, usually a pig or a lamb. Disputes would arise as to who had the right to this meat. Sometimes the greatest warriors would fight each other — at times to the death — to claim the right to eat the Champion's Portion. Eating this meat gave great prestige to the man who ate it.

The Champion's Portion was always seasoned simply, if at all. However, the bones and fat that wrapped it gave the meat great flavor and succulence. Sometimes it would be cut from a whole roasted animal and at other times it was cut and roasted separately.

Our version of the Champion's Portion is absolutely delicious, and you don't have to fight anybody to eat it.

Serves 4 modern eaters (or one very hungry champion)

1 (2 to 3 pound) bone in grassfed rack of lamb, with natural fat cap

1 teaspoon coarse unrefined sea salt, crushed

1. Take the meat out of the refrigerator at least 1 hour before you plan to cook it, so it can come to room temperature.

2. Build a charcoal fire on one side of the cooker only. Bring your cooker to medium high heat, with all vents fully open. When your cooker is ready, sprinkle the meat lightly with salt. Place the roast, bone side down, in front of, but not over, the heat source. Cover, and cook at medium high heat for 15 minutes.

3. Reduce the heat to medium low by adjusting the top vents to half-closed, and cook for another 15 minutes at medium low heat.

4. Reduce the heat to low by closing all the top and bottom vents to only one-quarter inch open, and cook for another 10 minutes, or until done to your taste.

Serve and enjoy the feast of champions.

Roast Lamb Loin
with the Flavors of the Balkans

Romania, Hungary, Bulgaria, Greece, Serbia, Montenegro, Macedonia, and Bosnia all have two things in common. They are located in an area collectively known as the Balkans, and they were ruled by the Ottoman Empire for hundreds of years. Though the rule of the Ottomans could be quite harsh, they did introduce elements of Turkish cuisine into each and every one of these countries. The combination of European and Turkish cuisines has created some of the most delicious food on earth.

This recipe came from my experimentation with a Balkan chimichurri. This combination of dried herbs, garlic, and olive oil is absolutely fantastic as a marinade for grilled lamb.

Serves 2 to 4

1 (2 to 3½ pound) grassfed lamb loin roast, with fat cap

For the Balkan Herb Rub
2 cloves organic garlic, finely chopped

2 imported bay leaves, preferably Turkish, crushed and crumbled

2 teaspoons organic dried thyme, crushed between your fingers

2 teaspoons organic dried parsley, crushed between your fingers

½ teaspoon coarse unrefined sea salt, crushed

½ teaspoon freshly ground organic black pepper

2 tablespoons unfiltered organic extra virgin olive oil

1 tablespoon dry sherry, preferably Spanish

1. At least 1 hour before you plan to cook the meat, make the Balkan Herb Rub. Combine all ingredients, and mix well.

2. Cover all surfaces of the roast (including the meat, fat, and bones) with the herb rub. Place the roast in a glass bowl large enough to hold it. Cover, and let rest at room temperature for at least 1 hour.

3. Build a charcoal fire on one side of the cooker only. Bring your cooker to medium high heat, with all vents fully open. Place the roast, fat side up, in front of, but not over, the heat source. Cover, and cook for 30 to 40 minutes, depending on how you like it.

Serve hot and enjoy the wonderful flavors.

Roast Lamb Loin
with the Flavors of Spain

Lamb loins are almost always cut into chops. Traditionally, they were more often cooked as a roast, together with the bone and fat encasing the meat as it roasted, providing wonderful flavor and tenderness. The Spanish love good lamb, and this recipe uses several traditional Spanish flavors to make this old-fashioned roast taste even better. If you have never had a lamb loin roast, you will be astonished at how tender, juicy, and flavorful this magnificent cut of meat can be.

Serves 4

1 (2½ to 3½ pound) untrimmed grassfed lamb loin roast, with bones and fat

For the Seasoning Paste

2 teaspoons fresh organic rosemary leaves, finely chopped

2 teaspoons fresh organic thyme leaves, finely chopped

2 teaspoons fresh organic parsley leaves, finely chopped

2 tablespoons unfiltered organic extra virgin olive oil

4 cloves organic garlic, very finely chopped

1 tablespoon dry sherry, preferably Spanish

½ teaspoon freshly ground organic black pepper

1 teaspoon coarse unrefined sea salt, crushed

1. At least 1 hour before you plan to cook the meat, mix all the seasoning paste ingredients together until they are well combined. Rub the seasoning paste all over the lamb roast, coating the meat, fat, and bones. Let rest at room temperature, covered, for 1 hour.

2. Build a charcoal fire on one side of the cooker only. Bring your cooker to medium high heat, with all vents fully open. Place the roast in front of, but not over, the heat source, bone side down (fat side up). Cover, and cook for 20 minutes.

3. Reduce the heat to medium low by adjusting the top vents to half-closed, and cook for another 20 to 30 minutes, or until done to your taste.

Serve and enjoy the wonderful flavors of this magnificent roast.

Charcoal-Roasted Lamb

Lamb is one of the oldest meats enjoyed by humankind. It was quite common to roast a whole lamb to celebrate an important occasion. The seasonings ranged from almost nothing to elaborate marinades. One of the favorite methods was to build a hot fire and roast the lamb on a spit in front of the fire. The lamb would first be seared by a hot fire, then would cook more and more slowly as the fire burned down, until it reached a state of tender perfection. My recipe here is less ambitious, as I use a boneless leg of lamb, and a covered grill instead of a spit. Nevertheless, it is absolutely delicious and uses the High-Low Method to achieve traditional tenderness and flavor.

This recipe is designed to be cooked with lump charcoal, which has been used to cook lamb for thousands of years.

Serves 8 to 12

1 (4 to 6 pound) boneless grassfed leg of lamb, with a fat cap
4 tablespoons sherry wine, preferably Spanish
2 teaspoons coarse unrefined sea salt, crushed

1. Take the meat out of the refrigerator about an hour before you plan to cook it, so it can come to room temperature.

2. Rub the sherry wine all over the meat, on all surfaces. The meat will absorb some of the wine.

3. Build a charcoal fire on one side of the cooker only. Bring your cooker to medium high heat, with all vents fully open. When the fire is ready, rub the salt into all surfaces of the meat.

4. Place the meat fat side up, in front of, but not over, the heat source. Cover, and cook for 15 minutes.

5. Rotate the meat, so the other side faces the heat source. Cover, and cook for another 15 minutes.

6. Add 2 small handfuls of fresh lump charcoal to the fire. Reduce the heat to medium low by adjusting the top vents to half-closed, cover, and cook for 30 minutes at medium low heat.

7. Test the meat for doneness. If it is not done to your taste, add a handful of lump charcoal to the fire. Cover, and continue to cook at medium low heat, testing for doneness at 10 minute intervals.

Serve and enjoy the wonderful flavor of this charcoal-roasted lamb.

Lamb with Garlic and Parsley — Medieval-Style

One medieval seasoning method that has almost disappeared in modern times is to stuff meat with parsley sprigs. I have come across several recipes for medieval roasts that are seasoned only with parsley sprigs and salt. It is very hard for me not to use garlic when seasoning lamb. Garlic is often combined with parsley, so I decided to try this combination, but with a twist. The roast is not only stuffed with garlic and parsley, but is also coated with a garlic-parsley marinade on the outside. The marinade also contains the traditional Middle Eastern seasoning of puréed or liquid onion, which does wonderful things to lamb. This roast has magnificent flavor, which is enhanced by the smoldering charcoal.

Serves 4 to 8

1 small (4 to 5 pound) boneless grassfed leg of lamb, (or half of a large leg of lamb)

For the Stuffing
2 cloves organic garlic, cut into quarters
2 sprigs organic Italian parsley, cut into quarters

For the Marinade
2 cloves organic garlic, minced
2 sprigs organic Italian parsley, minced
1 medium organic onion, puréed in a blender
1 teaspoon freshly ground organic black pepper
1 teaspoon coarse unrefined sea salt, crushed
3 tablespoons unfiltered organic extra virgin olive oil

1. The day before you plan to cook the meat, cut 8 deep slits into the lamb. Place a piece of parsley and a piece of garlic into each slit, pushing it into the hole with your finger.

2. Prepare the marinade by combining all ingredients, and stirring well. Place the lamb in a glass bowl large enough to hold it, and coat all surfaces with the marinade. Cover, and refrigerate overnight.

3. Remove the meat from the refrigerator at least 1 hour before you plan to cook it, so it can come to room temperature.

4. Build a charcoal fire on one side of the cooker only. Bring your cooker to medium high heat, with all vents fully open. Place the roast on the grill, in front of, but not over, the heat source. Cover the grill, and cook for 30 minutes at medium high heat, with all vents fully open.

5. Reduce the heat to medium low by adjusting the top vents to half-closed, and cook for another 30 minutes, or until done to your taste.

Serve and enjoy.

Roast Spring Lamb on the Bone

People welcomed the first spring lamb of the year. This lamb, nourished by the rich green grass of spring, had a tenderness and flavor that was exquisite, beyond compare.

Lamb is at its absolute best when cooked on the bone, with the flavor of the meat being enhanced by the marrow, and the internal cooking aided by the heat conducted by the bone. It is even better when naturally basted with a cap of its own natural fat.

No people honored lamb more than the Greeks, a tradition going back thousands of years. I have used Greek flavors with this wonderful grassfed lamb. Once you taste this lamb, you will understand why spring lamb was so valued.

Serves 4 to 8

1 (4 to 5½ pound) bone in grassfed leg of lamb, (or half leg of lamb of equivalent weight)

4 cloves organic garlic, quartered

1 medium-sized organic lemon, well washed

2 teaspoons fresh organic thyme leaves

1 teaspoon dried organic or imported oregano, preferably Greek or Italian

1 teaspoon freshly ground organic black pepper

1 teaspoon coarse unrefined sea salt, preferably French, crushed

4 tablespoons unfiltered organic extra virgin olive oil

1. The night before you plan to cook the roast, cut 16 slits, about an inch deep, all over the top and sides of the lamb. Push a garlic quarter into each slit, as deep as it will go.

2. Roll the lemon on a flat, hard surface, pressing down with your hand. This will help release the juice. Cut the lemon in quarters, and squeeze the juice into a glass bowl. Remove any seeds from the bowl. Reserve the lemon quarters.

3. Add the thyme, oregano, pepper, salt, and olive oil to the lemon juice, and mix well to make a marinade. Place the lamb in a glass bowl, and coat well with the marinade. Crush the lemon quarters a bit in your hand (warning, your hand will smell like lemon), and press the outside of the lemon quarters into the meat. Cover, and refrigerate overnight.

4. Remove the lamb from the refrigerator an hour before you plan to start cooking it, so it can come to room temperature.

5. Build a charcoal fire on one side of the cooker only. Bring your cooker to medium high heat, with all vents fully open. Place the lamb in front of, but not over, the heat source. Cover, and cook for 30 minutes.

6. Cover, and reduce the heat to medium low by adjusting the top vents to half-closed. Cook for another 30 minutes at medium low heat.

7. Add a handful of lump charcoal to the fire, cover, and cook for another 30 minutes, or until done to your taste.

Serve and enjoy! Remember that lamb tastes best when it is hot, not warm.

Slow-Roasted Leg of Lamb

The combination of grassfed lamb and natural charcoal is ancient, and delicious. Ancient peoples would often roast the lamb in front of a low fire, which gave it a wonderful smoky flavor. This recipe celebrates this old tradition, using traditional seasonings to recreate the traditional taste.

Serves 4 to 12

1 (4 to 6 pound) bone in grassfed leg of lamb, with fat cap
4 cloves organic garlic, quartered lengthwise into 4 long slivers

For the Marinade

3 tablespoons unfiltered organic extra virgin olive oil
1 tablespoon freshly squeezed organic lemon juice
1 tablespoon filtered water
1 teaspoon freshly ground organic black pepper
3 cloves organic garlic, finely chopped
1 teaspoon coarse unrefined sea salt, crushed

1. At least 2 hours before you plan to cook the meat, use a sturdy knife to poke holes all over the leg of lamb, for a total of 16 holes. The holes should be deep near the bone, and shallow elsewhere. Place a garlic sliver into each hole.

2. Combine the ingredients for the marinade and mix well. Place the lamb in a glass container, and coat thoroughly with the marinade. Cover, and let rest at room temperature for 2 hours.

3. Build a charcoal fire on one side of the cooker only. Bring your cooker to medium high heat, with all vents fully open.

4. When the cooker is ready, place the meat on the grill, in front of, but not over, the heat source. Cover, and reduce the heat to medium low by adjusting the top vents to half-closed. Cook for 1 hour at medium low heat.

5. Add two handfuls of lump charcoal to the fire. Cover, and cook for another 30 minutes, then check for doneness.

6. If the roast is not done, add another two handfuls of lump charcoal to the fire. Cover, and continue cooking until the lamb is done to your taste, checking for doneness at 15 minute intervals. (Add one handful of lump charcoal to the fire at 30 minute intervals, if necessary.)

Serve and enjoy the wonderful flavor of slow-roasted barbecued lamb.

Leg of Lamb in the Style of Sardinia

The Sardinians are famous for their roasted meat. The basic method is very simple. The meat is roasted in front of a fire of aromatic wood. When the roast is done, it is placed on a bed of myrtle leaves and left to sit for a while. At the time, I was unable to find unsprayed myrtle leaves in the United States, so I decided to try marinating the meat with comparable herbs, and roasting it. This recipe is so simple, it is hard to believe it can taste so wonderful, but it does.

Serves 4 to 8

1 small (4 to 5 pound) bone in grassfed leg of lamb, (or half leg of lamb of equivalent weight), with fat cap

For the Marinade

2 tablespoons unfiltered organic extra virgin olive oil

6 imported bay leaves, crushed between your fingers

1 tablespoon dried imported sage leaves, preferably Sardinian, crushed between your fingers

1½ teaspoons coarse unrefined sea salt, crushed

1. At least 2 hours before you plan to cook the lamb, prepare the marinade. Combine the ingredients, and mix well. Rub the marinade all over the lamb, cover, and let rest at room temperature for 2 hours.

2. Build a charcoal fire on one side of the cooker only. Bring your cooker to medium high heat, with all vents fully open. Place the lamb in front of, but not over, the heat source. Cover, and cook for 30 minutes.

3. Reduce the heat to medium low by adjusting the top vents to half-closed, and cook for 1 more hour, or until the roast is done to your taste, checking at 10 minute intervals. (Add two handfuls of lump charcoal to the fire if you cook for more than an hour at medium low heat.)

Serve hot and enjoy the wonderful flavor of this Sardinian-style roast.

Very Tender Lamb Shoulder

Grassfed lamb is naturally tender. However, traditional methods of marinating lamb can make it even more tender, while enhancing its flavor. Yogurt is often used to marinate lamb in Turkey, the Balkans, and the Caucasus region. Crushed onion, puréed onion, or onion juice is used to marinate lamb all over the Middle East. Yogurt and onions have been used for this purpose for thousands of years. This simple recipe shows why great flavor combinations become a tradition. Most roast lamb recipes contain garlic, but not this one. Cooking lamb this way makes it wonderfully tender.

Serves 4 to 8

1 (4 to 6 pound) grassfed lamb shoulder roast, either bone in or boneless

For the Marinade

1 cup natural full-fat unflavored yogurt, organic or the equivalent

1 large organic onion, grated, (or puréed in a blender)

6 organic green onions, very finely chopped

3 tablespoons pastured butter, softened

1½ teaspoons coarse unrefined sea salt, crushed

1. The day before you plan to cook the roast, prepare the marinade. Combine all ingredients in a large bowl, using a large fork or a heavy spoon to blend the butter with the marinade, and mix well. Place the lamb in a large glass bowl. Cover all surfaces of the lamb completely with the marinade, then refrigerate overnight.

2. Take the lamb out of the refrigerator approximately 1 hour before you plan to cook the meat, so it can come to room temperature.

3. Build a charcoal fire on one side of the cooker only. Bring your cooker to medium high heat, with all vents fully open. Place the lamb in front of, but not over, the heat source. Cover, and cook for 15 minutes.

4. Rotate the lamb so the other side of the meat is facing the fire. Cover, and cook for 15 more minutes.

5. Reduce the heat to medium low by adjusting the top vents to half-closed, and continue cooking the lamb until done to your taste, (which could take anywhere from 30 minutes to an hour and a half, depending on the size of your roast).

6. After 30 minutes, check the roast. If it is not done, add two handfuls of lump charcoal to the fire, and continue cooking, checking for doneness at 10 minute intervals.

Serve and enjoy the wonderful taste of this very tender lamb.

Lamb Shoulder with Cape Malay Style Marinade

South African cuisine is very diverse, influenced by the many different peoples who live in that country. The first European settlers were of Dutch descent. They called themselves Boers after the Dutch word for "farmer." When the Protestants were expelled from France, a number of them immigrated to South Africa. The Dutch imported workers from their Indonesian and Malayan colonies. These workers were known as Malays. There were also indigenous peoples, who hunted, raised cattle, and had a long tradition of cooking with charcoal. This led to a cuisine that had influences from all of these groups, along with the British and Indian immigrants that came much later.

This had led to some rather unique ways of marinating and barbecuing meat. After looking at some of the most traditional marinades, I decided to try something different. The idea of combining European meats, Malaysian spices, and fruit, with the African tradition of roasting meat in front of a charcoal fire is very appealing. So I came up with my own recipe, which made a huge substitution of fresh pears for the traditional dried apricots. The lamb came out unbelievably tender, with a unique and wonderful flavor.

Serves 4 to 6

1 (3 to 6 pound) grassfed lamb shoulder roast, either bone in or boneless

For the Marinade
2 ripe pears, peeled, and puréed
1 small onion, puréed
2 tablespoons unfiltered organic extra virgin olive oil
2 tablespoons sherry, preferably Spanish
2 cloves organic garlic, very finely chopped
1 teaspoon freshly ground organic black pepper
1 teaspoon coarse unrefined sea salt, crushed
1 teaspoon organic ground coriander
1 tablespoon organic curry powder

1. The day before you plan to make the roast, prepare the marinade. Combine all ingredients for the marinade, and mix well. Place the lamb in a glass bowl. Pour the marinade over the meat, making sure that all surfaces are covered by the marinade. Cover, and refrigerate overnight.

2. Remove the roast from the refrigerator at least 1 hour before you plan to cook it, so it can come to room temperature.

3. Build a charcoal fire on one side of the cooker only. Bring your cooker to medium high heat, with all vents fully open. Place the meat in front of, but not over, the heat source, fat side up. Cover, and cook for 30 minutes.

4. Reduce the heat to medium low by adjusting the top vents to half-closed, and cook for 1 more hour. Check for doneness. If it is not done, add two handfuls of lump charcoal to the fire, and continue cooking, checking for doneness at 10 minute intervals.

Denver Lamb Ribs with Armenian Marinade

Once, when I was a small boy, my mother took me to an Armenian restaurant in San Francisco that was owned by a friend of hers. Somehow, I wound up with some unbelievably tender and flavorful lamb ribs. The flavor was exquisite, a slightly sweet and tart marinade that combined perfectly with the tender lamb to create a taste that was so good that I could not believe it. We only went to that restaurant once, and I never learned its name. But I never forgot the taste of those ribs, and I can remember it to this day.

I tried for years to find the restaurant, with no success. I tried various Armenian restaurants, but none of them even served lamb ribs. I tried various recipes, but nothing was even close.

I finally tried to recreate the recipe by analyzing the taste I remembered. I wound up with a combination of pomegranate, onion, white wine, and barbecue. This recipe is close to my memory, and it is truly delicious.

Serves 4

3 pounds grassfed Denver-cut lamb ribs

⅓ cup pure pomegranate concentrate, preferably organic or imported

½ cup dry sherry, preferably Spanish

1 medium organic onion, puréed

1½ teaspoon coarse unrefined sea salt, crushed

1. The day before you plan to cook the ribs, combine all ingredients in a large glass bowl, and mix well (making sure that all surfaces of the meat are coated). Cover, and refrigerate overnight.

2. Remove the ribs from the refrigerator 1 hour before you plan to cook them, so they can come to room temperature.

3. Build a charcoal fire on one side of the cooker only. Bring your cooker to medium high heat, with all vents fully open. Place the ribs on the grill, bone side down, in front of, but not over, the heat source. Cover, and cook for 30 minutes.

4. Turn the ribs over. Cover, and cook for 20 more minutes.

5. Turn the ribs bone side down again. Cover, and reduce the heat to low by closing all the top and bottom vents to only one-quarter inch open. Cook for 20 minutes at low heat.

Serve and enjoy some of the most delicious lamb ribs you will ever have.

Lamburger with Georgian Flavors

This recipe is unusual and takes some extra effort, but the result is one of the most delicious burgers I have ever eaten. The flavors are typical of the Republic of Georgia, where good food is very much appreciated and cherished. Caramelizing the onion and garlic gives a wonderful flavor to these burgers.

Serves 4

1 pound grassfed ground lamb

2 tablespoons pastured butter

1 medium organic onion, finely chopped

2 organic garlic cloves, finely chopped

¼ cup fresh organic Italian parsley, finely chopped

1 teaspoon dried organic dill

1 organic egg, preferably pastured

½ teaspoon coarse unrefined sea salt, crushed

½ teaspoon freshly ground organic black pepper

¼ teaspoon organic garlic powder

1. Heat the butter over medium heat in a medium-sized, heavy-bottomed pan. When the butter is hot and bubbly, add the onion and garlic. Continue cooking over medium heat until the onion shrinks and starts to caramelize. Put the contents of the pan in a glass bowl. Add all the other ingredients, and mix well. When all the ingredients have been thoroughly combined, form into 4 equally sized hamburger patties about 1 inch thick.

2. Build a charcoal fire on one side of the cooker only. Bring your cooker to medium high heat, with all vents fully open. When the cooker is ready, place the burgers in front of, but not over, the heat source. Cover, and cook for 5 minutes.

3. Turn the burgers over. Cover, and cook for 5 more minutes.

Serve and enjoy.

Basil Lamburger

Grassfed lamb has a natural, mild flavor that is really enhanced by the right choice of seasonings. Fresh basil is one of my favorite flavors for lamb. Fresh basil has no substitute, and it must be used soon after being bought, because it does not last very long. But when basil is freshly picked, it has a wonderful aroma and flavor that goes so well with grassfed lamb. This lamburger is simple and utterly delicious.

Serves 4

1 pound grassfed ground lamb
¼ cup fresh organic basil, very finely chopped
1 clove organic garlic, very finely chopped
¼ teaspoon freshly ground organic black pepper
1 teaspoon coarse unrefined sea salt, crushed

1. Mix all ingredients together so the herbs and spices are evenly distributed throughout the meat. Form the mixture into 4 equally sized hamburger patties, approximately 1 inch thick.

2. Build a charcoal fire on one side of the cooker only. Bring your cooker to medium high heat, with all vents fully open. When the cooker is ready, place the burgers in front of, but not over, the heat source. Cover, and cook for 5 minutes.

3. Turn the burgers over. Cover, and cook for 5 more minutes.

Serve and enjoy.

Pastured Pork

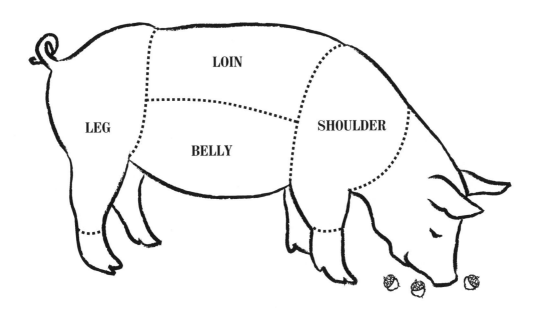

Judging Doneness in Pastured Pork

Unfortunately, most pork in the United States has been bred to be very lean. It is almost impossible to get great results with lean pork, as the meat will usually dry out by the time it is ready. Lean pork has very little flavor, because it is missing the tastiest and most nutritious part of the pig — the fat. For this reason, it is important to go to the trouble of getting pastured pork, pork with fat in it and on it, preferably from a heritage breed.

Pork must be cooked long enough to kill the parasites that can cause a disease known as trichinosis. While trichinosis is very rare in the United States, it is important to cook the meat to at least 140 degrees, which the government says will prevent trichinosis.

Doneness for Pastured Pork

The temperature to which pastured pork should be cooked varies greatly, depending on the cut.

- More expensive cuts such as loin, rib, sirloin, and tenderloin, are best at a temperature of about 150 to 160 degrees.

- Classic barbecue cuts, such as spareribs and pork shoulder, can be absolutely wonderful at higher temperatures, even up to 180 degrees, if cooked slowly on a barbecue for a long time.

Obviously, you cannot use a meat thermometer to test the doneness of spareribs, since they are just too thin. But because they are thin, they will be fully cooked if you follow the times given in the recipes.

The time it takes to reach a particular internal temperature for pork can vary widely, depending on the outside temperature, the thickness of the cut, the density of the meat, and the breed. Even brining pork changes the amount of time it takes to reach a particular internal temperature. Until you develop a feeling for when a particular cut is done, a good instant-read meat thermometer is invaluable.

The color of cooked pork can vary. Pork cooked with traditional barbecue fuels tends to turn pink inside, even when it has been completely cooked. The pink color is created by the interaction of the barbecue fuel and the meat. If the pink color is on the outside edges of the meat (once you cut into it), it is often called a smoke ring. Cooked pork should never look rare or raw, though some interior pinkness is okay, as long as the meat is at the proper temperature. Fully cooked pork usually has a grayish-white color, but can also take on a pink color as described above.

Georgian Pork Chops

The Republic of Georgia is a small country with a huge cuisine. Georgia is located in the Caucasus Mountains, and is an ancient country with a very long history, full of wars, foreign domination, and conflict. Somehow, through all their troubles, the Georgians developed one of the most varied and delicious cuisines in the world. I ate at a Georgian restaurant in San Francisco as a child, and still cannot forget how good the lamb was, and how good everything was. I picked up a very important cooking tip during this visit. The owner told my mother to never marinate good meat in wine or vinegar, as that would toughen the meat. I have found this to be absolutely true with grassfed beef and grassfed bison.

The Georgians are also famous for their robust good health and extreme longevity. Their traditional diet is the reason for their remarkable health and longevity. One of the favorite Georgian foods is fatty pork, which is often roasted with a marinade similar to the one here. The flavors may seem unusual, but they go perfectly with pork and charcoal — and the results are wonderful.

Serves 2 to 4

2 thick pastured pork chops, approximately 1 pound each

For the Marinade

2 teaspoons organic whole black peppercorns

1 teaspoon organic coriander powder

1 teaspoon organic dried sage

1½ teaspoons coarse unrefined sea salt, crushed

4 cloves organic garlic, coarsely chopped

2 tablespoons filtered water

2 tablespoons unfiltered organic extra virgin olive oil

1. At least 1 day before you plan to cook the chops, prepare the marinade. Combine all the marinade ingredients and mix well. Place the chops in a glass bowl, and coat all sides of the meat with the marinade. Cover, and let rest for 1 hour, then refrigerate overnight.

1. Remove the meat from the refrigerator at least 1 hour before you plan to cook it, so it can come to room temperature.

2. Build a charcoal fire on one side of the cooker only. Bring your cooker to medium high heat, with all vents fully open. Scrape the marinade off the meat. It's okay if some bits remain. Place the meat in the cooker, in front of, but not over, the heat source. Cover, and cook the chops for 5 minutes on each side.

3. Reduce the heat to medium low by adjusting the top vents to half-closed, and cook for 10 minutes, or until done to your taste. Remember that pork must be thoroughly cooked to a temperature above 140 degrees.

Serve and enjoy the magnificent flavors of Georgia.

Pork Chops in
Spanish Chimichurri-Style Marinade

Chimichurri is a hot, spicy Argentine condiment that is often served with grilled meats. There are many variations, but it usually contains herbs, fresh or dry, and a good deal of hot red peppers, powdered, dried, or fresh.

Sometimes it is used as a marinade as well. It can be very hot, too hot for the taste of many people.

The idea came to me to make a Spanish-style chimichurri-type marinade, with typical Spanish flavors, and without the hot peppers. Pork is the favorite meat in Spain, so I decided to make the marinade for pork. This flavorful marinade is redolent with the flavors of Spain, and goes perfectly with grilled pork chops.

Serves 2 to 4

2 thick pastured pork chops, approximately 1 pound each

For the Marinade

4 cloves organic garlic, crushed

1 teaspoon freshly ground organic black pepper

2 teaspoons organic dried thyme

2 teaspoons organic dried parsley

2 teaspoons organic dried oregano

4 tablespoons unfiltered organic extra virgin olive oil

1 tablespoon dry white wine, such as Spanish sherry

1 teaspoon coarse unrefined sea salt, crushed

1. At least 3 days before you plan to cook the chops, prepare the marinade. Combine all the marinade ingredients and mix well. Place the chops in a glass bowl, and coat all sides of the meat with the marinade. Cover, and let rest for 1 hour, then refrigerate for 3 days.

2. Remove the meat from the refrigerator at least 1 hour before you plan to cook it, so it can come to room temperature.

3. Build a charcoal fire on one side of the cooker only. Bring your cooker to medium high heat, with all vents fully open. Place the meat in the cooker, in front of, but not over, the heat source. Cover, and cook the chops for 5 minutes on each side.

4. Reduce the heat to medium low by adjusting the top vents to half-closed, and cook for 10 minutes, or until done to your taste. Remember that pork must be thoroughly cooked to a temperature above 140 degrees.

Serve and enjoy the magnificent flavors of this wonderful pork.

Charcoaled Pork Roast with French Brine

The French are famous for the superb flavors of their cooking, but not for barbecued pork. I decided to add typical French flavors to a light brine, hoping that the brine would carry the flavors deep into the meat. This recipe uses both fresh and dried thyme, which gives a deep flavor. The result was pork that was soft and tender, with a deep, yet subtle flavor that was both outstanding and unique.

Serves 3 to 6

1 (3 pound) bone in pastured pork loin roast, with fat cap

For the Brine

1 quart filtered water

1 tablespoon coarse unrefined sea salt, preferably from France

1 tablespoon dried organic thyme leaves

12 sprigs fresh organic thyme

4 cloves organic garlic, slightly crushed

2 imported bay leaves, crushed

8 sprigs fresh organic Italian parsley

1 teaspoon organic mustard seeds

20 organic whole black peppercorns

1. The day before you plan to cook the roast, prepare the brine. Pour the water in a glass or stainless steel bowl large enough to hold the roast. Add the salt and stir vigorously until the salt dissolves. Add the rest of the brine ingredients, and stir well. Add the roast to the bowl, bone side up. Add more filtered water if necessary to cover the roast. Cover the bowl, and refrigerate overnight.

2. Remove the bowl from the refrigerator 1 hour before you plan to cook the meat, so it can come to room temperature.

3. Build a charcoal fire on one side of the cooker only. Bring your cooker to medium high heat, with all vents fully open. Place the roast on the grill, fat side up, with one of the meat sides of the roast facing the heat source. in front of, but not over, the heat source. Cover, and cook for 20 minutes.

4. Rotate the roast so the opposite side faces the heat source. Cover, and reduce the heat to medium low by adjusting the top vents to half-closed. Cook for 30 minutes at medium low heat.

5. Add two handfuls of charcoal to the fire. Cover, and cook for another 30 minutes to 1 hour, or until the pork is fully cooked and done to your taste. Add another two handfuls of charcoal if you want to keep cooking after an hour. Check for doneness at 10 minute intervals.

Serve and enjoy the classic French flavors.

Roast Pork with Mediterranean Myrtle, in the Style of Sardinia

It is said that the Sardinians are the true masters of barbecue in Italy. Since Italy is famous for the magnificent quality of its cuisine, this is quite a compliment. I studied all I could find on Sardinian barbecue (which was not much), but I did find out a few things. Everyone agreed that the Sardinians like to use myrtle leaves, lots of myrtle leaves, to flavor barbecued meats. The species of myrtle used is not crepe myrtle, which is common in the U.S., but the myrtle that grows naturally in the Mediterranean, especially Sardinia. As far as I know, no one uses myrtle for barbecuing meat, except the Sardinians.

The myrtle leaves could be used as a flavoring, usually after the meat was cooked, when it would be set to rest in a bed of myrtle leaves. Myrtle branches and leaves would often be part of the cooking fire.

I could not find the right kind of myrtle leaves, so I developed a substitute by combining bay leaves and dried sage leaves. This resulted in some delicious barbecue. Then I found a source of organic Mediterranean myrtle leaves. I decided to use the leaves in a marinade before cooking the meat. The result was this recipe, which produced some of the very best pork I have ever had. This recipe is so simple, and so tender, savory, and delicious.

Try to get the best fatty, pastured pork you can find for this one. It is really something special.

Serves 6 to 8

1 (3 to 4 pound) bone in pastured pork loin roast, with fat cap

½ cup dried organic Mediterranean myrtle leaves, or more if needed

2 tablespoons unfiltered organic extra virgin olive oil

3 cloves organic garlic, crushed and quartered

1 teaspoon coarse unrefined sea salt, crushed

1. At least 4 hours before you plan to cook the meat, cover the bottom of a glass bowl with a layer of myrtle leaves, and one-quarter of the garlic. Pierce the fat cap of the roast many times with a fork. Place the roast directly on the leaves, fat side down. Coat the two meat sides of the roast with the olive oil. Press the remaining garlic into the meat. Cover each of the two meat sides with a layer of myrtle leaves. Cover the bone side of the roast (which will be on top) with a layer of myrtle leaves. Cover the bowl, and let rest in a cool place for at least 4 hours.

2. Build a charcoal fire on one side of the cooker only. Bring your cooker to medium high heat, with all vents fully open.

3. Remove the myrtle leaves and garlic from the roast, and reserve (if you want to add them to the fire). Sprinkle the salt on the meat sides of the roast, and put the roast on a plate, fat side up.

4. Place the roast on the grill, fat side up, in front of, but not over, the heat source. One of the meat sides should face the heat source. (See **note** below.) Cover, and cook for 15 minutes at medium high heat.

5. Rotate the roast so the opposite side faces the heat source. Cover, and cook for another 15 minutes.

6. Move the roast to the center of the grill. Cover, and reduce the heat to medium low by adjusting the top vents to half-closed. Cook for 30 minutes at medium low heat.

7. Add two handfuls of charcoal to the fire. Cover, and cook for another 30 minutes. Test for doneness. If the roast is not fully cooked, continue cooking, checking for doneness at 10 minute intervals.

Serve and enjoy the exotic Mediterranean flavor.

NOTE: You can try adding the remaining myrtle leaves to the fire see *Herbal Smoke* (pages 29 – 30).

Charcoaled Pork Shoulder with Polish Brine

Few Americans know that Poland was once one of the largest, most free, and most powerful nations on earth. This helped the Poles develop a cuisine worthy of an empire, with a huge variety of magnificent dishes. The Poles love meat, and have developed some wonderful ways to flavor it. This brine is based on traditional Polish seasonings for pork. It has a terrific flavor, especially when barbecued.

Serves 4 to 6

1 (3 to 4 pound) pastured pork shoulder roast

For the Brine
1 quart filtered water
1 tablespoon coarse unrefined sea salt
½ teaspoon organic dried marjoram
1 teaspoon sweet paprika, preferably Hungarian
1 teaspoon caraway seeds, preferably organic
1 teaspoon organic dried sage
1 teaspoon freshly ground organic black pepper
1 medium organic onion, sliced
4 organic garlic cloves, crushed

1. The day before you plan to cook the meat, make the brine by combining all ingredients in a glass bowl large enough to hold the roast. Mix well until the salt dissolves. Place the roast in the bowl, fat side up. The brine should cover the roast, though it is fine if the fat at the top is not covered. Add more filtered water if necessary. Cover, and refrigerate overnight.

2. At least 1 hour before you plan to cook the roast, remove it from the refrigerator, so it can come to room temperature.

3. Build a charcoal fire on one side of the cooker only. Bring your cooker to medium high heat, with all vents fully open.

4. Place the roast on the grill, in front of, but not over, the heat source, fat side up. Cover, and cook for 15 minutes.

5. Rotate the roast so the other side is facing the heat source. Cover, and cook for another 15 minutes.

6. Move the roast to the center of the grill. Cover, and reduce the heat to medium low by adjusting the top vents to half-closed. Cook for 1 hour at medium low heat.

7. Check for doneness. If the roast is not done, add two handfuls of charcoal to the fire and continue to cook until done, checking for doneness at 10 minute intervals. Remember that pork must be thoroughly cooked to at least 140 degrees. Pork shoulder is better at 160, or even 170 degrees.

Serve and enjoy the magnificent Polish flavor.

Roast Pork Shoulder with the Flavors of Germany

Most Americans do not realize that Germany has its own barbecue heritage. Most German barbecue is pork, which creates a problem. Most pork in the United States is so industrialized and lean that it lacks flavor. My previous book, *Tender Grassfed Meat*, had no pork recipes because I could not find good pork. Fortunately, there is some good, traditionally raised pork available at my local farmers' market from time to time. This pork has plenty of good fat, and is raised in oak woods, and the pigs are allowed to root in organic vegetable fields. This type of pasture-raised pork can be wonderful, especially if it is a heritage breed, such as Berkshire.

This recipe uses flavorings typical of German barbecue, and is superb. The use of fresh garlic and green onion together with powdered garlic and onion provides a very deep flavor.

Serves 4

    1 (3 pound) boneless pastured pork shoulder roast, rolled and netted

    2 organic green onions, with the root end trimmed off

    2 organic garlic cloves, whole

For the Rub

    1 teaspoon organic onion powder

    1 teaspoon organic garlic powder

    1 teaspoon dried organic mustard powder

    1 teaspoon freshly ground organic black pepper

    1 teaspoon organic white pepper

    ½ teaspoon organic ground nutmeg

    1½ teaspoons unrefined sea salt, crushed

1. At least 1 hour before you plan to cook the meat, remove it from the refrigerator so it can come to room temperature.

2. Insert the green onions and the garlic cloves into the space at the center of the roast, where it has been rolled. Leave the netting on.

3. Combine the rub ingredients. Rub the mixture all over the surface of the pork roast.

4. Build a charcoal fire on one side of the cooker only. Bring your cooker to medium high heat, with all vents fully open.

5. Place the roast in front of, but not over, the heat source. Cover, and reduce the heat to medium low by adjusting the top vents to half-closed. Cook for 1 hour at medium low heat.

6. Add two handfuls of charcoal. Cover, and cook for 30 more minutes. Check for doneness. Pork should be at least 140 degrees, but it would be even better at 150 to 160 degrees. If the roast is not ready, continue cooking at medium low heat, testing the temperature at 10 minute intervals until it is done.

Mediterranean Pork Roast

The so-called "Mediterranean Diet" has very little to do with the actual diet of the peoples along on the coast of the Mediterranean Sea. The favorite food of many of these peoples was roast pork, the fattier the better. The pork was always made with the local herbs, which gave a wonderful flavor to the meat.

This pork shoulder roast borrows from the traditions of several Mediterranean peoples, but is faithful to all of them. All of these peoples dried herbs in the sun, and this recipe celebrates the use of such herbs.

Serves 4 to 6

1 (3 to 4 pound) boneless pastured pork shoulder roast, with skin and fat

For the Marinade

3 tablespoons unfiltered organic extra virgin olive oil

1 teaspoon organic dried sage, crumbled between your fingers

1 teaspoon organic dried thyme, crumbled between your fingers

½ teaspoon organic dried oregano, crumbled between your fingers

1 teaspoon organic ground coriander

1 teaspoon organic granulated garlic powder

1 teaspoon freshly ground organic black pepper

1 teaspoon organic hot red pepper flakes (optional)

1½ teaspoons coarse unrefined sea salt, crushed

For Cooking

2 large organic garlic cloves, quartered

1. The day before you plan to cook the pork, score the fat side of the pork and skin by slicing through the skin and fat lengthwise all the way through the skin and fat of the pork, but stopping short of cutting into the meat, at half-inch intervals. Be sure to use a sharp, sturdy knife and be very careful. The knife can slip on the pork skin, so make sure the knife edge is angled away from your other hand at all times. This step is absolutely crucial to the success of this recipe.

2. Prepare the marinade by mixing all ingredients together, stirring well to combine them. The marinade will be quite thick. Using a narrow blade, poke eight holes deep into the meat side of the pork roast. Take a garlic sliver, coat it with the marinade, and push the garlic sliver into one of the holes you have cut into the pork, pushing the garlic sliver deep into the hole. Repeat with the other seven garlic slivers.

3. Place the roast in a glass bowl, and coat with the rest of the marinade, pressing the marinade into every side of the meat, and putting some on the fat. Cover, and let rest at room temperature for 1 hour, then refrigerate overnight.

4. Remove the roast from the refrigerator 1 hour before you plan to cook it, so it can come to room temperature.

5. Build a charcoal fire on one side of the cooker only. Bring your cooker to medium high heat, with all vents fully open. Place the roast fat side up, in front of, but not over, the heat source. Cover, and cook for 15 minutes.

6. Rotate the roast so the opposite side is facing the heat source (still fat side up). Cover, and cook for another 15 minutes.

7. Reduce the heat to medium low by adjusting the top vents to half-closed, and cook for 30 minutes at medium low heat.

8. Add two handfuls of charcoal to the fire. Cover, and cook for 30 more minutes at medium low heat. Test for doneness. Pork should be cooked to at least 140 degrees, but the meat will be even better at a temperature of 150 to 160 degrees. Keep cooking at medium low heat until the desired temperature is reached, checking at 10 minute intervals.

Serve and enjoy this fabulous pork roast.

Pork Roast with Traditional Italian Flavors

I love traditional Italian cooking. Very often just a few simple, well chosen ingredients are combined to provide fantastic taste. The combination of rosemary and garlic, for instance, is a favorite in Italy, and does wonderful things for pork. The recipe that follows has only five ingredients, but these five combine perfectly to create one of the most delicious pork roasts you will ever have.

It is very important to score the pork fat on this roast.

Serves 4

1 (3 to 4 pound) pastured boneless pork shoulder roast with fat and skin

For the Seasoning Paste
2 teaspoons coarse unrefined sea salt, crushed

6 cloves organic garlic, crushed and finely chopped

Leaves from 2 large sprigs organic rosemary, very finely chopped

2 teaspoons freshly ground organic black pepper

3 tablespoons unfiltered organic extra virgin olive oil

1. The day before you plan to cook the roast, combine all the other ingredients in a bowl, and stir well to make a seasoning paste. Using a sharp, sturdy knife, score the fat of the pork roast. (Be sure to have a firm grip on the pork when you score it, and make sure to angle the edge of the blade away from the hand that is holding the pork.) Make long parallel cuts all the way through the skin and the fat, but stopping short of cutting into the meat, at half-inch intervals.

2. Place the pork roast in a glass bowl, and rub the seasoning paste all over the roast. Cover, and let rest at room temperature for 1 hour, then refrigerate overnight.

3. Remove the roast from the refrigerator at least 1 hour before you plan to cook it, so it can come to room temperature.

4. Build a charcoal fire on one side of the cooker only. Bring your cooker to medium high heat, with all vents fully open. Place the roast on the grill, fat side up, in front of, but not over, the heat source. Cover, and cook for 15 minutes.

5. Rotate the roast so the opposite side is facing the heat source. Cover, and cook for another 15 minutes.

6. Move the roast to the center of the grill. Cover, and reduce the heat to medium low by adjusting the top vents to half-closed. Cook for 30 minutes at medium low heat.

7. Add two handfuls of charcoal to the fire, and continue cooking for 1 hour. Check for doneness. Continue checking for doneness at 10 minute intervals until the roast is fully done. Add more fuel if necessary to keep the temperature at medium low heat.

8. When the roast is done, reduce the heat as low as possible by closing all the top and bottom vents completely, and let the roast remain in the cooker for 5 to 10 minutes.

Spicy Georgian Pork Shoulder

This is not the Georgia in the United States, but the other Georgia. The nation of Georgia is located in the Caucasus, a mountainous area between Iran and Russia. It is a very old nation, and its cuisine is rich and complex. Food is very important in Georgian culture. In fact, there is a tradition there that a girl is not ready for marriage until she can perfectly prepare a particular traditional chicken dish. The Georgians are also noted for their longevity, leading long, healthy, and productive lives. Georgian cuisine has an incredible variety of offerings, ranging from meat grilled with no seasoning whatsoever to complex dishes made with a huge array of exotic spices, including some (like marigold) that seem to be used only in Georgia. The Georgians love meat, especially fatty pork. This recipe uses typical Georgian flavors to give a hot and intense flavor to barbecued pork.

Serves 4 to 6

1 (3 to 4 pound) pastured pork shoulder roast, with fat cap

For the Wet Rub

1½ tablespoons sweet paprika, preferably imported

1½ tablespoons hot paprika, preferably imported

1 tablespoon organic garlic powder

1 teaspoon Jamaican allspice

1 teaspoon organic ground coriander

½ teaspoon organic ground cumin

1 teaspoon coarse unrefined sea salt, crushed

2 tablespoons filtered water, or as needed

1. The day before you plan to cook the meat, combine the ingredients for the wet rub, adding just enough water to give you a thick, spreadable paste. Place the roast in a glass bowl, and spread the rub all over the pork roast. Be careful not to touch your eyes before you have washed all the rub off your hands. When the roast is well coated, cover and refrigerate overnight.

2. Remove the roast from the refrigerator 1 hour before you plan to cook it, so the roast can come to room temperature.

3. Build a charcoal fire on one side of the cooker only. Bring your cooker to medium high heat, with all vents fully open.

4. Place the roast on the grill, in front of, but not over, the heat source, fat side up. Cover, and cook for 15 minutes.

5. Rotate the roast so the other side is facing the heat source. Cover, and cook for another 15 minutes.

6. Move the roast to the center of the grill. Cover, and reduce the heat to medium low by adjusting the top vents to half-closed. Cook for 1 hour at medium low heat.

7. Check for doneness. If the roast is not done, add two handfuls of charcoal to the fire and continue to cook until done, checking for doneness at 10 minute intervals. Remember that pork must be thoroughly cooked to at least 140 degrees. Pork shoulder is better at 160, or even 170 degrees.

Rediscovered Ribs

Restaurants used to be much, much better than they are now. Back when just about every family had a good home cook, a restaurant had to have really outstanding food, or it wouldn't have any customers. One of the restaurants I remember had outstanding barbecued pork ribs. The restaurant chain had been founded in 1928. The secret of their success was a baste that was supposed to have been invented by a member of the Kiowa Tribe and was based on Native American cooking traditions. The barbecue in that restaurant had a unique and absolutely wonderful taste and texture. It was a sad day when the founder sold the restaurants to a large corporation which made the restaurants mediocre and then sold them.

I have tried for many years to find a recipe for the baste they used on their meats and have had absolutely no success. This year, I decided to take a different approach. I researched how Native Americans roasted meat. I put a few clues together and came up with this recipe. This baste is not the baste used at that restaurant, but it does include the most important ingredient — melted animal fat. I'm just about certain that the Kiowa used bison fat. I am just as certain that the restaurant used melted pork lard. The ribs in this recipe look just like the ribs used to look at that restaurant, and the taste is very similar, though not identical. These just might be the finest spareribs I have ever made.

Important Note: It is vital to get the right kind of spareribs for this dish, or it will not work. The ribs should be actual spareribs, not baby back ribs. They must not be overtrimmed. In other words, all of the bones must be covered by meat, and hopefully some fat. Many butchers trim off so much fat that you can actually see the bones with a very thin covering of meat. Those ribs are not worth buying.

Serves 2 to 4

1 (2½ to 3½ pound) rack pastured pork spareribs

For the Brushing Baste
½ cup homemade bone broth, preferably *Beef Bone Broth* (page 50)
¼ cup unhydrogenated natural pork lard
½ teaspoon coarse unrefined sea salt, crushed
1 teaspoon freshly ground organic black pepper

1. About an hour before you plan to cook the ribs, remove them from the refrigerator, so they can come to room temperature.

2. Heat the broth and pork lard together over low heat until the pork lard melts. Remove the pot from the heat and pour into a bowl. Add the salt and pepper, and mix well.

3. Brush a generous coating of the baste on the meat side of the ribs, covering all the meat. Let the baste dry on the meat.

4. Build a charcoal fire on one side of the cooker only. Bring your cooker to medium high heat, with all vents fully open.

5. Place the ribs in the cooker, meat side up, in the middle of the grill. Cover, and reduce the heat to medium low by adjusting the top vents to half-closed. Cook for 1 hour at medium low heat.

6. Add two handfuls of charcoal to the fire. Brush another coating of the baste onto the ribs. Turn over the ribs. Cover, and reduce the heat to low by closing all the top and bottom vents to only one-quarter inch open. Cook for 1 hour at low heat.

7. Add one more handful of charcoal to the fire. Turn over the ribs again, then brush a final coating of the baste onto the ribs. Cover, and cook at low heat for 30 more minutes.

8. Turn the ribs over for the final time. Cover, and cook for 10 more minutes at low heat.

It would be a crime to put barbecue sauce on these ribs. Serve and enjoy the wonderful taste of the rediscovered ribs.

Thai-Style Spareribs

There is more than one way to cook spareribs. Actually, there are hundreds of ways. But there are two main ways to barbecue them. One way is to cook them low and slow for hours with low heat. Another is to cook them at a higher heat, which is a lot quicker. This recipe uses the latter method. It is so good that I defy anybody to claim that low and slow is better. This recipe is based on my memory of some wonderful spareribs I used to enjoy in a Thai restaurant in Berkeley, California, several decades ago. Those ribs were so good that they were the favorite food of a number of local chefs, according to a newspaper poll. They had a unique flavor from the Thai seasonings and were very tender.

When I came across a genuine recipe for these ribs, I did not like the ingredients or the cooking method. So I decided to invent my own using traditional Thai ingredients and my own cooking method. These ribs do not taste the same, but they have a wonderful flavor of their own. I like them even better.

Serves 2 to 4

1 (3 to 4 pound) rack pastured pork spareribs

For the Marinade
   ¼ **cup organic cilantro stems, finely chopped**
   4 cloves organic garlic, finely chopped
   1 (2 inch) piece ginger, very finely chopped
   3 tablespoons Thai fish sauce
   2 tablespoons dry white wine, preferably Spanish sherry
   2 tablespoons organic grade B maple syrup
   2 tablespoons organic peanut butter
   2 tablespoons unrefined organic toasted sesame oil

1. The night before you plan to cook the ribs, prepare the marinade. Combine all the ingredients in a bowl, stirring vigorously until the peanut butter has dissolved completely into the marinade. Place the ribs in a glass bowl, and coat all sides of the ribs with the marinade. Cover, and refrigerate overnight.

2. Remove the ribs from the refrigerator at least 1 hour before you plan to cook them, so they can come to room temperature.

3. Build a charcoal fire on one side of the cooker only. Bring your cooker to medium high heat, with all vents fully open.

4. When the cooker is ready, place the ribs in front of, but not over, the heat source, bone side down. Baste with some of the marinade remaining in the bowl, cover, and cook for 30 minutes.

5. Baste the ribs once more with the remaining marinade. Turn the ribs bone side up, cover, and cook for 20 minutes.

6. Turn the ribs bone side down. Cover, and cook for 10 minutes.

Serve and enjoy the wonderful flavor of these tender ribs.

Pork Burger with Two Garlics

The flavors for this pork burger are Italian, but it contains a unique twist, which, once again, was the result of a mistake.

I couldn't decide whether to use fresh garlic or garlic powder for this recipe. While making the mixture, I got distracted and I ended up using both of them. The combination of fresh garlic and garlic powder gives this burger a depth of flavor that complements the other ingredients perfectly, and makes it truly wonderful. This is an absolutely delicious burger, especially if you can find ground pork from a pastured pig. The mixture should include plenty of pork fat. Lean just does not taste good when it comes to pork.

Serves 4

1 pound pastured ground pork

1 organic egg, preferably pastured

2 tablespoons fresh organic basil leaves, finely chopped

2 cloves organic garlic, finely chopped

1 teaspoon organic granulated garlic powder

¼ cup grated Parmesan and/or Romano cheese

¼ cup fine organic bread crumbs

4 thin slices Havarti or mozzarella cheese

1. Add all ingredients (except the sliced cheese), and mix well. Form the mixture into 4 equally sized hamburger patties, about 1 inch thick.

2. Build a charcoal fire on one side of the cooker only. Bring your cooker to medium high heat, with all vents fully open. When the cooker is ready, place the burgers in front of, but not over, the heat source. Cover, and cook for 6 minutes.

3. Turn the burgers over. Cover, and cook for another 5 minutes.

4. Place a slice of cheese on each burger. Cover, and cook for 1 more minute. Remember that pork should be thoroughly cooked.

Serve and enjoy.

Swedish Hamburger

Swedish meatballs are famous. Traditionally, different kinds of ground meat would be combined with various spices, a large amount of bread crumbs, and other ingredients, formed into tiny meatballs, and cooked in a sauce. I decided to try a number of traditional flavors to make a hamburger for grilling. To me, these burgers taste much better than tiny meatballs. You can just use beef, if you prefer, but pork adds a wonderful richness to these burgers. The spicing is unusual, but gives a wonderful and different flavor to the meat.

Serves 4 to 6

1 pound grassfed ground beef

½ pound pastured ground pork

2 tablespoons fresh organic Italian parsley leaves, very finely chopped

½ small organic onion, very finely chopped

1 organic egg, preferably pastured

½ teaspoon ground organic ginger

½ teaspoon ground organic nutmeg

½ teaspoon ground allspice, preferably Jamaican

½ teaspoon dried organic dill

¼ cup fine organic breadcrumbs of your choice

¼ cup pastured cream

1 teaspoon coarse unrefined sea salt, crushed

½ teaspoon organic white pepper

1. Mix all ingredients together thoroughly. Form into 4 to 6 hamburger patties, about 1 inch thick.

2. Build a charcoal fire on one side of the cooker only. Bring your cooker to medium high heat, with all vents fully open.

3. When the cooker is ready, place the burgers in front of, but not over, the heat source. Cover, and cook for 6 minutes.

4. Turn the burgers over. Cover, and cook for another 6 minutes. This should give you burgers that are medium, and utterly delicious. Remember that pork should be thoroughly cooked.

Serve and enjoy the wonderful flavors of these illustrious burgers.

Bastes

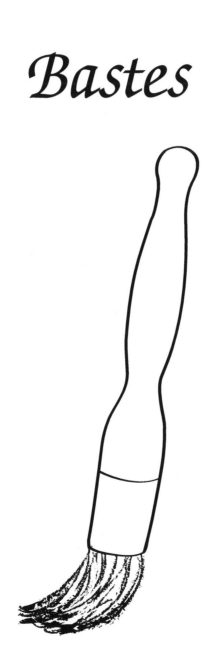

The Lost Art of Basting

One of my main motivations for writing this book is to help preserve some wonderful traditional cooking techniques that are being lost and forgotten. The ancient art of basting is one of these endangered techniques. This is truly a shame, because basting is one of the best ways to make grassfed meat into something truly special. Basting is one of the oldest cooking techniques for meat, and has been used for thousands of years. Today, most American cooks have never basted anything.

Basting meat greatly enhances its tenderness and flavor, especially when it is barbecued.

Basting is the act of pouring or brushing a particular liquid over meat before and during the cooking process. The composition of the liquid can be very simple or complex, but the very best traditional bastes are based on melted animal fat.

Traditional Fats for Basting

Melted animal fat, with nothing else, can be a wonderful baste. All you have to do is melt the fat. These are some of the best traditional fats for basting:

- Pastured butter
- Grassfed beef tallow
- Grassfed bison tallow
- Grassfed lamb tallow
- Unhydrogenated natural pork lard
- Chicken fat
- Duck fat
- Goose fat

All of these wonderful fats have been used as bastes for thousands of years.

The recipes in this chapter are some of the very best bastes I have ever used, and go magnificently with barbecued meat. Many of the recipes in this book contain detailed instructions on how to use a particular baste. (See "**bastes**" in the index on page 229.)

Bone Broth Baste

It is an old American tradition to use bone broth to baste barbecued meats. The addition of beef tallow really makes this baste ideal for barbecue.

¼ **cup grassfed beef tallow**
½ **cup homemade bone broth, preferably** *Beef Bone Broth* **(page 50)**
½ **small organic yellow onion, finely chopped**
1 **teaspoon freshly ground organic black pepper**

1. Melt the beef tallow in a small saucepan over medium low heat.

2. Add the broth, onions, and black pepper.

3. Heat the mixture to a slow simmer. Simmer for 5 minutes. Mix well.

Keep warm while using as a baste, or else the fat will solidify.

Native American Bison Baste

While most of my cooking background is European, this baste is perfect for grassfed bison. It makes the meat more tender, brings out the natural sweetness of the bison, and combines perfectly with the flavors of real charcoal. Grassfed bison suet or grassfed bison fat is absolutely necessary for this recipe. Only bison suet or fat will bring out the true sweet flavor of grassfed bison. There is no substitute. I have found that some sellers of grassfed bison will sell bison suet or bison fat, even if it is not listed on their website.

This baste has only two ingredients, but they create so much tenderness and flavor that nothing else is needed.

¼ cup grassfed bison suet, (or ¼ cup grassfed bison fat)

½ cup homemade bone broth, preferably *Bison* or *Beef Bone Broth* (pages 50 - 51)

1. First, render the bison fat as follows:

2. Break the bison suet into small pieces. (If you are using bison fat, cut the bison fat into small pieces about half an inch long.) Place the bison suet (or fat) in a single layer on a heavy-bottomed pan. Turn the heat to medium.

3. After a few minutes, most of the fat should have melted down to a clear liquid. Turn the heat down to medium low, and continue to heat the fat, stirring occasionally, until most of it has melted. There will be some hard, crisp pieces that remain solid. These are cracklings, and many people like to snack on them. Use a metal strainer to strain the liquid fat into a glass or ceramic bowl. Save the cracklings for eating.

4. Place the rendered bison fat and the broth in a small saucepan.

5. Heat the mixture over low heat until the bison fat melts into the broth. Mix well.

Keep warm while using as a baste, or else the fat will solidify.

Garlic Basil Baste

Butter is one of the best and most traditional mediums for basting meat. The most traditional way to cook a steak was to either fry it in lots of butter (if cooked on the stove), or to baste it with lots of butter (if cooked on the grill). Garlic and basil are a traditional flavor combination, especially in Italy. The Georgians of the Caucasus, a people known for their health and longevity, also combined basil and garlic.

These ingredients work wonderfully with butter, to make an especially flavorful baste. It is very important that the basil be fresh and fragrant. Dried basil has a totally different taste, and just will not do as a substitute. This is a particularly good baste for meat that has been stripped of its fat cap.

½ cup homemade bone broth, preferably *Beef Bone Broth* (page 50)

4 tablespoons pastured butter

2 tablespoons fresh organic basil leaves, finely chopped

4 cloves organic garlic, finely chopped

½ teaspoon coarse unrefined sea salt, crushed

½ teaspoon freshly ground organic black pepper

1. Add all ingredients to a small saucepan. Heat over low heat until the butter melts completely.

2. Simmer gently for 5 minutes, and remove from the heat.

This baste should be kept warm during use, as the butter can solidify if it gets too cold.

Romanian Garlic Butter Baste

Transylvania is now part of Romania. Transylvanians use garlic for other things besides scaring off Dracula. Garlic is heavily used in the cuisine of Transylvania. In fact, all of Romania values garlic and it is often used to flavor meat. This baste, combining garlic with butter and homemade beef bone broth, provides an absolutely wonderful flavor to barbecued steak. The olive oil is not traditional, but unites the ingredients and helps keep the fat in the baste from solidifying.

2 tablespoons pastured butter

¼ cup homemade bone broth, preferably *Beef Bone Broth* (page 50)

4 cloves organic garlic, very finely chopped

1 tablespoon unfiltered organic extra virgin olive oil

½ teaspoon freshly ground organic black pepper

1. Combine the butter, broth, and garlic in a small saucepan. Heat over low heat just until the butter melts completely. Remove from the heat and pour the mixture into a bowl. Add the olive oil and black pepper. Stir well.

See *Romanian Garlic Strip Steak* recipe on page 67.

Raw Vegetable Condiments

Chimichurri Sauce

Beef is THE food in Argentina. Many Argentines regularly eat beef two to three times a day. Grilled beef is usually served with a spicy parsley sauce known as chimichurri. There are an incredible number of versions of this condiment, which can be flaming hot, or just mildly scorching. This is my version. The amount of salt, pepper, and hot pepper is to taste. I have included the amount I use, which would be too hot for many people, but not hot enough for some. This spicy combination of raw vegetables and spices goes very well with any kind of barbecued meat. Chimichurri is usually used as a table condiment, like a salsa, but can also be used as a baste or marinade.

1 small organic onion, very finely chopped

1 small bulb organic garlic, very finely chopped

Leaves from 1 bunch organic Italian parsley, very finely chopped

1 teaspoon organic dried oregano

¾ cup unfiltered organic extra virgin olive oil

¼ cup unfiltered raw organic apple cider vinegar

Coarse unrefined sea salt, crushed

Freshly ground organic black pepper

Red pepper flakes (or crushed red pepper)

1. Chop the onion, garlic, and parsley as small as possible, and mix well. Add the remaining ingredients, and whisk together. The amount of salt, pepper, and red pepper is based on your taste. I use 2 teaspoons salt, 1 teaspoon pepper, and 2 teaspoons red pepper.

2. Let it sit for a couple of hours at room temperature before serving, so the flavors have a chance to blend. It should be used on the same day it is made.

This recipe can also be used as a tenderizing marinade (see recipe on page 99). If you use it as a marinade, do not add any salt, as salt can toughen grassfed meat.

Contra Costa Salsa

The original Spanish settlers of California, known as Californios, raised huge herds of cattle. They ate a lot of beef, and often served a salsa with it. This is my take on a Californio-style salsa. I named it after the county I live in, which used to be cattle country. The Californios did not use Thai fish sauce, but I really like the flavor provided by this anchovy-based condiment. They did not use piquillo peppers either, but those wood-smoked mild peppers are perfect for this dish, which goes so well with barbecued meat.

½ **cup organic green onions, finely chopped**

½ **cup organic celery, finely chopped**

½ **cup organic fresh cilantro, very finely chopped**

1½ **cups organic diced tomatoes**

½ **cup piquillo peppers, (or ½ cup organic Anaheim peppers), finely chopped**

1 **tablespoon unfiltered organic extra virgin olive oil**

1 **tablespoon unfiltered raw organic apple cider vinegar**

1 **tablespoon Thai fish sauce**

¼ **teaspoon organic dried oregano, crushed between your fingers**

A few dashes (or more if you like) organic hot sauce of your choice

1. Combine all the vegetables in a bowl, and mix well.

2. Combine the oil, vinegar, fish sauce, oregano, and hot sauce in another bowl. Stir briskly until these ingredients are well combined. Pour this mixture over the vegetables, and mix well. Refrigerate for a few hours before serving, so the flavors have a chance to mingle and form a delicious combined taste.

Fermented Cilantro Salsa

Cilantro is widely used in cooking, especially in Latin America and Asia. The combination of cilantro and tomatoes is one of the most traditional and popular condiments in Latin America. I am convinced that food combinations become traditional because they are beneficial for both taste and health.

This version is fermented. Fermentation increases the nutrient value, besides adding beneficial probiotics. This recipe was inspired by and based on a salsa recipe contained in *Nourishing Traditions*, Sally Fallon Morell's magnificent cookbook. It is also based on the ingredients contained in traditional Latin American condiments.

I recommend that you chop the ingredients by hand. Not only is this traditional, but it really seems to taste better.

The hot peppers are traditional, but optional. If you do include the hot peppers, be sure to be careful, using gloves when you handle them and never touching your eyes until your hands have been carefully washed. An alternative would be to add 1 to 4 teaspoons of bottled hot sauce (preferably thick and organic) after the fermentation is complete, and stir well. This avoids the problem of handling fresh hot peppers.

3 medium ripe organic tomatoes

2 organic green onions

1 large or 2 small bunches of organic cilantro

4 cloves organic garlic

4 serrano peppers, or 4 jalapeño peppers, preferably organic or the equivalent, (optional)

4 tablespoons whey

2 teaspoons coarse unrefined sea salt

1. Wash all the vegetables thoroughly, and dry them. Chop the tomatoes, green onions, cilantro, and garlic very fine. Place the chopped vegetables in a large glass bowl.

2. If you are using the hot peppers, protect your hands by using disposable gloves. Remove the seeds, unless you really like it hot. Slice the peppers into small circular pieces, and add to the rest of the vegetables. Be sure never to touch your eyes until you wash your hands thoroughly.

3. Add the whey and the salt to the vegetables, and mix well.

4. Pour the mixture into a quart-sized Mason jar. There should be at least one inch of space between the top of the jar and the mixture. It is important that the mixture does not touch the lid.

5. Cover the jar, move to a dark place (I use the inside of a cupboard), and let rest for two days while the fermentation takes place, then refrigerate.

Pebre

Pebre is a traditional Chilean condiment, which is served with almost everything. It goes beautifully with barbecued meats. This raw vegetable condiment is full of enzymes and other beneficial nutrients. I am often impressed by how often traditional food combinations combine meat with a good serving of vegetables, which provides a balanced group of nutrients in the meal.

You can reduce or increase the amount of hot sauce according to your taste. Pebre is traditionally very hot.

The use of a mortar and pestle really makes a difference, but it is a lot more work than using a blender. You can use a blender, and it will still be delicious.

Leaves from 1 bunch organic cilantro

5 medium organic tomatoes

4 large cloves organic garlic

3 organic green onions

2 teaspoons coarse unrefined sea salt, crushed

1 teaspoon freshly ground organic black pepper

3 tablespoons unfiltered organic extra virgin olive oil

1 tablespoon unfiltered raw organic apple cider vinegar

2 teaspoons organic hot sauce of your choice, (or to taste)

1. Finely chop the cilantro and tomatoes together. Be sure to chop by hand.

2. Finely chop the garlic and salt together.

3. Finely chop the green onions.

4. Crush the tomato/cilantro mixture in batches with a mortar and pestle.

5. Crush the garlic/salt mixture in batches with a mortar and pestle.

6. Crush the green onions in batches with a mortar and pestle.

7. Mix all ingredients together in a bowl. Cover the bowl, and let sit for 2 hours at room temperature.

Low-Carb
Side Dishes

About Low-Carb Side Dishes

Many people have chosen to control their weight by going on low-carb diets. Many others avoid carbohydrates because of the high glycemic index of such foods, which can lead to a rise in blood sugar.

I want to thank my friend, low-carb advocate Jimmy Moore, for educating me about the world of low-carb through his podcasts, blogs, websites, and books.

Many people who avoid carbohydrates eat grassfed and pastured meats, and this chapter is designed to provide delicious low-carb side dishes that will go with these meats. These dishes are based on traditional recipes and food combinations, and go wonderfully with grassfed meat.

Eggs have been a favorite side dish for meat for a very long time, and steak and eggs are a very traditional combination. These side dishes rely on eggs, often combined with cheese, and are nourishing and delicious. While I do not consciously follow a low-carb diet, my diet is much lower in carbohydrates than the Standard American Diet (SAD), and my family has enjoyed all of these side dishes with our grassfed meat.

(See **note** below.)

NOTE: These dishes are low-carb, not no-carb. They may not be suitable for the induction phase of an Atkins-type diet, as they do contain some carbohydrates.

The Jimmy Moore

This recipe was inspired by my friend, low-carb advocate Jimmy Moore. Jimmy's website and podcasts are a treasure trove of information on low-carb diets and nutrition in general. I had the pleasure of being interviewed by him about my first book, *Tender Grassfed Meat*.

This recipe is based on a diet that Jimmy was on. He called the diet "Egg Fest." The recipe is very nutrient-dense and absolutely delicious. It goes very well with grassfed meat.

This is also a wonderful dish for breakfast, and I find it really energizes me. And it tastes very good indeed. The stirring is very important as it really combines all the ingredients well. It may look like ordinary scrambled eggs, but wait until you taste it!

Serves 4 as a side dish

4 ounces pastured full-fat cheese, preferably cheddar

4 organic eggs, preferably pastured

4 tablespoons pastured butter

1. Chop the cheese into very small pieces.

2. Break the eggs into a bowl, and mix well with a fork.

3. Add the cheese to the eggs, and mix well.

4. Heat the butter in a medium-sized skillet over medium heat until the butter melts.

5. Add the egg/cheese mixture to the butter. Start stirring the mixture in a clockwise direction with a fork as it cooks.

6. Continue to cook and stir until the eggs set. They should set within a few minutes.

Serve and enjoy.

Quick Mushroom Soufflé in a Pan

This is not a classic soufflé, but it is quick, easy, low-carb, and delicious. The combination of butter, mushrooms, pastured eggs, and cheese blend beautifully to provide a delicious dish.

This goes well with any meat, and can also be used for a nourishing breakfast.

Serves 4 as a side dish

¼ **cup pastured butter**
½ **pound sliced fresh mushrooms, preferably crimini**
6 organic eggs, preferably pastured
¼ **cup full-fat pastured cheddar cheese, chopped**
2 tablespoons full-fat organic cream

1. Heat the butter in a heavy pan over medium high heat until hot and bubbly. Add the mushrooms and cook, stirring frequently, until the mushrooms are well browned, but not burned.

2. Turn the heat down to low. Break the eggs into a bowl. Beat lightly with a fork until well combined and you can see some bubbles. Add the cheese and cream to the eggs. Mix well. Pour the mixture over the mushrooms.

3. Turn the heat up to medium. Cover, and cook for 5 minutes, or until the eggs are no longer runny.

Serve and enjoy.

Garlic-Cheese Eggs

Cheese and eggs are two of the most nutrient-dense foods available. Adding pastured butter to them not only gives great flavor, but makes them even more nutritious. Lots of melted cheese makes this dish especially delicious. The garlic makes this something special. This goes so well with steak, but it is good with all meat.

Serves 4 as a side dish

⅓ **cup pastured butter**

2 organic garlic cloves, very finely chopped

6 organic eggs, preferably pastured, lightly beaten with a fork

½ **pound full-fat organic cheese of your choice, such as cheddar or Havarti, chopped into small pieces**

1. Melt the butter in a heavy pan (preferably cast iron) over medium heat.

2. Add the garlic, and cook for 1 minute.

3. Add the cheese to the eggs. Mix well.

4. Add the mixture to the pan. Stir well, cover, and cook at medium heat for 5 minutes, or until the eggs have set.

Serve and enjoy with the grassfed meat of your choice.

Cheese and Eggs with Onions and Butter

Onions are one of the most traditional side dishes eaten with meat. Here, the lovely taste of onions caramelized in butter is combined with eggs and melted cheese to make a delicious side dish, which is also good for breakfast.

Serves 4 as a side dish

4 tablespoons pastured butter

1 medium organic onion, sliced

1 cup full-fat natural cheese of your choice, chopped into small pieces, (cheddar and Havarti are very good with this dish)

4 organic eggs, preferably pastured, with the yolks, beaten with a whisk or a fork until many small bubbles appear

1. Heat the butter over medium heat in a 10-inch pan, preferably cast iron. When the butter is melted, add the onion, and sauté for 5 minutes.

2. Add the cheese to the eggs and mix well. Pour the mixture over the onions. Reduce the heat to medium low. Cover, and cook until the eggs have set, about 5 minutes.

Serve with the grassfed meat of your choice, or enjoy for breakfast.

Cheese and Egg Bake

Cheese and eggs have been two of the most popular foods in Europe for many generations. Many nations have their own version of a dish where cheese and eggs are baked together. For some reason, I could never get these recipes to turn out well — until I created this one. The ingredients combine to make a great side dish that is full of flavor and nutrition. It goes great with any kind of meat. It also makes a great lunch dish all by itself.

The combination of the soft interior and the flavorful crust is delicious. The small amount of curry powder is just what is needed to complete the dish.

Serves 4 as a side dish

1 cup drained full-fat plain yogurt (see Step 1)

¼ pound Gruyère, (or Monterey Jack, or sharp cheddar)

¼ pound full-fat natural cheddar

¼ cup grated Parmesan or Romano cheese

4 organic eggs, preferably pastured

2 tablespoons pastured butter, melted, (or 1 tablespoon organic extra virgin olive oil)

½ cup organic Italian parsley, finely chopped

½ teaspoon organic curry powder

1. Place a strainer on a bowl. Place some natural, unbleached cheesecloth on the strainer. Place the yogurt on the cheesecloth. Let the yogurt drain for 1 hour. (This step can be done in advance. Keep the drained yogurt refrigerated until you are ready to cook the dish.) Save the whey in the bottom of the bowl for another purpose.

2. Finely chop and/or crumble the two hard cheeses into tiny pieces. Combine the drained yogurt, the two hard cheeses, and the grated cheese in a large bowl.

3. Break the eggs into a mixing bowl. Use an egg beater to beat the eggs well for a couple of minutes until they are quite fluffy and bubbly.

4. Preheat the oven to 350 degrees. Place the butter (or olive oil) in an 8-inch square baking dish. Spread the butter (or olive oil) over the bottom of the dish.

5. Add the beaten eggs slowly to the cheese mixture, stirring until well mixed. Add the parsley and the curry powder, and mix well.

6. When the oven is preheated, carefully remove the baking pan from the oven and pour the mixture into the pan. Return the pan to the oven and bake for 30 minutes.

Serve and enjoy. Be careful because the interior will be very hot.

Side Dishes

The Magic of Meat and Potatoes — and Fat

Meat and potatoes were once so popular that the very term came to mean the very essence, the indispensible part of anything, the "meat and potatoes." In terms of a good main meal, meat and potatoes were always there, and anything else was optional.

The attempts to ram grain and vegetables down people's throats, as exemplified by the ridiculous food pyramid, changed this. Meat has been demonized as unhealthy in a myriad of ways. Potatoes, with their high glycemic index and starch content, have also come under attack, and are avoided by the low-carb movement.

Yet the combination of meat and potatoes is a very old tradition in Europe, one that goes back centuries. The European tradition had a third component, perhaps the most important of all — fat. Fat that was almost always from animal sources, like butter, bacon, lard, beef tallow, lamb tallow, etc. Of course, animal fat is the most demonized food of all, today.

Demonization aside, the combination of meat, potatoes, and fat is one of the most nutritious and delicious combinations you can have in a meal. Most of my family's main meals feature this combination, and we thrive on it.

But it is crucial to use traditional meat, traditional potatoes, and traditional fat. Together they create a wonderful balance, both in nutrition and pH balance, and are one of the tastiest food combinations.

- The traditional meat is grassfed meat.

- The traditional potatoes are organic potatoes, free of pesticides.

- The traditional fat is the fat of grassfed and pastured animals, and the fat from their milk.

Meat, Potatoes, and Fat Balance Each Other

I have come to understand that traditional food combinations stand the test of time because they are beneficial. Time and time again, science has confirmed the wisdom of these traditions.

For example, it is known that it is important to maintain a body pH balance that is not too acidic or alkaline, with slightly alkaline being ideal. Meat is acidic, and potatoes are one of the most alkaline foods you can eat. They are a perfect balance for each other. This may explain why the meat and potato combination was so popular, as traditional peoples always seemed to know what foods should be eaten together.

The adverse effects of the high glycemic index of potatoes are avoided when the potatoes are eaten with plenty of good fat. The fat changes the way that high glycemic foods are digested and absorbed. Again, traditional peoples seemed to know this. In Europe, potatoes were always eaten with plenty of good, natural, traditional fat. Potatoes were baked with cream and milk, fried in lard, fried in butter, fried with bacon, made into casseroles with butter and cheese, covered with sour cream or butter, and combined with cheese and baked into pies. These are just a few of the thousands of ways fat and potatoes were combined.

Here is one of the most basic barbecue potato recipes:

Charcoal Roasted Potatoes

One of the oldest ways of cooking potatoes is to cook them in or over a charcoal fire — very simple, but absolutely delicious with butter and/or sour cream.

All you need is to wash some potatoes, leaving the skins on. Cook them directly over the heat source, turning at least once, until the skins are dark, and the potatoes are soft to the touch. This can take anywhere from 30 minutes to 1 hour, depending on the size of the potatoes. The skins may be burned black (and should not be eaten), but the interior will be soft and very hot, with a delicious barbecue flavor.

Serve with plenty of butter and/or sour cream.

Home Fries with Hungarian Flavors

The traditional flavor combinations of various countries have always fascinated me. Very often, the traditional flavor base consists of three ingredients. Some examples would be: onions, carrots, and celery in France; ginger, garlic, and green onions in China; onions, bell peppers, and celery in Cajun country. The Hungarian trio contains onions, paprika, and bacon fat.

This basic Hungarian flavor base is made by sautéing onions in bacon fat until lightly colored, lowering the heat, and adding paprika. It is very important not to burn the paprika. This combination gives a truly wonderful flavor, one that is quite distinctive. I have been able to find real Hungarian bacon only a couple of times. It has a depth of flavor and taste that goes far beyond anything I have had elsewhere. This recipe is absolutely wonderful with smoked uncured bacon, and I can only imagine how good it would be if I could get real Hungarian bacon.

Serves 4 as a side dish

Filtered water for boiling
1 teaspoon coarse unrefined sea salt
6 medium organic potatoes, peeled, and chopped into small cubes
4 tablespoons melted bacon fat, (or unhydrogenated natural pork lard)
1 medium organic yellow onion, sliced
2 teaspoons organic or imported sweet paprika, preferably Hungarian

1. Heat a medium-size pan of filtered water to boiling. Add the salt and the potatoes, boil at medium high heat for 10 minutes. Remove the potatoes from the water.

2. Place the bacon fat (or lard) in a heavy-bottomed frying pan over medium heat. Add the onions and sauté over medium heat for about 5 minutes, stirring occasionally.

3. Turn the heat down to low. Add the paprika and mix well into the onions. Cook over low heat for 2 minutes, being careful not to burn the paprika.

4. Add the potatoes and stir well, making sure that all the potatoes are coated by the fat and paprika.

5. Turn the heat back up to medium and stir. Cook for another 5 minutes, stirring to make sure that nothing burns.

6. Cover the pan, and turn the heat to low. Cook for another 10 minutes, lifting the lid and stirring occasionally.

Serve and enjoy.

Even Better French Fries

I thought the recipe for Old Fashioned French Fries contained in *Tender Grassfed Meat* made the best fries I ever had, by far. The fries from this recipe are even better.

Perhaps I should have entitled this recipe "Even Better Belgian Fries," but few people would know what I was talking about. Belgian fries, which are quite similar to the much better known French fries, are perhaps the very favorite dish of the Belgian people. Belgian towns and cities are full of handcarts selling these fries to passersby, and they are very popular. Unfortunately, they are fried nowadays in modern vegetable oils, but there is a much better fat. I use grassfed beef tallow, which gives a wonderful, almost nutty flavor to the fries.

These are the best fries, French, or Belgian, or American, that I have ever had.

Serves 4 to 8 as a side dish

8 medium organic potatoes, they should be Idaho, or some other kind of russet potato, peeled, and cut into medium-sized French fries
2 cups grassfed beef tallow

First Frying:

1. Break the beef tallow into small chunks and place in a deep, heavy cast iron casserole, or a deep-fat fryer. (If you use a deep-fat fryer, you may need more tallow, depending on how large your fryer is.) Melt the tallow at medium heat. There should be at least 1 inch of fat in the pan, once the tallow has melted. More tallow is better.

2. When the tallow has melted and seems somewhat hot, drop a potato piece into the pan. Once the oil bubbles over the potato, the fat is hot enough for the first cooking stage.

3. Fry the potatoes in batches over medium heat, being careful not to crowd them too much. Each batch should cook for 4 minutes. Remove each cooked batch from the oil with a slotted spoon and place the fries in a wide, shallow pan.

4. When all the fries have been cooked, raise the heat to medium high. The oil should get significantly hotter in 2 to 3 minutes. It is now time for the second frying.

Second Frying:

5. Re-cook each batch of potatoes in the hot oil until they are nicely browned. This should take 1 to 3 minutes, depending on how hot the oil is.

6. As you complete each batch, place it on another shallow pan, and put the pan in an oven, heated to 250 degrees, to keep the fries hot. When all batches have cooked for the second time, serve and enjoy these magnificent fries.

Potatoes Sautéed in Lamb Fat

The fat of grassfed lamb is one of the most delicious mediums for cooking potatoes. I usually get lamb racks untrimmed, which means that I get wonderful flavor from the lamb fat. However, there is always a fair amount of beautifully browned lamb fat left over after we have finished eating the roast. This fat looked so good that I wanted to use it for frying potatoes. The potatoes came out crisp, and so full of flavor that it has become one of my favorite ways to cook them.

Serves 4 as a side dish

6 to 8 organic potatoes, peeled, and cut into cubes
Approximately ½ cup of leftover lamb fat, (or ¼ cup lamb tallow)

1. Place the lamb fat in a heavy-bottomed frying pan over medium heat. When most of the fat has rendered into the pan, add the potatoes, and stir well.

2. Cook for 5 minutes, stirring constantly.

3. Cover the pan, and cook for another 30 minutes or so, stirring the potatoes every 5 minutes, until the potatoes are crisp, and nicely browned.

Enjoy this wonderful side dish.

Italian Potato Cubes

These potatoes use the traditional Italian flavor combination of butter, olive oil, garlic, and rosemary. Yes, butter is a very traditional Italian ingredient and is used in all kinds of dishes. These potatoes are easy, and so very wonderful. This recipe is one of my family's favorites.

Serves 4 as a side dish

6 medium organic potatoes, peeled and cut into wedges approximately ½ inch wide

½ teaspoon coarse unrefined sea salt

Filtered water for boiling

2 tablespoons pastured butter

2 tablespoons organic extra virgin olive oil

1 sprig organic rosemary, on the stem, cut into several pieces

2 cloves organic garlic, coarsely chopped

1. Place the potato wedges in a pot, with the salt and enough filtered water to cover them. Bring the pot to a boil, and cook for 5 minutes. Let the potatoes drain for 5 minutes in a colander. Cut the wedges into ½ inch cubes.

2. Place the butter and olive oil in a large frying pan over medium heat. When the butter has melted, add the rosemary and garlic.

3. Cook over medium heat for about a minute or so.

4. Add the cubed potatoes, and cook uncovered over medium heat, stirring occasionally. Cook for 8 to 15 minutes until the cubes are crusty and browned.

Serve and enjoy.

Potatoes in Sour Cream

This recipe has both Polish and Russian roots. Both Poles and Russians loved to use sour cream and onions with potatoes. The finished dish looks a bit like a potato salad, but has a terrific taste of its own, where the ingredients blend perfectly to create a wonderful side dish for just about any meat.

Serves 4 as a side dish

2½ pounds organic potatoes, peeled and thinly sliced (no more than ¼ inch thick)

Filtered water for boiling

3 tablespoons pastured butter

2 medium organic red onions, coarsely chopped

1 cup organic full-fat sour cream

1 teaspoon organic dried dill

1 teaspoon coarse unrefined sea salt

½ teaspoon freshly ground organic black pepper

1. Place the potatoes in a pan with enough filtered water to cover the potato slices. Bring the pot to a boil, and cook the potatoes for 5 minutes. Drain the potatoes.

2. Melt the butter in a large frying pan over medium heat. When the butter has melted, add the onions and cook, stirring occasionally, for 10 minutes.

3. Add the potatoes to the pan, and mix well with the onions. Add the sour cream, dill, salt, and pepper, and mix well. Bring the mixture to a simmer.

4. Cover the pan, and simmer the mixture over low heat for 15 minutes.

5. Stir the mixture thoroughly, cover, and simmer for another 15 minutes.

Serve and enjoy the wonderful flavors of this very traditional dish.

Belgian Potatoes

This is my variation on a very old dish. I think there may be as many variations on this dish as there are cooks in Belgium. The Flemings are one of the two major population groups in Belgium. Their homeland, Flanders, has some of the richest and most productive farmland. Though they may be small in numbers, their culture is very large, including their magnificent cooking. The combination of lard and butter is unusual, but it gives a wonderful flavor to this dish.

Serves 4 as a side dish

8 medium-sized organic potatoes, peeled and cut into 1 inch cubes

1 teaspoon coarse unrefined sea salt

Filtered water for boiling

4 tablespoons unhydrogenated natural pork lard

2 tablespoons pastured butter

1 large organic onion, sliced

2 cups homemade bone broth, preferably *Beef Bone Broth* **(page 50)**

1. Place the potato cubes in a pan for boiling. Add the salt and enough filtered water to cover the potatoes. Bring the water to a boil, and cook for 3 minutes. Drain the potatoes.

2. Heat the lard and butter together in a large frying pan over medium heat. Add the onions and cook for 10 to 15 minutes, stirring occasionally, until the onions are a nice golden color and have softened.

3. Add the potato cubes to the onions and cook for about 1 minute, stirring well to ensure that all the ingredients are well mixed.

4. Add the broth, and heat the mixture until it is bubbling. Cover the pan. Reduce the heat to medium low, and cook for about 30 minutes.

5. Uncover the pan. If you see some visible liquid, turn the heat up to medium high, and keep cooking and turning over the mixture until the liquid has cooked off. The potatoes should still be moist, but there should not be any visible liquid.

Serve and enjoy the wonderful flavor of this very traditional dish.

Portuguese Roast Potatoes

Portuguese cuisine is delicious. This recipe combines traditional Portuguese ingredients into a marinade for potatoes, which come out crusty and full of exotic flavor.

Serves 4 as a side dish

8 medium organic potatoes, peeled and cut into circles about ½ inch thick

Seasoning Mixture

2 tablespoons organic Italian parsley, finely chopped

1 teaspoon freshly ground organic black pepper

2 teaspoons coarse unrefined sea salt, crushed

1 tablespoon sweet paprika, preferably Portuguese or Spanish

3 large cloves organic garlic, finely chopped

For Roasting

¼ cup organic extra virgin olive oil

1. Place the potato circles in a large bowl.

2. Combine the ingredients for the seasoning mixture. Mix well. Add the seasoning mixture to the potatoes. Use a spoon to mix the potatoes and the seasoning mixture until all the potatoes are well coated.

3. Preheat the oven to 350 degrees. Pour the olive oil into a flat-bottomed roasting pan that is large enough to hold all the potatoes in a single layer. Place the potatoes in the olive oil in a single layer.

4. When the oven has preheated, bake the potatoes for 25 minutes.

5. Remove the pan from the oven, turn all the potatoes over, and return the pan to the oven for another 25 minutes.

Serve and enjoy.

Vesuvio Potatoes

This dish was inspired by an old Chicago Italian dish called Chicken Vesuvio. This dish, of which there are many variations, involves cooking chicken and potatoes together in a spicy, tomato-based sauce. The potatoes in this dish were so good that I thought I could make the potatoes on their own and have a wonderful side dish. They turned out great.

Serves 4 as a side dish

2 pounds organic potatoes, peeled and sliced into circles about ½ inch thick

¼ cup organic extra virgin olive oil

4 cloves organic garlic, minced

1 cup organic tomato purée, or organic strained tomatoes

½ cup dry sherry wine, preferably Spanish

2 tablespoons finely chopped organic Italian parsley

1 teaspoon organic dried oregano

1½ teaspoons coarse unrefined sea salt, crushed

½ teaspoon freshly ground organic black pepper

1. Heat the olive oil over medium heat until it is hot. Add the garlic, and cook, stirring occasionally, for 2 minutes.

2. Add all the other ingredients (except for the potatoes) and stir well. Reduce the heat to low, and simmer the mixture for 10 minutes.

3. Preheat the oven to 400 degrees. Grease a roasting pan (large enough to hold the potatoes in one layer) with olive oil or butter. Place the potatoes in a single layer in the pan. Pour the sauce over the potatoes. Bake at 400 degrees for 20 minutes.

4. Remove the pan from the oven, turn the potatoes over, and bake for 20 more minutes.

Serve and enjoy.

Potato Casserole, Brussels Style

This is one of the most nutrient-dense side dishes I know, loaded with real cream, butter, milk, and cheese. The leeks add a nice flavor, and this combination of ingredients makes the potatoes taste terrific. This is a very old recipe that is supposed to have originated in Brussels, the capitol of Belgium.

This recipe is yet another example of a mistake that results in a better recipe. I am very lucky that way. For some reason, I used the wrong kind of cheese, and far more cheese than I intended to use. But the cheese improved the recipe.

This recipe is also extremely easy.

Serves 4 as a side dish

6 medium organic potatoes, peeled and cut into circular slices, about ¼ inch thick

2 organic leeks, white part only, carefully washed and thinly sliced in little circles

¼ cup pastured butter, sliced

¼ pound full-fat Havarti cheese, preferably from Denmark, coarsely chopped

½ cup full-fat organic unhomogenized milk

1 cup organic cream

1. Preheat the oven to 400 degrees. Grease a baking dish with some of the butter. Place half of the potatoes on the baking dish, spreading them out to cover the surface of the dish. Spread half of the leeks over the potatoes. Spread the remaining potatoes over the leeks. Spread the remaining leeks over the last of the potatoes.

2. Place the butter slices over the leeks. Place the cheese over the butter and the leeks. Pour the milk and cream over all.

3. Put the dish in the oven. Cook for 40 minutes at 400 degrees.

Serve and enjoy this wonderful dish.

Two Onion Sauté

Some of the most delicious dishes are also the simplest. Recipes do not get much simpler than this one. The secret is to use the best organic onions you can find, and good pastured butter. The combination of onions and butter is magical, resulting in a caramelized, slightly sweet, absolutely delicious, healthy side dish that will go with just about any meat. The use of two different kinds of onions makes a wonderful flavor combination.

Serves 4 as a side dish

1 large organic red onion, sliced
1 large organic yellow onion, sliced
3 tablespoons pastured butter

1. Melt the butter over medium heat in a heavy-bottomed frying pan, preferably cast iron.

2. When the butter is hot and bubbly, add the onions. Cook, stirring occasionally, for 10 minutes over medium heat. The onions should have shrunk considerably at this point.

3. Turn the heat down to low and continue cooking the onions, stirring occasionally, until they are nicely browned and caramelized. This will take another 5 to 10 minutes, depending on the water content of the onions. Be careful not to let them burn.

Enjoy this simple, yet delicious side dish.

Classic Vegetables in Butter

Carrots, onions, and celery are one of the oldest flavoring combinations in the culinary traditions of Europe. When you sauté these vegetables until they have softened and mingled their flavors, enhanced by pure butter, you have one delicious side dish. This dish will go with any grassfed meat.

Serves 4 as a side dish

2 large organic yellow onions, sliced
4 organic carrots, sliced
4 stalks organic celery, sliced
⅓ cup pastured butter

1. Melt the butter in a large heavy-bottomed frying pan over medium heat.

2. Add all the vegetables, and raise the heat to medium high. Cook for about 10 minutes, stirring constantly. The vegetables will shrink in size, and begin to brown.

3. Turn the heat down to medium low and cook for another 10 minutes, stirring occasionally. The vegetables should be very soft, caramelized, and redolent with the wonderful flavor of butter.

Serve and enjoy the deep combined flavor.

Quick Collard Greens with Bacon

While grassfed meat is my favorite food, part of the pleasure comes from eating it with delicious side dishes. Some of these side dishes are so good they become favorites, and are made time and time again. This recipe is one of my favorites, and I have made it often. It goes wonderfully with every kind of grassfed meat. I love to make this dish with collard greens that have deep green, firm leaves.

Collard greens originated in West Africa, and are loaded with nutrition, with many vitamins and minerals concentrated in their deep green leaves. They are a staple of traditional soul food. Traditionally, collard greens are cooked for a very long time, with some kind of fatty pork. More modern versions cut the fat, but not mine. I keep the pork fat, but reduce the cooking time.

Serves 4 as a side dish

2 thick slices fatty uncured bacon, or 4 thin slices, (if the uncured bacon is not salted, add 1 teaspoon of unrefined sea salt)

2 cups filtered water

1 large bunch fresh organic collard greens, with deep green leaves

3 tablespoons unfiltered raw organic apple cider vinegar

1 teaspoon thick red organic hot sauce of your choice

1. Wash the collard greens well with filtered water, making sure any soil or sand is washed off. Remove the leaves from the stem, tearing the leaves into 2 to 3 inch pieces. Discard the stems.

2. Pour 2 cups filtered water into a stainless steel pot with the bacon, and bring to a slow boil. Cover, and cook for 10 minutes. This will cook a lot of the fat into the water, where it will really flavor the greens.

3. Add the greens, vinegar, and hot sauce to the pot. Bring the pot back to a strong simmer. Cover, and cook for 20 minutes. Remove the greens to a serving dish with a slotted spoon.

Serve and enjoy with the grassfed meat or pastured pork of your choice.

Appendix

Sources

There are many sources of grassfed meat and other food. The sources listed here are sources I use for my family, which ship their products all over the Continental United States. Local sources are not listed on this page, but you may have some excellent grassfed ranches in your area.

I have used each of the sources listed on this page multiple times, and I am satisfied that their meat is truly grassfed and grass finished. Pigs do not eat grass, but I am satisfied that the source for pork is pastured, and properly raised. I have used these products many times because they are excellent, and the suppliers are good people who care about the quality of what they do.

Beef

Alderspring Ranch
www.alderspring.com
May, Idaho 83253

Gaucho Ranch
www.gauchoranch.com
Miami, FL 33138
(305) 751-0775

Homestead Natural Foods
www.homesteadnatural.com
Middleton, ID 83644
(208) 880-8923

U.S. Wellness Meats
www.grasslandbeef.com
Monticello, Missouri 63457
(877) 383-0051

Bison

NorthStar Bison
www.northstarbison.com
Rice Lake, Wisconsin 54868
(888) 295-6332

Lamb

Anderson Ranches
www.oregonlamb.com
Brownsville, OR 97327
(541) 466-5866

NorthStar Bison
www.northstarbison.com
Rice Lake, Wisconsin 54868
(888) 295-6332

U.S. Wellness Meats
www.grasslandbeef.com
Monticello, Missouri 63457
(877) 383-0051

Pastured Pork

Homestead Natural Foods
www.homesteadnatural.com
Middleton, ID 83644
(208) 880-8923

Unfiltered Extra Virgin Olive Oil

Chaffin Family Orchards
This oil is not certified organic, but is the equivalent, and the best I've ever had.
www.chaffinfamilyorchards.com
Oroville, CA 95965
(530) 533-8239

Herbs and Spices

Mountain Rose Herbs
My favorite source of organic herbs, including Mediterranean myrtle.
www.mountainroseherbs.com
Eugene, OR 97405
(800) 879-3337

Index

Made in the USA
Columbia, SC
06 January 2022

53667659R00135